Paths to Perfection
BUDDHIST ART AT THE FREER|SACKLER

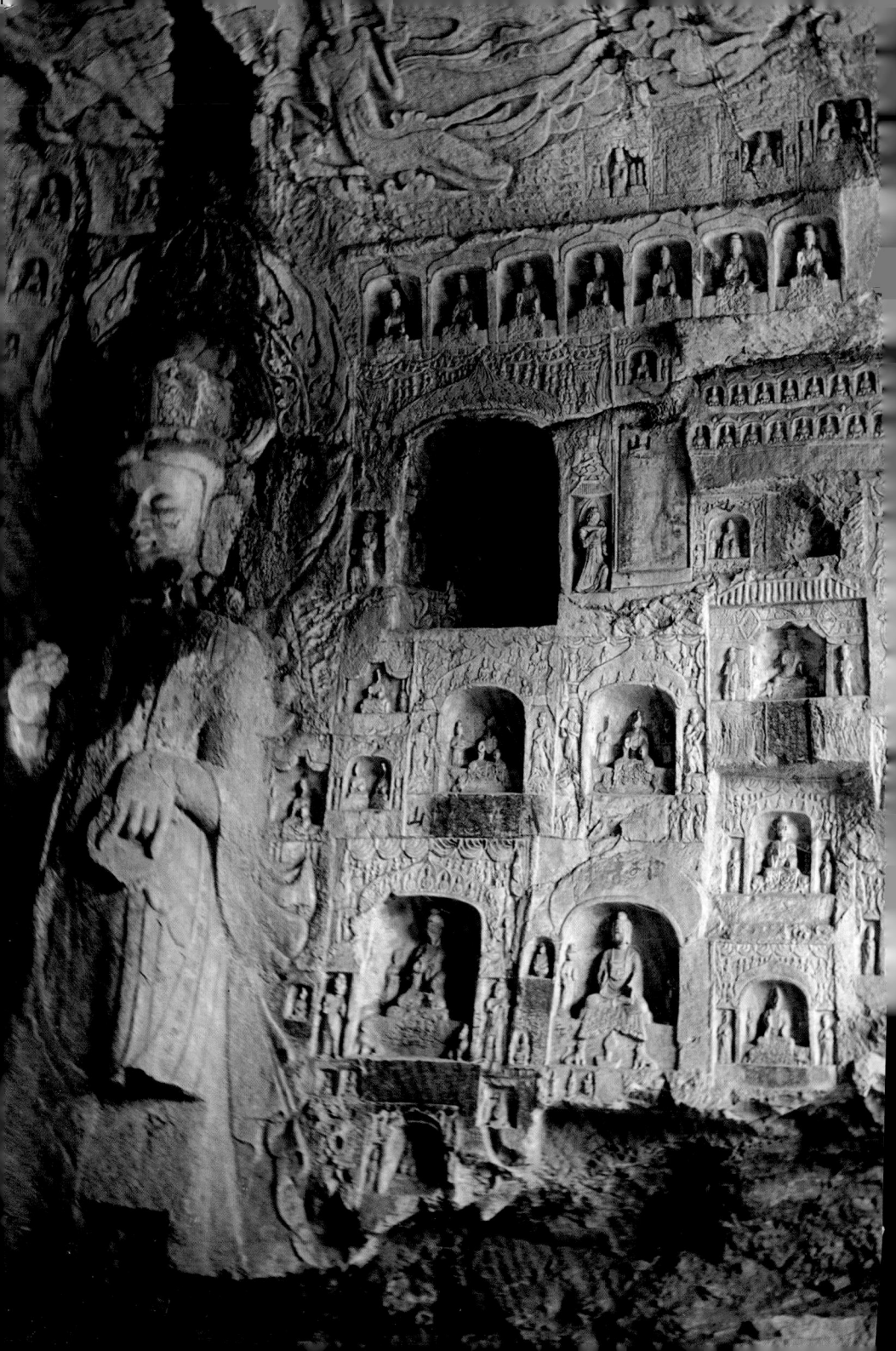

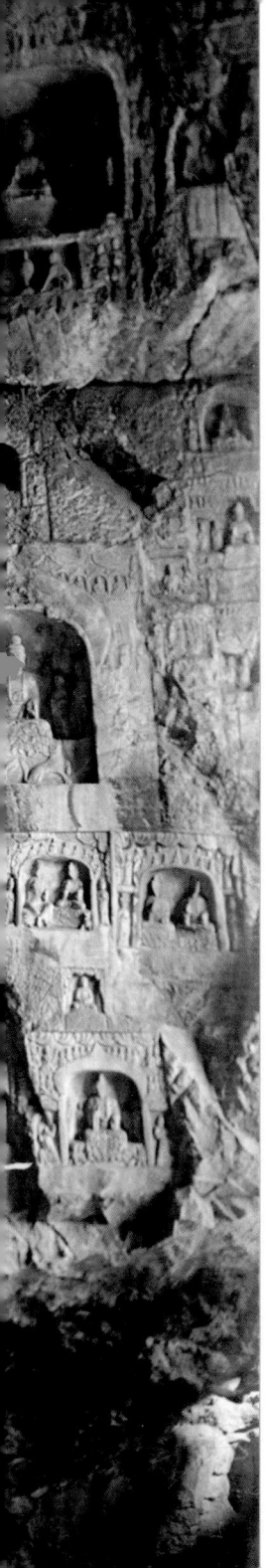

Paths to Perfection

BUDDHIST ART AT THE FREER|SACKLER

GILES

FREER|SACKLER

The Smithsonian's Museums of Asian Art,
Washington, DC

Paths to Perfection, Buddhist Art at the Freer|Sackler, © 2017,
Smithsonian Institution. All rights reserved.

Published by Freer|Sackler, the Smithsonian's museums of Asian art:
asia.si.edu

Distributed in the USA and Canada by
Consortium Book Sales & Distribution
The Keg House
34 Thirteenth Avenue, NE, Suite 101
Minneapolis, MN 55413-1007
USA
www.cbsd.com

GILES
An imprint of D Giles Limited
4 Crescent Stables
139 Upper Richmond Road
London
SW15 2TN
UK
www.gilesltd.com

Page II: North wall, Lianhuadong, Longmen cave temples; China, Henan Province, 1910; Charles Lang Freer Papers; Freer|Sackler Archives, FSA A.01 12.05.GN.150

Editor: Joelle Seligson
Content editor: Debra Diamond
Designer: Adina Brosnan McGee

Library of Congress Cataloging-in-Publication Data

Names: Freer Gallery of Art, author. | Arthur M. Sackler Gallery (Smithsonian Institution), author.
Title: Paths to perfection : Buddhist art at the Freer|Sackler.
Description: Washington, D.C. : Freer|Sackler, the Smithsonian's museum of Asian art ; London : Giles, [2017] | Includes index.
Identifiers: LCCN 2017013603 | ISBN 9781907804649 (pbk.)
Subjects: LCSH: Freer Gallery of Art--Guidebooks. | Arthur M. Sackler Gallery (Smithsonian Institution)--Guidebooks. | Buddhist art--Guidebooks. | Art--Washington (D.C.)--Guidebooks.
Classification: LCC N8193.A2 F74 2017 | DDC 709.753--dc23
LC record available at https://lccn.loc.gov/2017013603

Typset in Benton Sans
Printed and bound in Slovenia.

Contents

VI	Foreword: Robert Y.C. Ho
VII	Foreword: Julian Raby
IX	Note to the Reader
1	Introduction: Robert DeCaroli
22	Map
24	Buddhas
70	Bodhisattvas
116	Mandalas and Ritual Objects
154	Teachers and Teachings
196	Attendants and Protectors
220	About the Authors
223	Glossary
228	Index

Robert Y.C. Ho, chairman, The Robert H.N. Ho Family Foundation

The Robert H.N. Ho Family Foundation's support of the Freer|Sackler and its exhibition *Encountering the Buddha: Art and Practice across Asia*, on view from 2017 through 2020, grew from an earlier collaboration. In 2013, the foundation and the museums convened scholars, museologists, curators, conservators, historians, designers, and practitioners to discuss how to make Buddhist art more relevant and accessible. The exhibition and this guidebook to the museums' collections of Buddhist art have been informed by that discussion.

One of the foundation's aims is to help spread awareness and understanding of Buddhism and its relevance to contemporary society. Buddhist concepts have long influenced American artists and intellectuals, and outstanding visual art has broad appeal. I hope that this guidebook to the Freer|Sackler's Buddhist art collections will give a new generation deeper insight into the meaning and context of Buddhism.

It is an honor for The Robert H.N. Ho Family Foundation to collaborate with the Freer| Sackler. I wish to especially acknowledge director Julian Raby, the team behind the museums' Buddhist art exhibitions, and those who contributed to this publication. We applaud their vision and resolve to be innovative.

Julian Raby, The Dame Jillian Sackler Director of the Arthur M. Sackler Gallery and the Freer Gallery of Art

Let me welcome you, as you open this book, into a fascinating realm: the world of the Buddha, as glimpsed through the collections of the Freer Gallery of Art and the Arthur M. Sackler Gallery, the Smithsonian's museums of Asian art.

As Buddhist ideas and practices have inspired artists throughout Asia for millennia, it is not surprising that Buddhist art features in both museums' founding collections. Charles Lang Freer's trips to China and Japan before the First World War brought him into intimate contact with Buddhist art and monuments. Freer firmly believed that art could elevate the human spirit. In 1909, he commissioned autochromes of carefully selected groupings of his objects, including a wooden statue of Avalokiteshvara with objects that were not Buddhist in character. This is revealing: It emphasizes Freer's philosophy that "for those who have the power to see beauty, all works of art go together." It also reflects the fact that Freer himself never sought to make a broadly encompassing Buddhist collection.

Like Freer, Dr. Arthur M. Sackler never formed a collection focused exclusively on Buddhism. He was interested, though, in tracing the evolution and spread of artistic ideas, and he had a passion for the arts of ancient China, Iran, and India. Ultimately, Sackler collected many Buddhist items from China and Central Asia.

By combining in this book the two founding collections with acquisitions made over almost a hundred years, we can form a map of Buddhism's dissemination. In some cases, most notably through Alice S. Kandell's recent gift of Tibetan shrine objects, we also can take a focused look at regional practice.

Since the start of the present century, Buddhist art has featured prominently in numerous exhibitions at the Freer|Sackler. Among them are major loan exhibitions, notably *Return of the Buddha: The Qingzhou Discoveries* (2004), *In the Realm of the Buddha* (2010), and *Echoes of the Past: The Buddhist Cave Temples of Xiangtangshan* (2011). Smaller but important exhibitions drawn from our own collections include *Faith and Form: Selected Calligraphy and Painting from Japanese Religious Traditions* (2004), *Goryeo Buddhist Paintings: A Closer Look* (2012), *Promise of Paradise: Early Chinese Buddhist Sculpture* (2012), and *Body of Devotion: The Cosmic Buddha in 3D* (2016).

Encountering the Buddha: Art and Practice across Asia (2017) is our first more comprehensive look at pan-Asian Buddhism through the collections. This multiyear installation in the Sackler links to objects throughout the museums. It also uses digital technology to provide background information on many of the objects and to convey a sense of their vast geographical span. Visitors can journey from Korea to India through the eyes of an eighth-century Korean monk and experience a Buddhist site in Sri Lanka from dawn to moonrise.

This guidebook is another way to experience our Buddhist holdings. It has provoked for us, as we hope it will for you, spirited exchanges about connections among objects from across the Buddhist world and about the power of art to express the tenets of this faith.

The book has been a team effort, with illuminating entries by curators Stephen D. Allee, Louise Allison Cort, Debra Diamond, Jan Stuart, James Ulak, J. Keith Wilson, and Ann Yonemura, as well as by fellows Rebecca Bloom and Johannes Eijsermans. Special thanks are due to Buddhist art historian Robert DeCaroli for his enlightening introductory essay. We are also indebted to monks Kovida U and Ashin Ariyacara for translating a Burmese manuscript folio. For pulling together all the moving parts, I would like to express my sincere thanks to content editor Debra Diamond, editor Joelle Seligson, and designer Adina Brosnan McGee. None of this would have been possible without photographer Neil Greentree; staff members Brian Abrams, Nancy Eickel, Cory Grace, Tim Kirk, Amelia Meyer, and Christina Popenfus; and, last but not least, interns Sally Kendrick and Giorgi Medellin.

NOTE TO THE READER   IX

In the pages that follow, spectacular Buddhist objects from the Freer|Sackler collections are organized by type rather than by region, highlighting transregional similarities and inviting comparison. The works are ordered chronologically within each section.

Like the museums, the book covers a broad range of countries and cultures. For clarity and consistency, we have identified bodhisattvas and deities in Sanskrit, followed by identifications in the relevant language. For readability, we have omitted diacritics in favor of phonetic spellings. Visit the glossary on page 223 for a full list of terms and translations.

Freer|Sackler curators and fellows wrote the objects' descriptions. Authors are identified by their initials at the end of each entry. Find out more in the About the Authors section on page 220.

Stephen D. Allee (SDA)
Rebecca Bloom (RB)
Louise Allison Cort (LAC)
Robert DeCaroli (RDC)
Debra Diamond (DD)
Johannes Eijsermans (JE)
Jan Stuart (JS)
James Ulak (JU)
J. Keith Wilson (KW)
Ann Yonemura (AY)

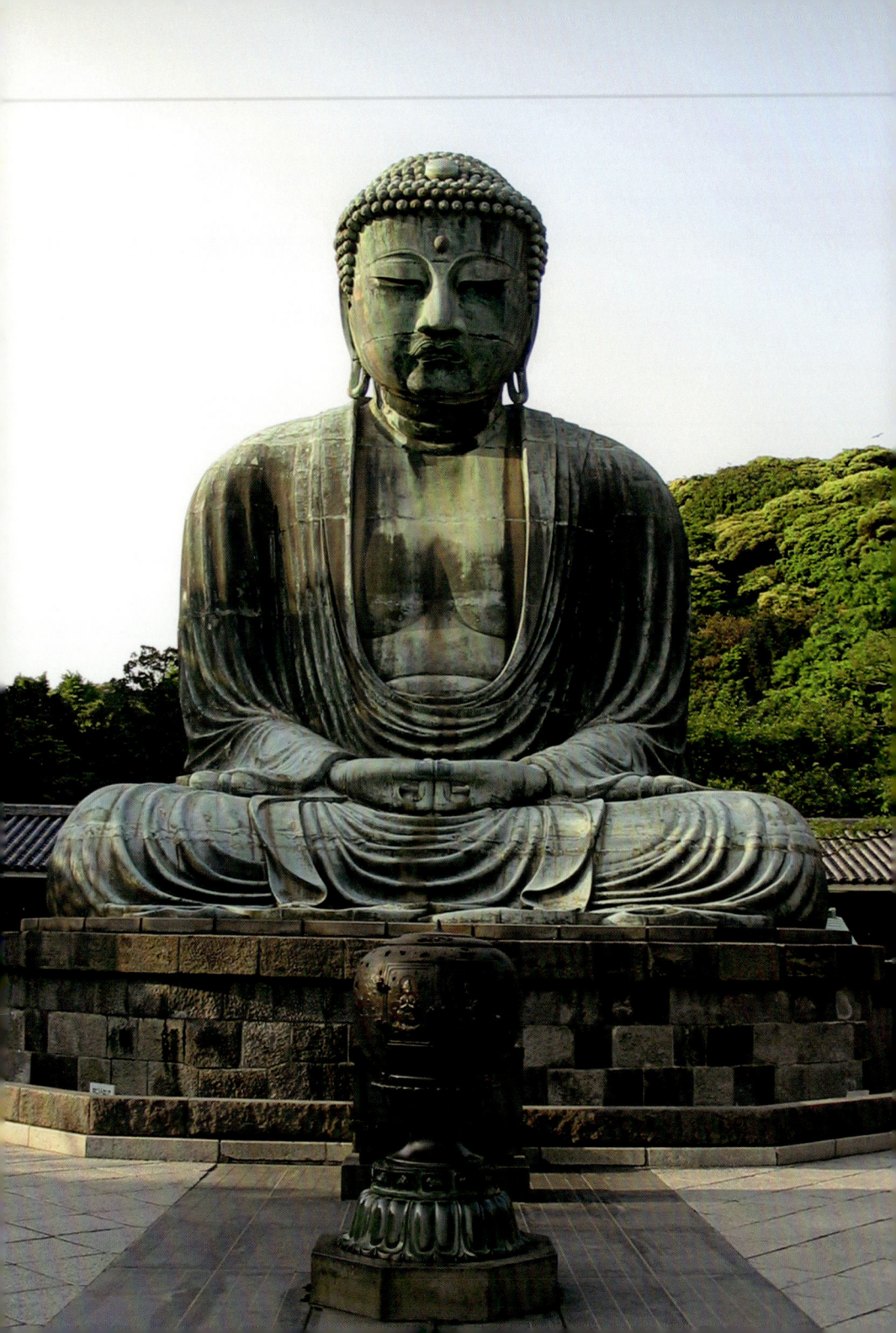

Introduction

In the history of world art, few figures are as familiar or widely depicted as the Buddha. For thousands of years, artists have shaped his image in metal and stone and painted his form on the walls of monasteries, temples, and caves. Today, we also see him represented in advertisements and serving as decoration for boutiques and restaurants.

Typically seated with crossed legs and downcast eyes in a state of calm introspection, the Buddha's form is easily identified (fig. 1). The abundance and relative consistency of his image may suggest a timeless uniformity or that representations of the Buddha hold the same meaning for all believers. History, however, tells a very different story—one in which meanings vary greatly according to period and place. The significance of the Buddha's image has never been fixed or static.

A Thai monk might recognize such an image as an empty reminder of the Buddha and his teachings (dharma) that holds no inherent connection to the teacher, who has passed into the state of nirvana. The artwork is a reminder and nothing more. Yet his fellow Thai Buddhist might travel great distances to seek out a potent Buddha image in hope of curing an illness. Certain representations of the Buddha have storied histories of miraculous and compassionate acts, offering refuge in times of need.

A Tibetan Buddhist might commission a painting of the Buddha so that she can donate it to the local monastery. The act earns her merit (good karma), which she then offers to her recently deceased father, attaining him a positive rebirth. To her, the image is the means to help a loved one. The nun who receives the painting, by contrast, might recognize the Historical Buddha as just one buddha among many through whom the dharma's eternal truths have been revealed.

For a Zen practitioner in Japan, seeing an image of the Buddha might call to mind the adage "If you encounter the Buddha, kill him." This saying is a reminder that attachments, even to the Buddha, can be a hindrance along the path to attaining enlightenment, or perfect wisdom into the nature of existence. Only personal striving can cultivate one's potential to become a buddha. By contrast, a newcomer to an

1
Great Buddha of Kamakura; Japan, Kamakura, Kotoku-in; courtesy Dirk Beyer, via Wikimedia Commons

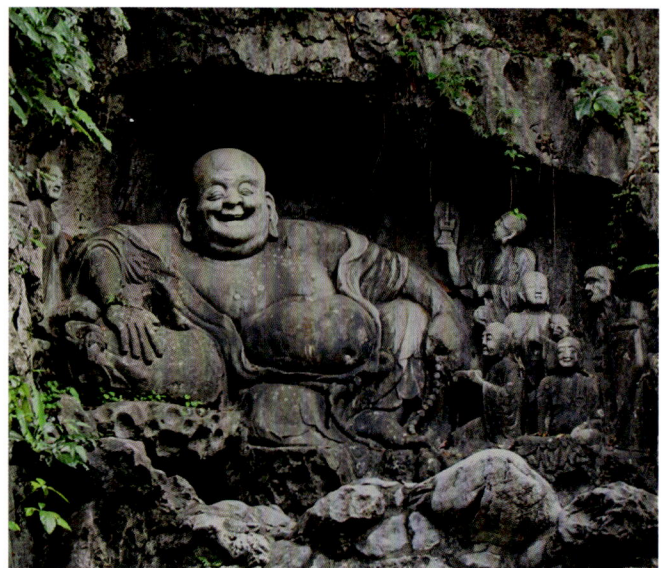

American meditation group might encounter the same image and be surprised that it isn't the rotund, jovial figure often represented as the Buddha in popular media. In fact, such "laughing buddha" images are not traditionally understood to depict the Historical Buddha at all (fig. 2).

These examples provide just a taste of the varied ways the image of the Buddha has been used and understood. In all cases, these objects are more than just decorative: their creation and veneration is believed to provide a range of benefits, both material and spiritual. There are many more examples throughout this book of Buddhist art from the Freer|Sackler, the Smithsonian's museums of Asian art. While not encyclopedic, this collection illuminates the incredible diversity of Buddhist art across time and space.

BASICS OF BUDDHISM

To get a sense of the rich history of Buddhist art, it is best to begin at the beginning. The Buddha can be identified with a man named Siddhartha Gautama who lived in northeastern India sometime after the fifth century BCE. Born to a royal family, he renounced his wealth

2
Laughing Buddha; China, Lingyin Temple; courtesy Stephen D. Allee

as a young man to pursue a life of asceticism and to grapple with the question of suffering, or *duhkha*.

For six years, Siddhartha Gautama practiced harsh austerities as a hermit, but they failed to bring him enlightenment. After taking food, he sat under a tree, determined to acquire insight. He came to realize that *duhkha* is tied to our desires and attachments to worldly things—including our own egos—which all inevitably decay. This realization, and his decision to share it with others, earned him the title of Buddha, or "Awakened One." He is also known as Shakyamuni, the Historical Buddha.

For Shakyamuni, not even death would end suffering. Like most South Asians of his time, he believed in the relentless cycle of life, death, and rebirth (samsara) and the power of karma to determine one's fate. Through karma, which literally means "action," selfless deeds lead to good results and malicious intentions produce negative consequences. The accrual of karma determines into which realm of existence an individual is reborn: among humans or animals, hungry ghosts or demigods, the hosts of heaven or those suffering in the hells. Yet none of these states is permanent, so even the best of existences is tinged with sorrow and the knowledge that it will one day end.

Shakyamuni overcame this suffering by attaining enlightenment and, ultimately, nirvana—a state beyond dualities, including that of life and death. In his first sermon, the Buddha expounded on the Four Noble Truths: (1) life is suffering; (2) suffering is caused by ignorance and desire; (3) ignorance and desire can be overcome; (4) the way to overcome them is by following the eightfold path: right view, resolve, speech, action, livelihood, effort, mindfulness, and concentration. These precepts are the foundation of all forms of Buddhism.

Even though Shakyamuni accepted the existence of gods and regional deities, he recognized that they too were trapped in the cycle of rebirth and could therefore benefit from his teachings. Many deities and spirits did convert to Buddhism, often becoming protectors of the faith. For humans, this means that while gods may help with worldly concerns, enlightenment can be achieved only through personal commitment to the dharma.

SCHOOLS OF PRACTICE
Within a generation or two of the Buddha's death, disagreements developed over how best to pursue the spiritual goals he had established. And as the monastic order (sangha) of monks and nuns formed and grew, divisions began to emerge and new schools developed. While we cannot delve into the full history of this complex process, it is helpful to classify these schools within three broad categories of Buddhism: Nikaya, Mahayana, and Vajrayana.

Scholars often describe Nikaya (sometimes called Theravada or Hinayana) as the most conservative branch of Buddhism because it focuses on nirvana and the monastic community. Nikaya currently predominates in Sri Lanka and Southeast Asia, where it has replaced other traditions.

Mahayana schools typically identify buddhahood, rather than nirvana, as their ultimate aim. Unlike Nikaya Buddhists, most Mahayana schools believe that buddhas remain active in the world even after they die. Therefore, devotees often make room for practices honoring both buddhas and bodhisattvas. Bodhisattvas are future buddhas who have attained advanced spiritual states and, out of compassion, vow to stay in the world to help all other beings. Mahayana Buddhism has been practiced in many locations, but traditionally its presence has been strongest across East Asia.

Vajrayana or tantric Buddhism also holds buddhahood as the ultimate spiritual goal, but practitioners attain it through specialized techniques transmitted from teacher to pupil. This training involves special initiations and teachings not typical of the other branches of Buddhism. Vajrayana Buddhists honor buddhas and bodhisattvas as well as a complex array of teachers, guardians, and deities. These initiatory or esoteric (secretive) schools took root in many parts of the world; today, they are found predominantly in the Himalayas and, to some degree, Japan.

BEGINNINGS OF BUDDHIST ART
The earliest Buddhist centers developed in India around monastic residences and large burial mounds (fig. 3) containing relics of the Buddha or of his important disciples. Devotees frequently decorated

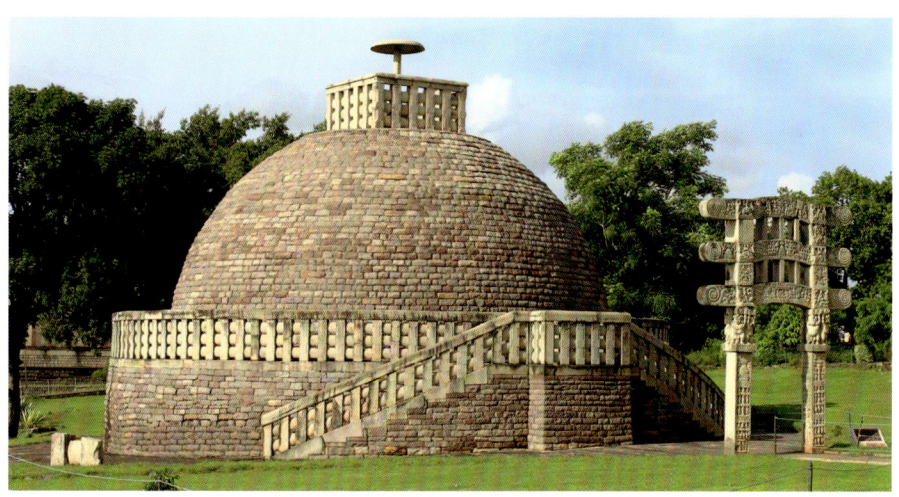

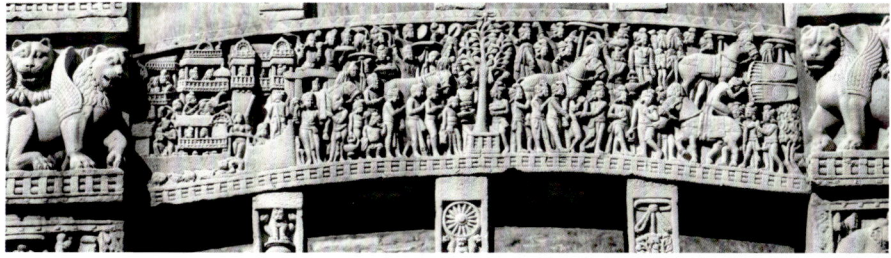

3
Sanchi Stupa no. 3; India, Madhya Pradesh, Sanchi; 2nd century BCE; courtesy Suyash Dwivedi via Wikimedia Commons

4
The "Great Departure" of Shakyamuni from Sanchi Stupa no. 1; India, Madhya Pradesh, Sanchi; 2nd–1st century BCE; Huntington Archive, 1306

these structures, known as stupas, with sculptural ornamentation, often including regional deities that had been converted into Buddhist guardians. The decoration also featured narrative scenes detailing the Buddha's life and past lives (jataka tales).

For approximately four hundred years after his death, the Buddha was not represented directly in art. Rather than emerging from strictly Buddhist prohibitions, this intentional omission seems to have derived from the idea that figural art could influence the individual who was depicted. Such imagery was therefore deemed inappropriate for religious figures. Instead, artists indicated Shakyamuni's presence with a notable absence, such an empty throne or a riderless horse (fig. 4), or with a symbol, such as a spoked wheel.

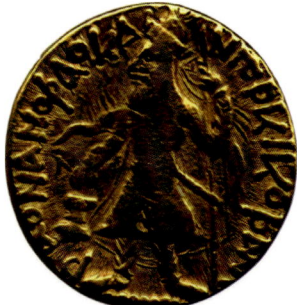
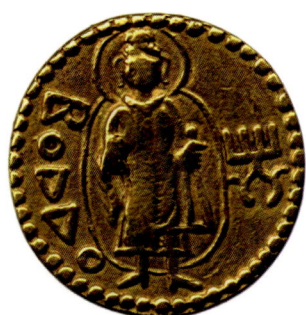

By the first century, South Asia had experienced a tremendous burst of artistic innovation, catalyzed by the arrival of kings with cultural ties to other regions. These rulers embraced portrayals of themselves and a wide variety of religious figures in sculpture and on coins (fig. 5). It is in this context that the first images of the Buddha appeared.

Although the style of these first-century images varies by region, they share a great deal of iconography. The Buddha is immediately recognizable by his simple monastic robes and distended earlobes, the result of the heavy golden earrings he wore before abandoning his life as a prince. His body also displays a range of unique marks (*lakshana*), among which the cranial bump (*ushnisha*) and the mark or swirl of hair between his brows (*urna*) are the most common. Artists also used postures and hand gestures (mudras) to indicate specific actions, such as teaching or meditating, or to reference particular events in his life.

While these iconographic traits are typical of Shakyamuni, the Historical Buddha, they are associated with other buddhas as well. In fact, all schools of Buddhism acknowledge, to varying degrees, the existence of multiple buddhas.

5
Gold coin with King Kanishka and the Buddha; South Asia, ca. 127–50; The British Museum IOC.289

BUDDHAS AND BODHISATTVAS
One concept that Buddhism borrowed from wider South Asian

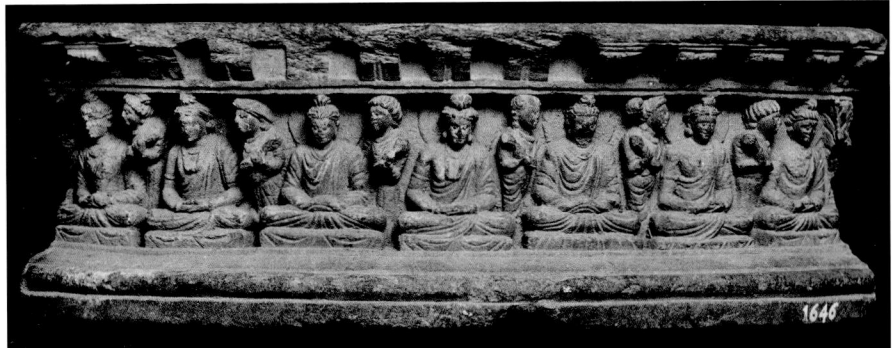

tradition is that the world passes through ages (kalpas) lasting billions of years. At the close of each age, the world ends, and after a time, a new one is formed. Early Buddhist thinkers postulated that buddhas had existed in past ages and revealed the dharma to their respective worlds (fig. 6). In this system, Shakyamuni did not technically invent his teachings; rather, he was the first in our age to rediscover timeless truths.

This concept of time also allows for the existence of a Future Buddha, who is waiting for the next age to arrive. This figure, known as Maitreya, generally is depicted in a pensive pose and richly adorned, residing in heaven until his next and final rebirth. Of the alternate forms of Maitreya, the most notable is a plump, plainly dressed, wish-granting sage. This so-called "laughing buddha" gained popularity in parts of East Asia and in the West.

Whereas buddhas typically wear simple monastic robes, we can easily distinguish bodhisattvas by their rich garments and jewels. Artists often include symbols or traits to identify particular bodhisattvas. For example, Avalokiteshvara, the bodhisattva of compassion, frequently holds a lotus blossom or medicine flask and wears a small buddha image in his headdress. Such attributes allow us to distinguish him from other important bodhisattvas such as Manjushri, Kshitigarbha, and Samantabhadra.

6
Row of past buddhas; Pakistan, ca. 100–299 CE; blue schist; American Institute of Indian Studies, Varanasi; 51572

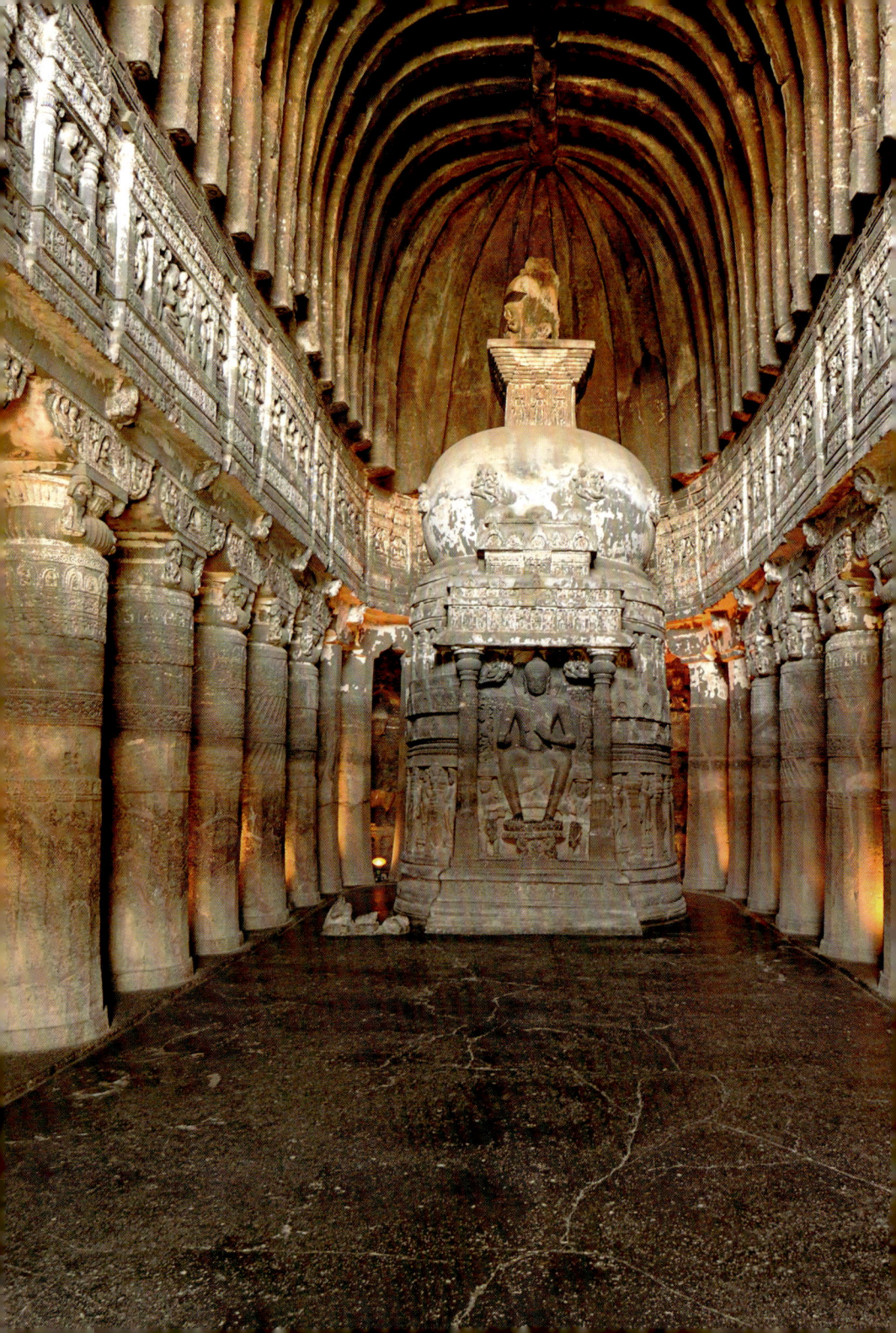

Although buddhas and bodhisattvas are the most prominent, Buddhism has other categories of advanced spiritual beings. For example, arhats are figures who have attained nirvana—or come close to it—based on a buddha's teaching. While Nikaya texts often praise such individuals, some Mahayana and Vajrayana traditions view the arhats as having fallen short of true buddhahood. At times, they are therefore depicted as eccentric or outlandish figures. Nevertheless, all Buddhist traditions acknowledge arhats as defenders of the dharma, particularly when no buddha is actively teaching in the world. Fortunately, arhats' spiritual attainments assure that they have the immensely long lifespans necessary to accomplish this task.

THE SPREAD OF BUDDHISM

It is hard to say if the visual arts helped Buddhism to spread or if the religion's growing popularity encouraged artistic patronage. Regardless, both dynamics contributed to Buddhism's success. From the third century BCE to the fifth century CE, kings and commoners in South Asia increasingly supported the faith. Eventually, however, competition from Hinduism—together with political, military, and religious pressures from within South Asia and abroad—led to a decline. By the twelfth century, Buddhism had all but disappeared from the Indian subcontinent.

Yet long before this recession, merchants and monks had carried Buddhism abroad along with the luxury goods of the Silk Road, the overland trade networks stretching across Central Asia. In the form of texts and images, the religion had journeyed from the ancient region of Gandhara to Afghanistan and into western China.

7
Cave 26; India, Maharashtra, Ajanta; courtesy Dey.sandip, via Wikimedia Commons

8
following pages
Seated Buddha with disciples and bodhisattvas; China, near Dunhuang, Mogao, Cave 45; Tang dynasty, 705–81; terra-cotta; Dunhuang Research Institute

In many oasis towns along these trade routes, monasteries were carved into the mountainsides that encircled the desert. This tradition of rock-cut architecture had begun in India (fig. 7) before reaching Central Asia and parts of China (fig. 8). Today, these caves, decorated with Buddhist murals, are among the earliest remaining examples of Buddhism's eastward expansion.

BUDDHISM IN CHINA

The exact date of Buddhism's arrival in China is difficult to pin down. Buddhist texts were being translated into Chinese as early as the mid-second century, whereas the earliest dated Chinese-made

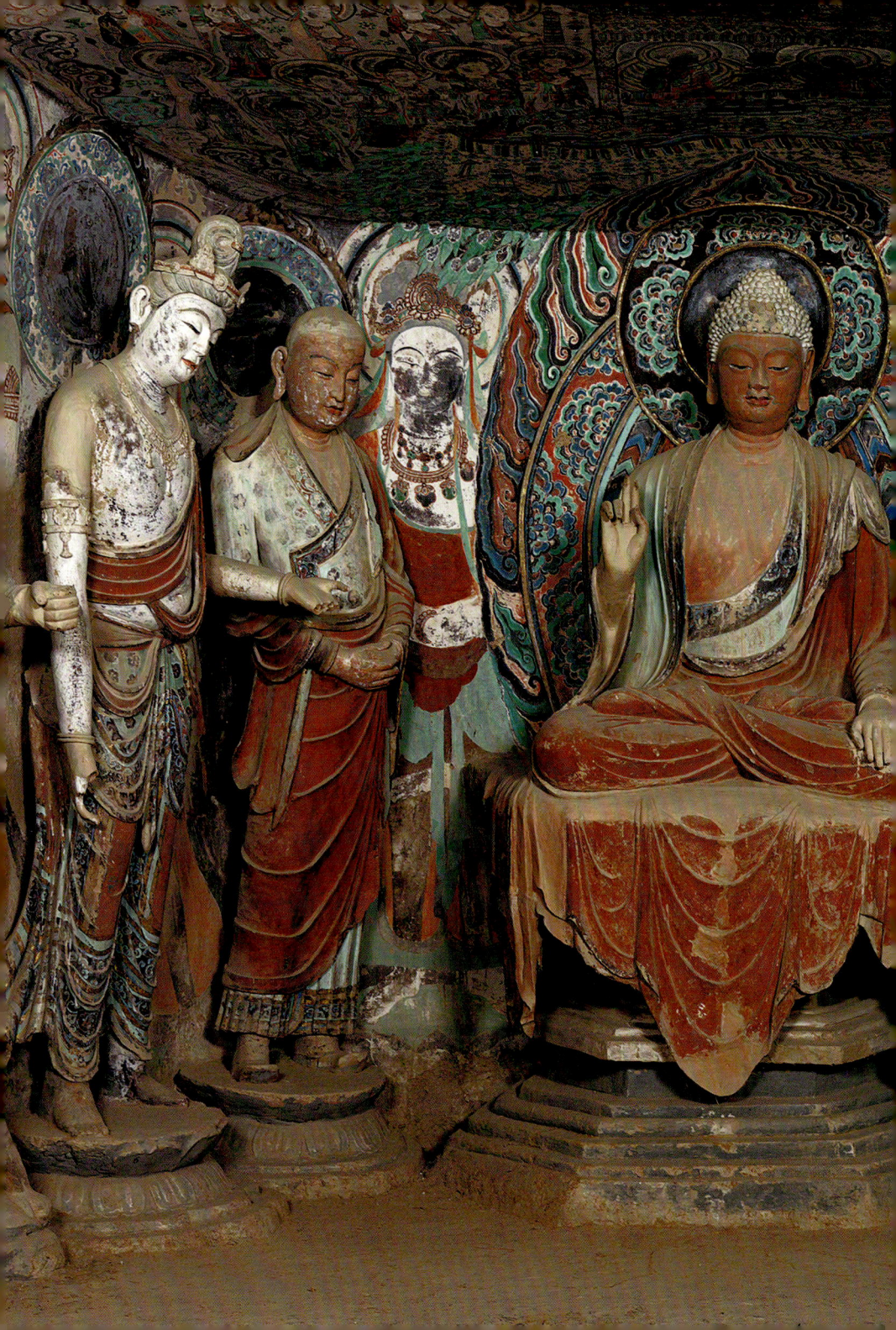

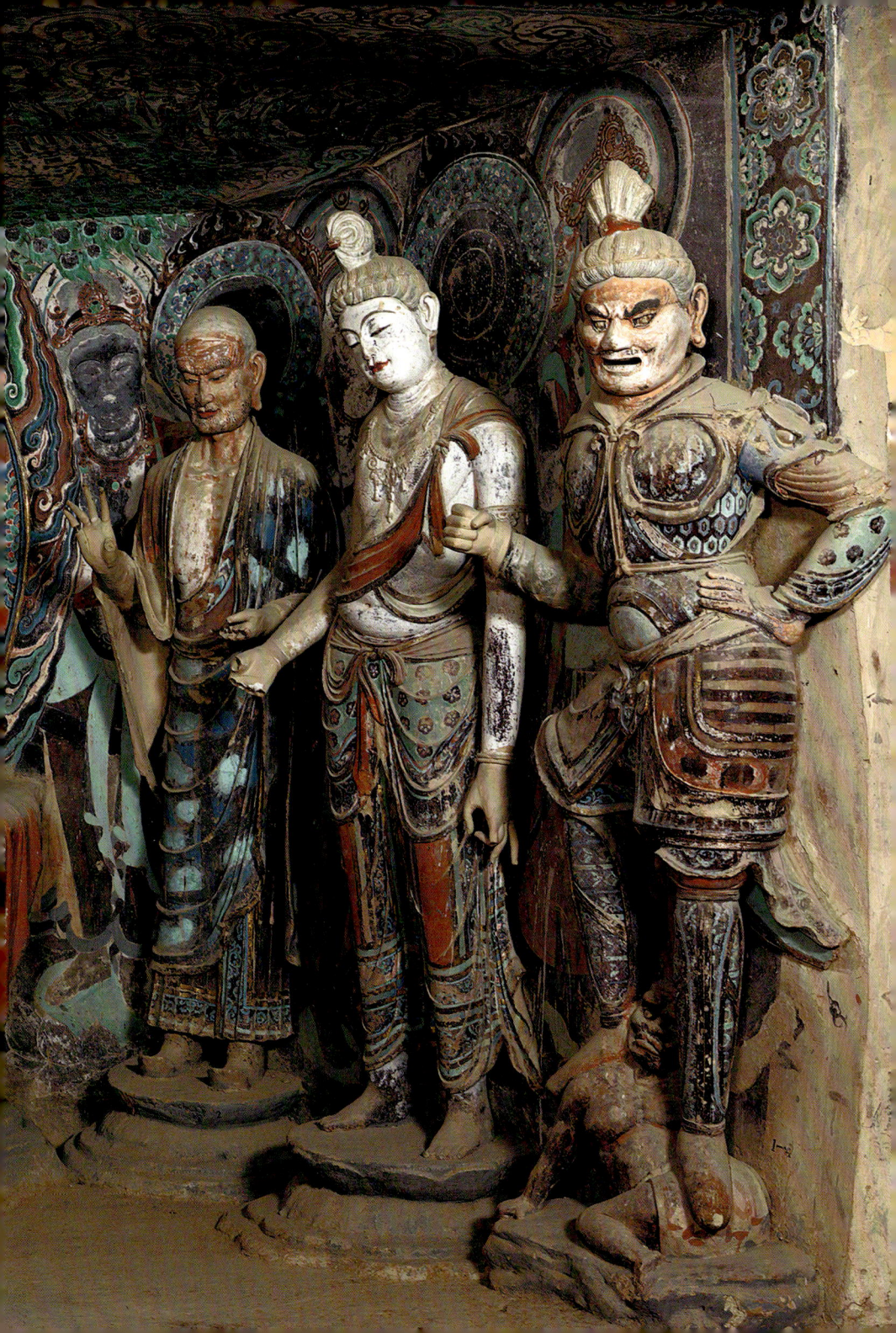

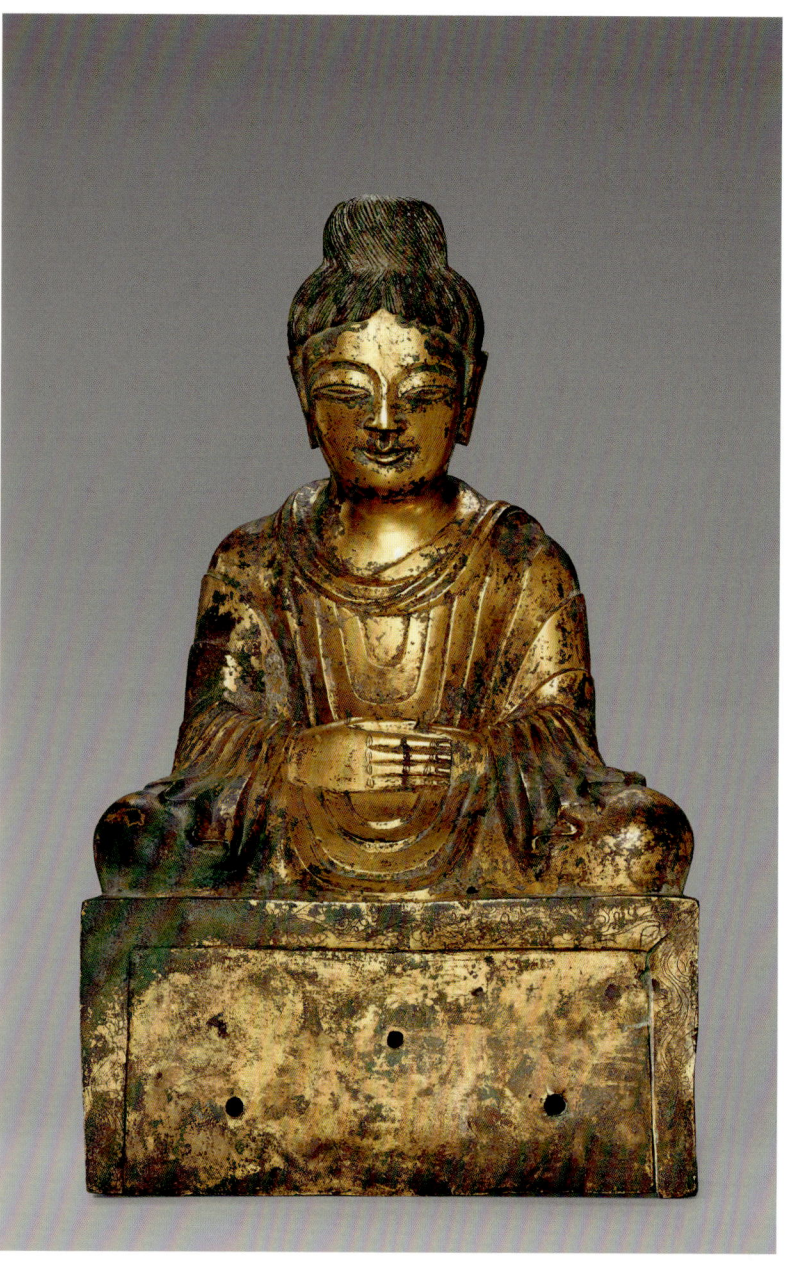

buddha image dates to 338 CE (fig. 9). The Northern Wei dynasty (386–535 CE) may have been the first regional state to legally recognize Buddhism as an official religion.

Buddhism developed a stronger hold in the area over time, but it had a tumultuous relationship with the Chinese courts. Imperial powers alternated between supporting and persecuting the faith. As a foreign import, some people viewed Buddhism and its emphasis on monasticism as corrupting and hostile to Confucian notions of family. This turbulent history influenced Chinese Buddhist art, which fluctuates between grandiose, public displays and modest objects intended for private use.

As sutras and other texts representing diverse South Asian Buddhist schools entered China, scholars struggled to reconcile their contradictory perspectives. The challenge gave rise to the Tiantai school, which ranked the Buddha's teachings based on the premise that audiences heard different sermons depending on their level of spiritual attainment. According to Tiantai scholars, the *Lotus Sutra*, which presents a sermon as a conversation between two buddhas, is at the apex.

Another school of Buddhism that emerged in China focused on Amitabha, the celestial buddha of infinite light. Followers of the Pure Land school of Mahayana Buddhism believe that Amitabha took a special vow to create the Western Paradise, or Pure Land (Sukhavati). Those who call upon Amitabha are reborn from lotuses into this heavenly realm, where they perpetually practice the dharma. Images of Amitabha and his palace-like monastery are especially popular in China, Korea, and Japan.

After death, devotees are guided to the Pure Land by Avalokiteshvara (in Chinese, Guanyin), the bodhisattva of compassion. Attentive to those in need, Avalokiteshvara holds a central place in many East Asian Buddhist traditions. Many of this bodhisattva's forms are male or ambiguously gendered. Over time, however, the female form of Guanyin, a healer and provider for children, became preeminent across East Asia.

Chan Buddhism existed alongside these devotional traditions in China, but it differs from them in significant ways. Chan, better

9
Seated Buddha; China, 338; gilded bronze; The Avery Brundage Collection, Asian Art Museum of San Francisco, B60B1034

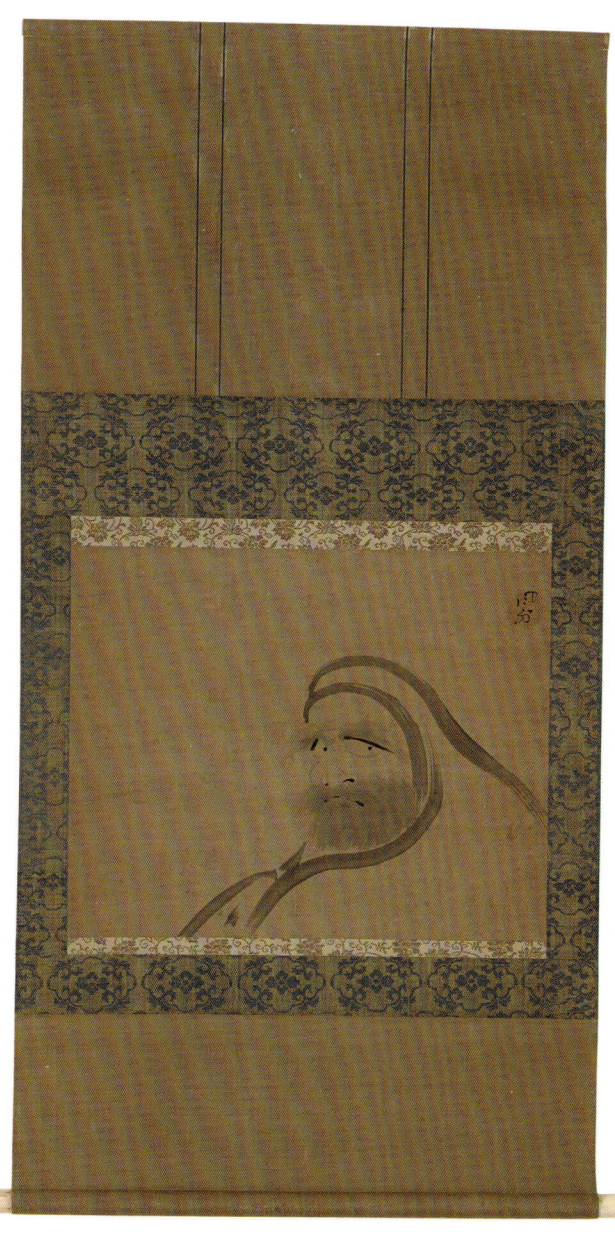

10
Bodhidharma; Japan, Edo period, 17th century; ink on paper; Gift of Peggy and Richard Danziger in honor of Kurt Gitter; Freer Gallery of Art, F1997.12

known in the West by its Japanese name, Zen, is attributable to the Indian master Bodhidharma (fig. 10). He traveled to China in the fifth or sixth century and shocked people with practices that greatly contrasted with mainstream Buddhism. Instead of relying on texts, he advocated a direct "mind to mind" transmission of the dharma, in which teachers, considered living buddhas, lead pupils to a moment of insight.

Although Chan practitioners venerate the school's patriarchs (leaders of the monastic lineage), they eschew traditional depictions of important figures in favor of monochrome, abbreviated, and often-unflattering portraits. Such images emphasize the patriarchs' mundane humanity. Their visual imperfections remind viewers of both the accessibility of enlightenment and the need for non-attachment, even to revered religious teachers.

BUDDHISM IN KOREA

Chinese monks introduced Buddhism to the Korean peninsula in the late fourth century CE. Within two hundred years, the faith was flourishing under court patronage that lasted nearly a millennium. Many of the most remarkable examples of Korean Buddhist art are the result of this elite support. Though some were inspired by Chinese subjects and compositions, these works are distinctly Korean achievements.

The Future Buddha Maitreya (in Korean, Mireuk), who pensively waits to be reborn as a buddha, quickly became a popular subject in Korean art (fig. 11). Images of the Future Buddha gathered new meaning in the sixth and seventh centuries with the rise of social movements that identified Maitreya's heaven, Tushita, as a model for social harmony and an idealized state. Such images reveal the growing connections between Buddhism and political power in Korea.

The Korean imperial court and its powerful officials often sponsored elaborate temple complexes and monasteries. In the eleventh century, the Goryeo court turned its attention and wealth to a new art form: lavishly decorated woodblock-printed editions of Buddhist texts. Requiring a massive commitment of time and money, these compilations were considered valuable religious resources that could protect the state from misfortune. They still serve as important resources for both devotees and historians.

BUDDHISM IN JAPAN

Although merchants and travelers had already brought Buddhism into Japan, in the mid-sixth century it arrived formally as an official "gift" from a Korean kingdom. Under the nurturing guidance of the powerful Soga clan, Buddhism developed close ties to the Japanese state. Over time, the connections between monastery and palace became very close, and the imperial family initiated large-scale Buddhist projects.

However, Buddhist influence on the court eventually attracted criticism. When the imperial capital was relocated, monasteries were outlawed within the capital city of Heiankyo (modern Kyoto). Still, support flourished for the Shingon (a Vajranaya sect) and Tendai (the Japanese form of Tiantai) schools, which built monasteries in the hills outside the city.

Fortunes changed again in the late twelfth century, when the shogunate, or military government, rose to power. The shogunate's martial ideals matched well with Zen Buddhism, the Japanese version of China's Chan Buddhism, which emphasizes austerity and self-control. Zen monasteries attained new levels of support and popularity. The school's focus on human effort also inspired artists to represent traditional Buddhist subjects, such as teachers and guardian deities, with elevated drama and intensity.

Just as Buddhism had appropriated ideas from the indigenous religions of India and China, it also drew on Japanese concepts, which inspired innovative artwork. For centuries, some Japanese devotees believed that Buddhist deities and certain native gods were manifestations of one another. In 1868, however, the Meiji court, seeking to separate Buddhism from indigenous faiths, challenged and ultimately outlawed this coexistence. This decision and a later one forbidding the government from favoring any religion profoundly impacted Buddhism's connections to the state. Despite these setbacks, Buddhism retains a prominent role in Japanese society.

BUDDHISM IN SOUTHEAST ASIA

Texts tell us that Buddhism traveled to parts of Southeast Asia in the third century BCE. This is certainly possible given the region's

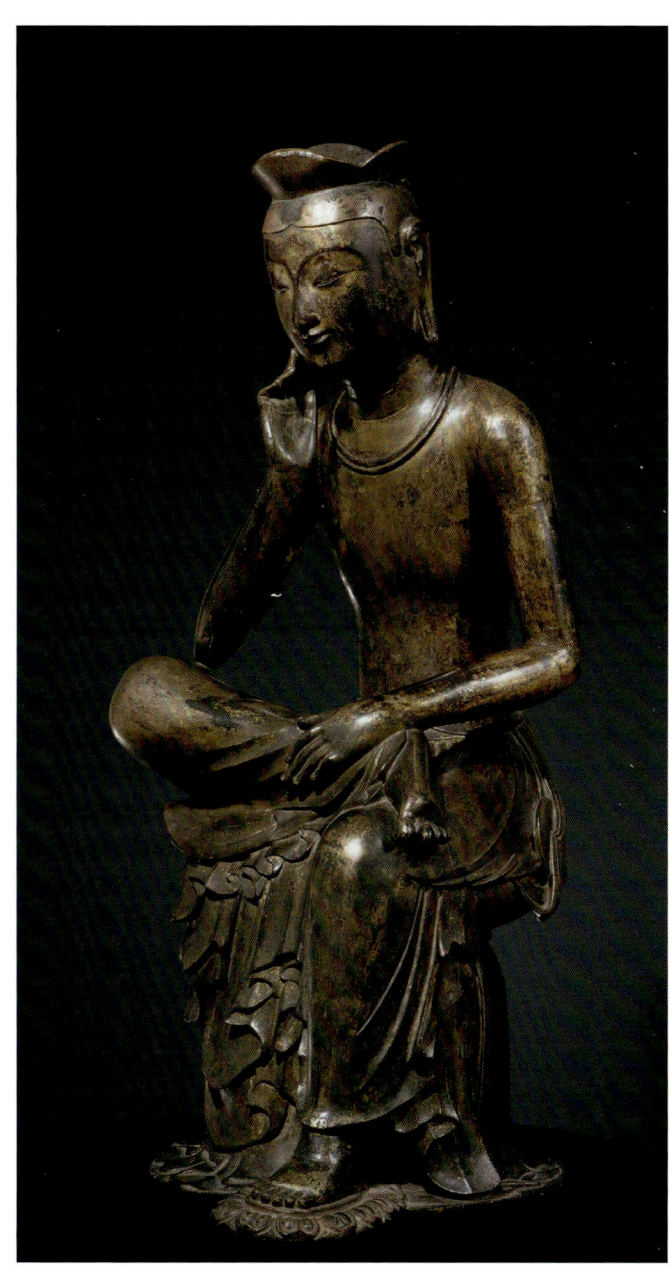

11
Pensive Bodhisattva;
Korea, Three Kingdoms
Period; gilt bronze;
National Museum
of Korea, Bongwan
-002789-000

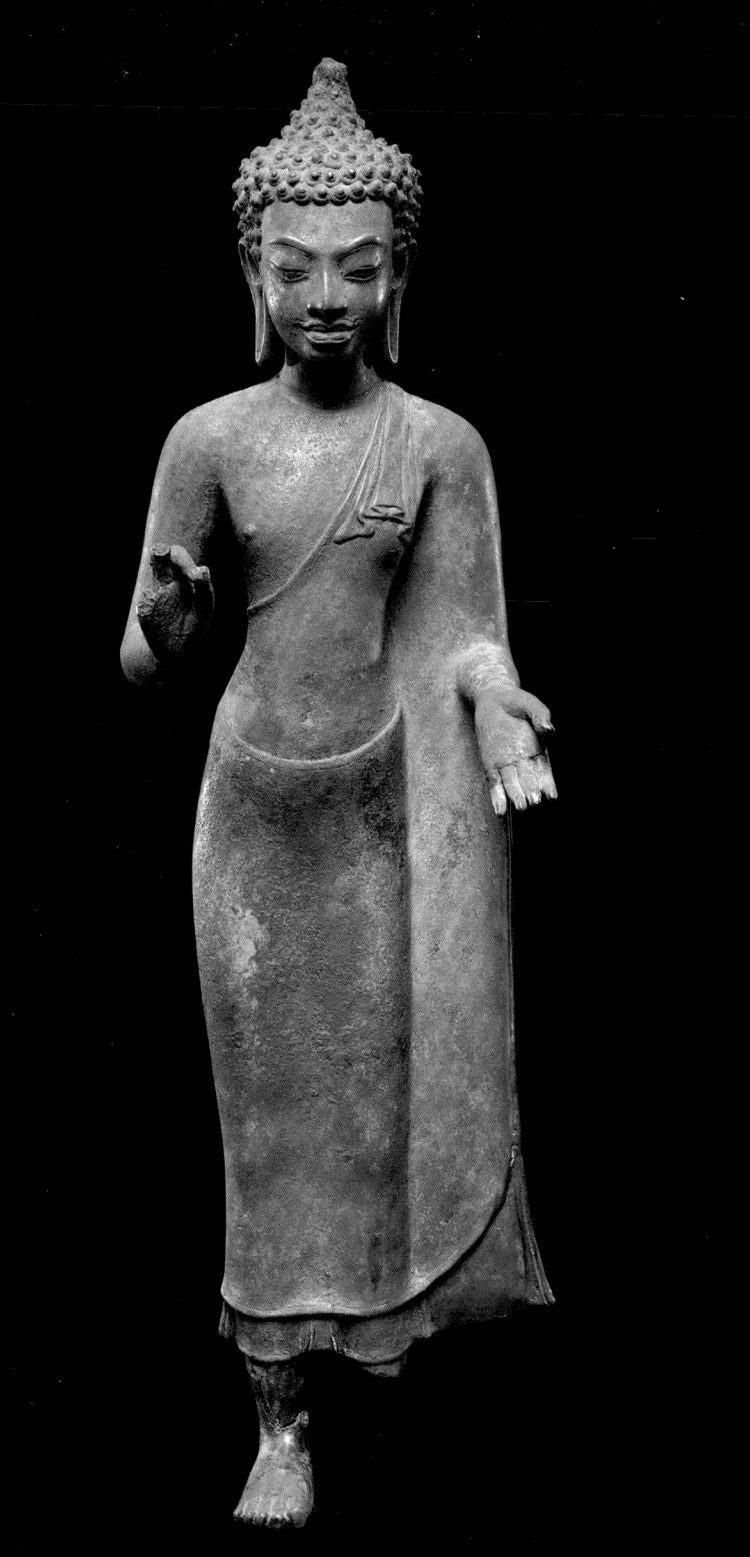

proximity to the Buddha's homeland. The earliest artistic evidence of Buddhism in Southeast Asia, however, dates to much later: the sixth century CE, when Buddhist artworks first appeared in the Malay Peninsula and in what is now central Thailand. These small images appear to be based on portable bronze prototypes that seafaring Indian traders carried across the Indian Ocean.

Buddhism gained regional prominence in the royal courts of such places as Ayutthaya in Thailand (fig. 12), Angkor in Cambodia, and Srivijaya in Indonesia. The faith's fortunes at these courts rose and fell over the centuries according to royal preferences. Eventually, a more durable and consistent dedication to the Buddha's teachings developed and thrived among non-elite Southeast Asian communities.

BUDDHISM IN THE HIMALAYAS

Although the Himalayas also are located near the Buddha's birthplace, the region's challenging topography led Buddhism on a circuitous journey to the Tibetan plateau. The initial wave of Buddhism did not arrive until the seventh century. By that time, later Vajrayana schools predominated in India, and these esoteric traditions took root in Tibet.

Although the ninth-century collapse of the Tibetan empire caused Buddhism to lose imperial backing, the tradition survived and even thrived on the periphery. New teachings from India caused a second dissemination of Buddhism in Tibet beginning in the eleventh century. Over time, Tibetan Buddhism developed four lineages or schools: Nyingma, Sakya, Kagyu, and Geluk. The oldest, Nyingma, is linked to the eighth-century arrival of the great Indian teacher Padmasambhava. But Geluk, which originated in the fifteenth century, became the most politically powerful due to the support of the Mongol khans, who granted a Geluk leader regional authority and the title of Dalai Lama (fig. 13).

THE COLLECTION

The preceding paragraphs have offered a brief overview of the rich diversity and complexity of Buddhism and its art. The discussions that accompany the objects in this volume will provide more specific insights. We hope this guidebook enables you to explore the history of Buddhism and to engage with the ideas that have inspired, and continue to inspire, Buddhist art across the globe.

12
Buddha Preaching; central or northeastern Thailand, 8th–early 9th century; silver alloy, Gift of Enid A. Haupt; The Metropolitan Museum of Art, 1993.387.6

13
following pages
Potala Palace; Tibet Autonomous Region, Lhasa; courtesy Coolmanjackey, via Wikimedia Commons

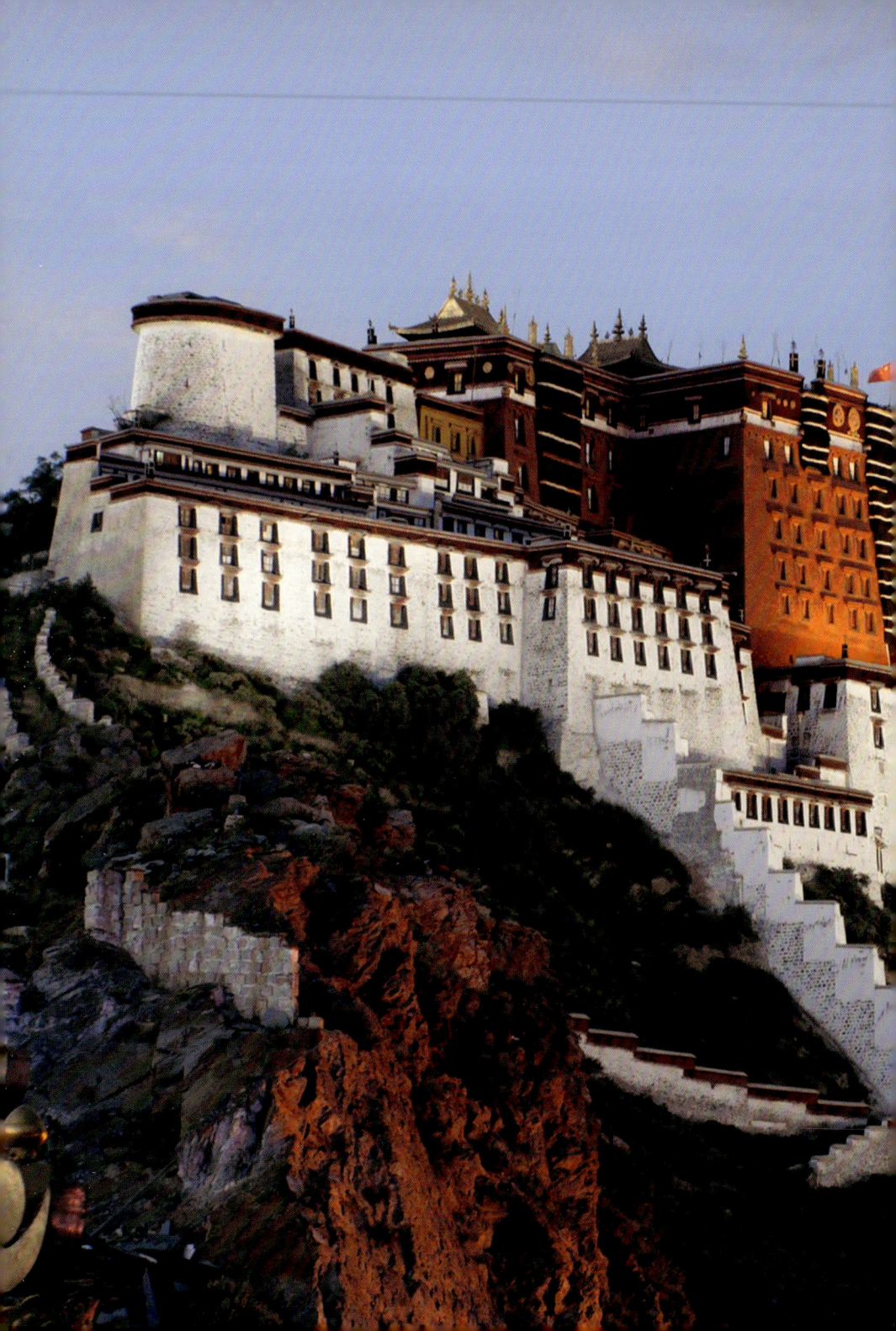

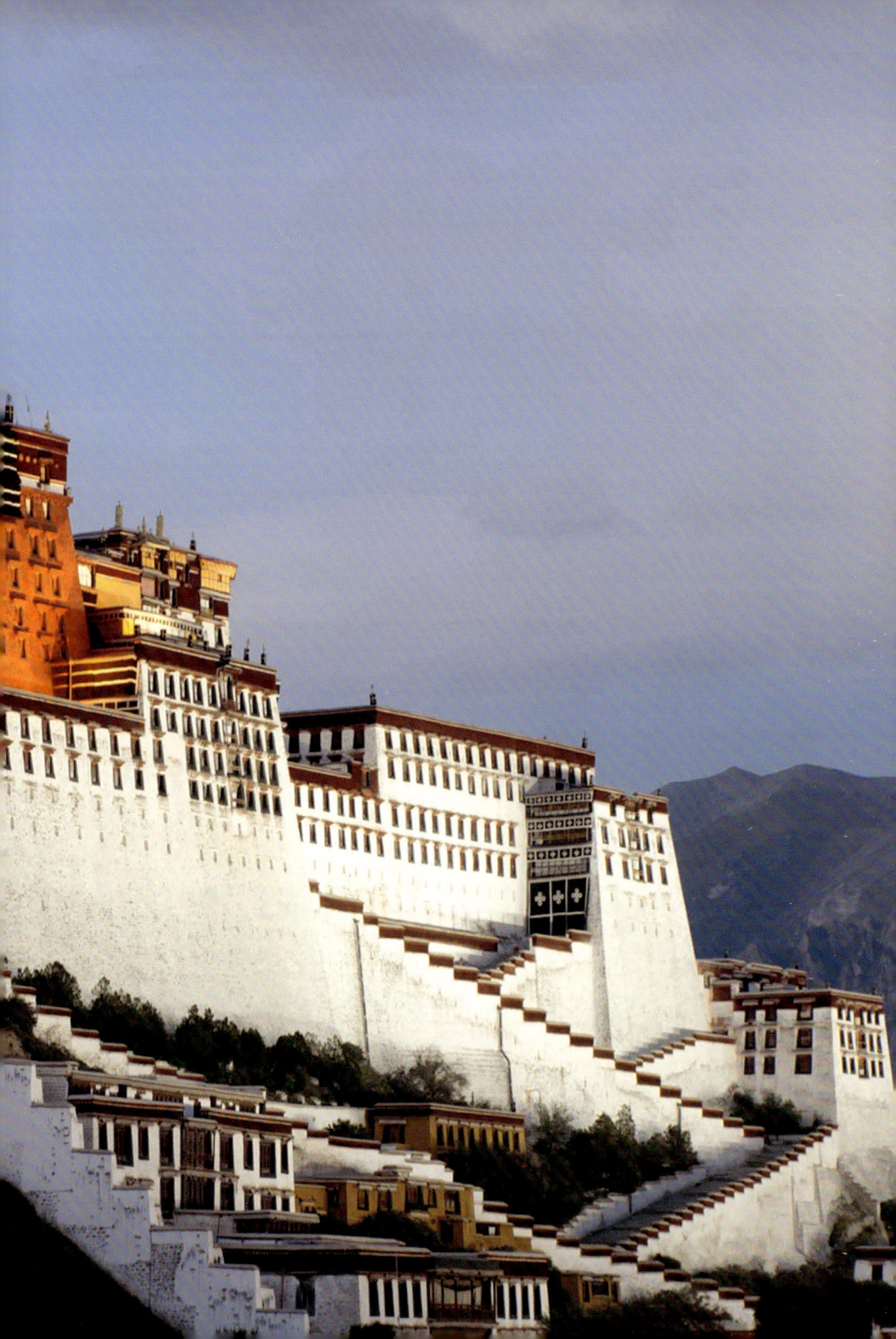

MAP

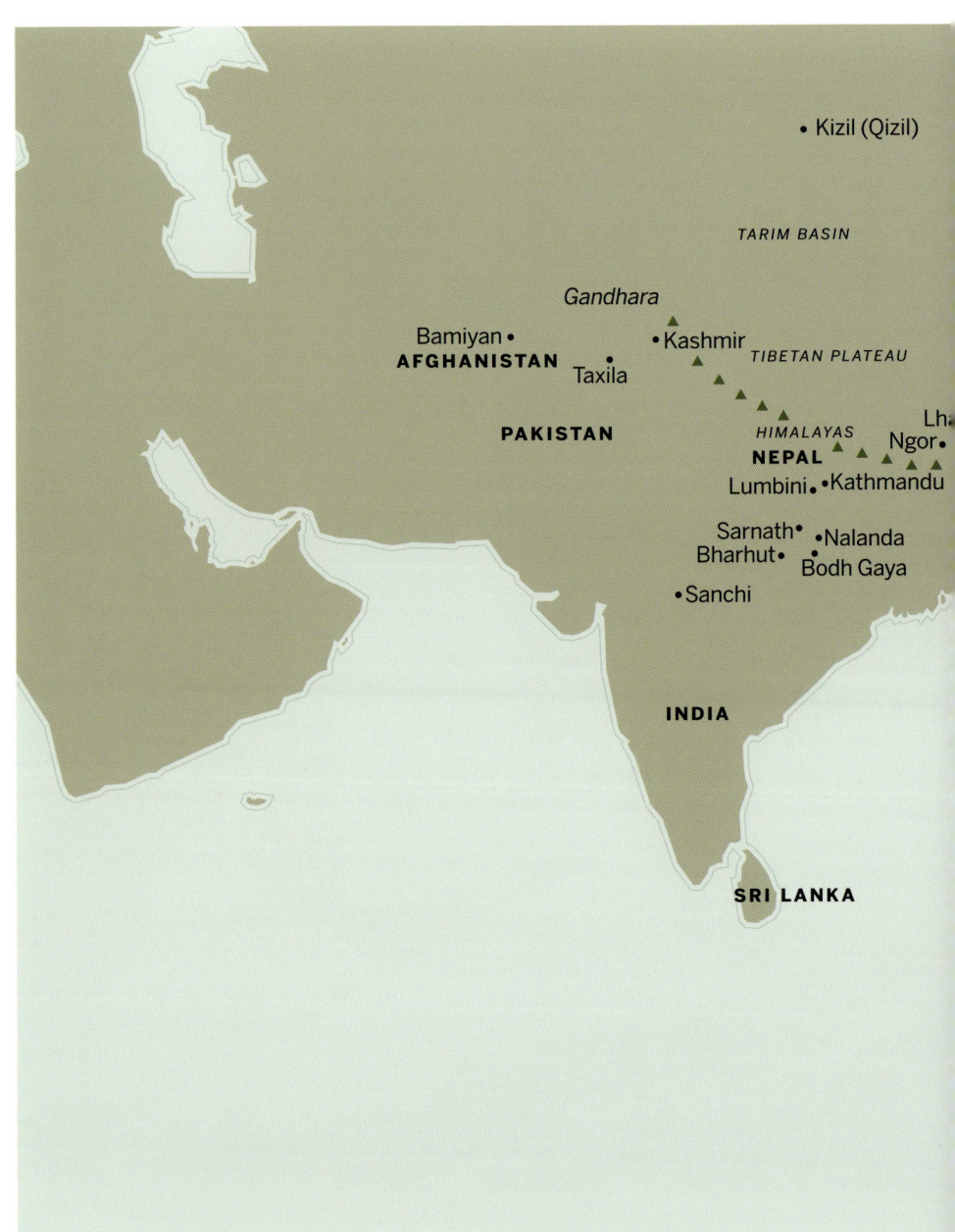

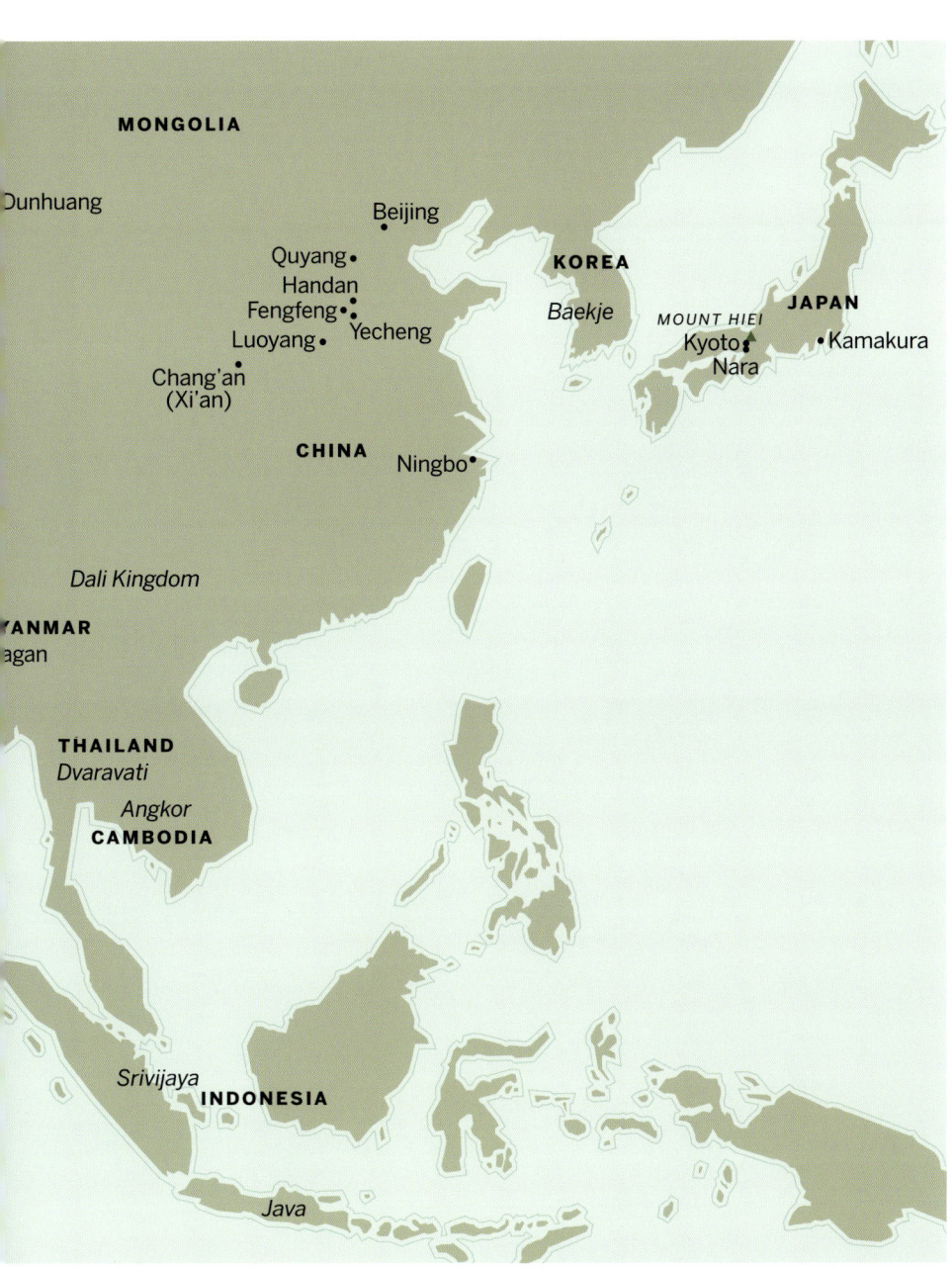

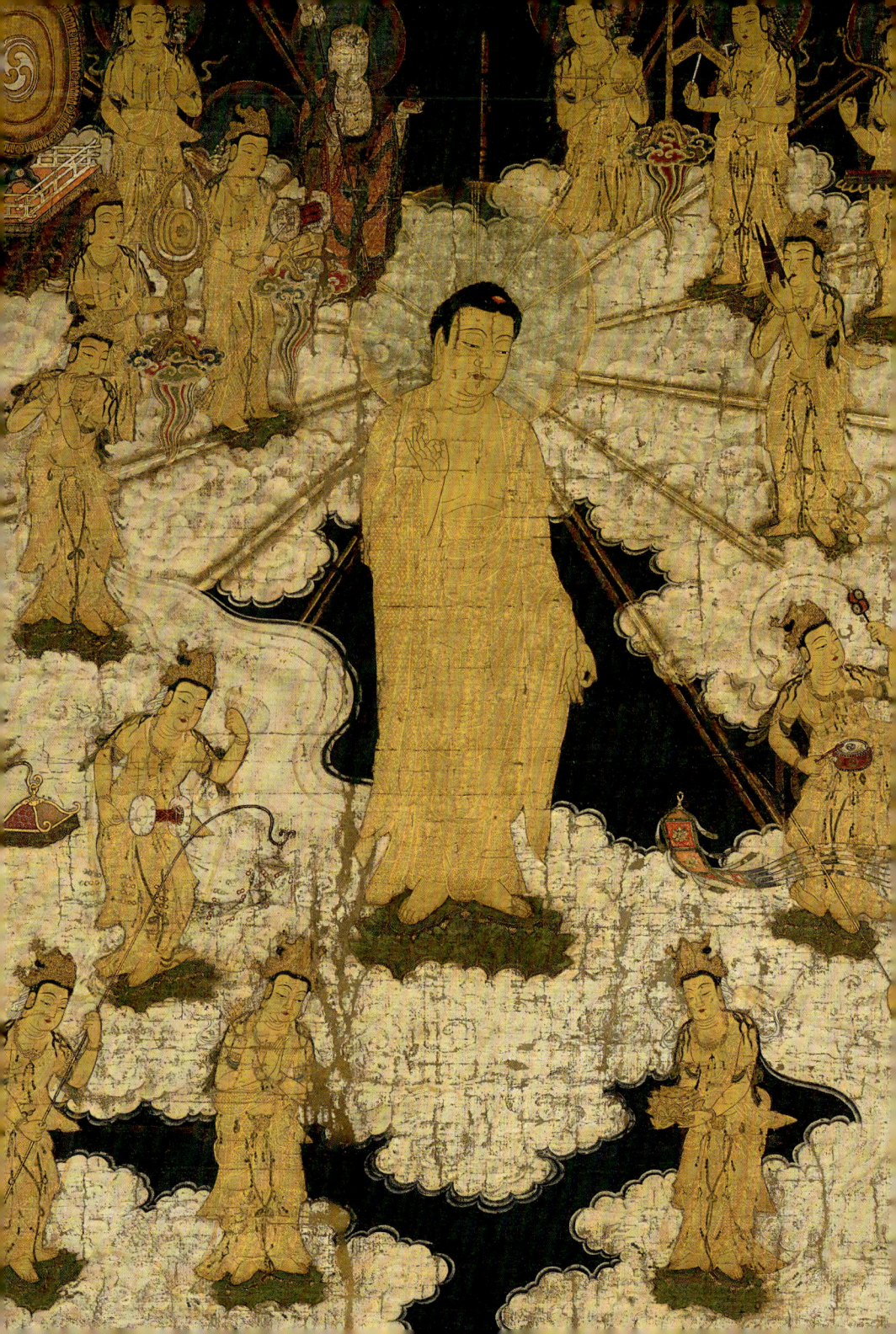

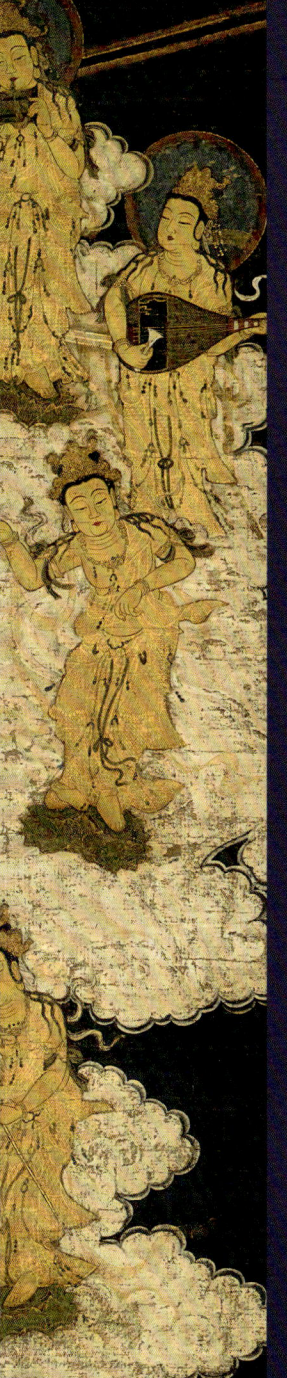

Buddhas

After abandoning both his opulent palace life and the harsh austerities he had practiced among the hermits, Shakyamuni sat under a tree with the unshakable intention of acquiring insight. He found his Middle Way, a path between excess and self-punishment, and attained a profound realization about the world and the causes of suffering. Through this enlightenment, he earned the designation of Buddha, or "Awakened One."

According to most Buddhist traditions, Shakyamuni, the Historical Buddha, reenacted a process that has occurred and will continue to occur countless times. He is one of many past buddhas who have reintroduced the dharma to our world after it had been forgotten. Even now, Maitreya, the Future Buddha, waits in heaven for his next lifetime and his chance to reveal the dharma.

Unlike Nikaya schools, which insist only one buddha may be active in the world at a time, Mahayana thinkers allow for many. Buddhahood therefore became the idealized goal for all beings, who can be aided on their paths by those who have already become buddhas.

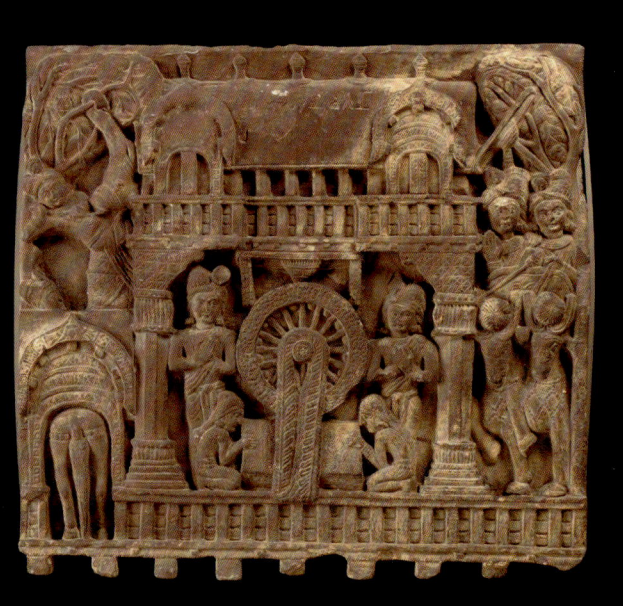

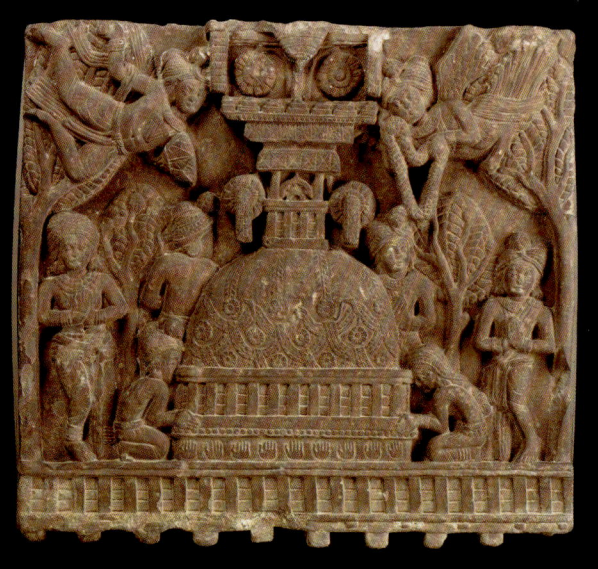

Worship at a Stupa and Worship of the Buddha
India, state of Madhya Pradesh, Bharhut, Shunga dynasty,
early 2nd century BCE
Sandstone, 48 × 52.8 × 8.9 cm; 47.5 × 51.9 × 8 cm
Purchase, Freer Gallery of Art, F1932.25–26

After the passing of the Buddha Shakyamuni (circa 400 BCE), his followers faced an immense challenge. How could the teachings be conveyed without the charismatic presence of the great sage?

Monks divided and ritually buried the Historical Buddha's relics (ashes and belongings) in hemispherical mounds known as stupas. Because relics retain the Buddha's sacred power, stupas gained importance as pilgrimage centers. Gradually glorified through donations from nuns, monks, and laypeople, stupas evolved from earthen domes circled by wooden fences to become, by the first century CE, India's first freestanding stone monuments.

The earliest extant Buddhist imagery appears on stupa gateways and fence railings such as this one. Carved in warm, red sandstone, this two-sided panel features what may be the oldest representations of the Buddha in a US museum. For approximately four hundred years after the Historical Buddha's death, artists refrained from creating icons that depicted his body. Instead, they conveyed the Buddha's presence through depictions of stupas, as well as thrones he had sat on, trees under which he had meditated, and paths on which he had walked.

On one side of this panel (bottom left), the Buddha, represented by a flower-garlanded stupa, is venerated by worshippers and celestial beings who swoop down from the sky. On the other, the Buddha takes the form of a flower-strewn throne and an eight-spoked wheel, adorned with a massive garland. A couple is depicted twice as they circle the shrine to honor him. The inscription, which appears at the top of the panel on the shrine's roof, somewhat cryptically states that the panel was a gift and "made by himself," indicating that the donor was perhaps an artist.

DD

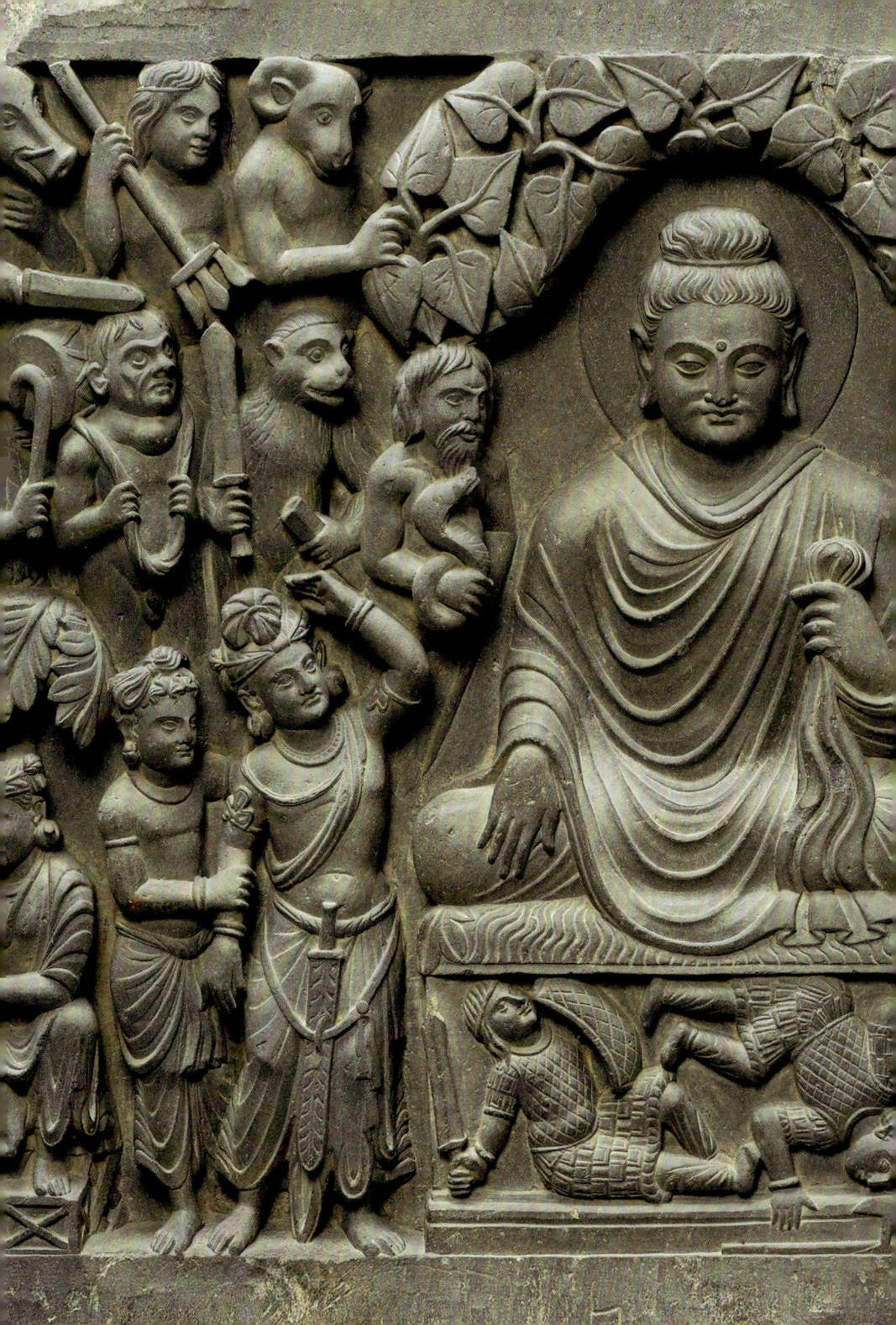

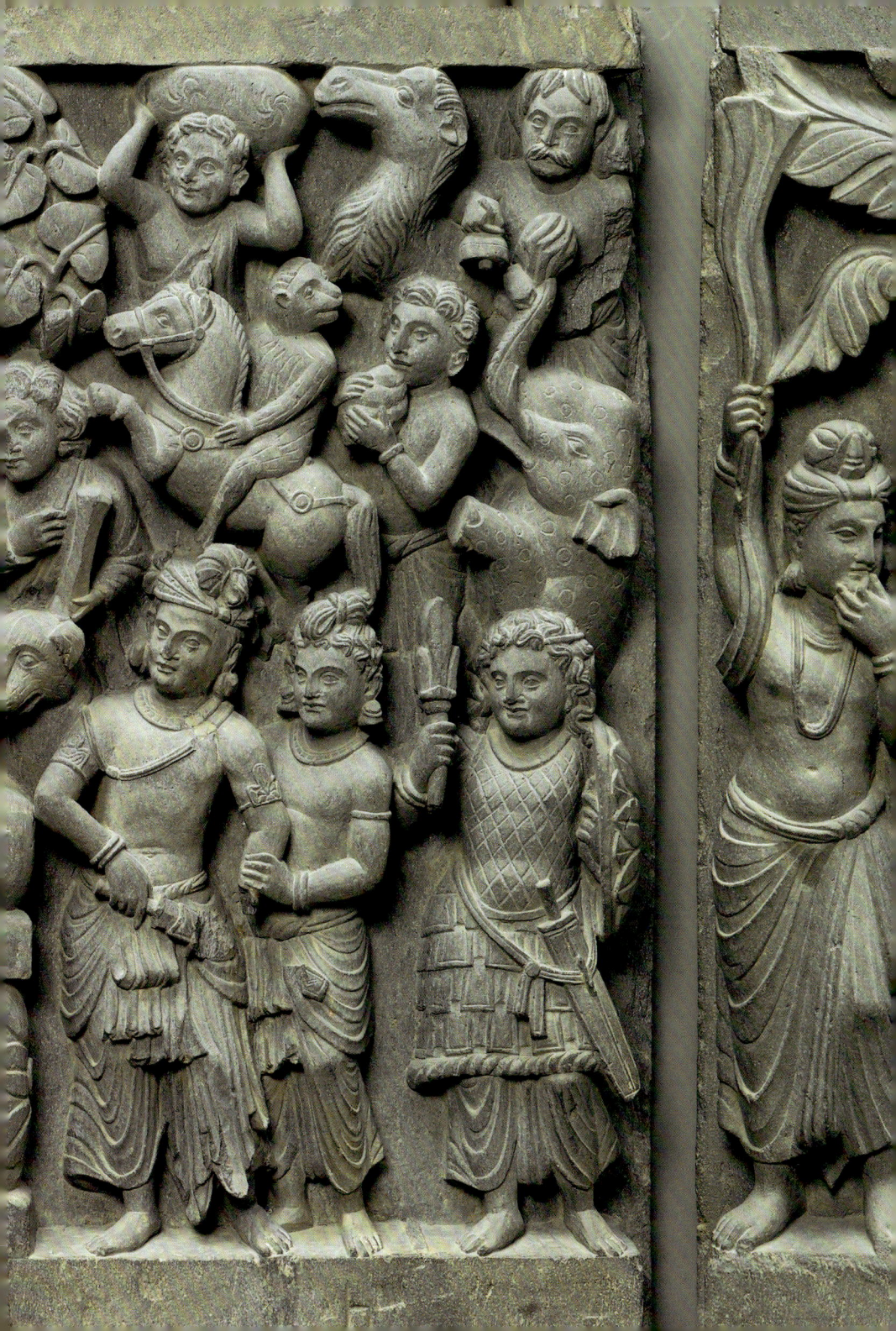

Four great events from the life of Buddha Shakyamuni
Ancient Gandhara (modern Pakistan/Afghanistan),
Kushan dynasty, late 2nd–early 3rd century CE
Schist
67 × 289.8 × 9.8 cm
Purchase, Freer Gallery of Art, F1949.9.a–d

In the third century, Gandhara was a cosmopolitan region with cultural and economic ties to India, western Asia, and the Hellenistic world. To represent stories of the Buddha's life, Gandharan artists combined the visual vocabulary of Greco-Roman art with Indian Buddhist concepts and iconography. Commissioned for a monumental stupa, these panels are among the earliest representations of the four central events in the life of the Historical Buddha.

The sequence begins at right as the baby Buddha miraculously emerges from the side of his mother, Queen Maya. Dressed and coiffed like a Roman matron, she stands clasping a tree branch in the posture of an Indian nature spirit.

The second relief represents the great moment of awakening. After meditating for forty days beneath a tree, the Buddha approaches

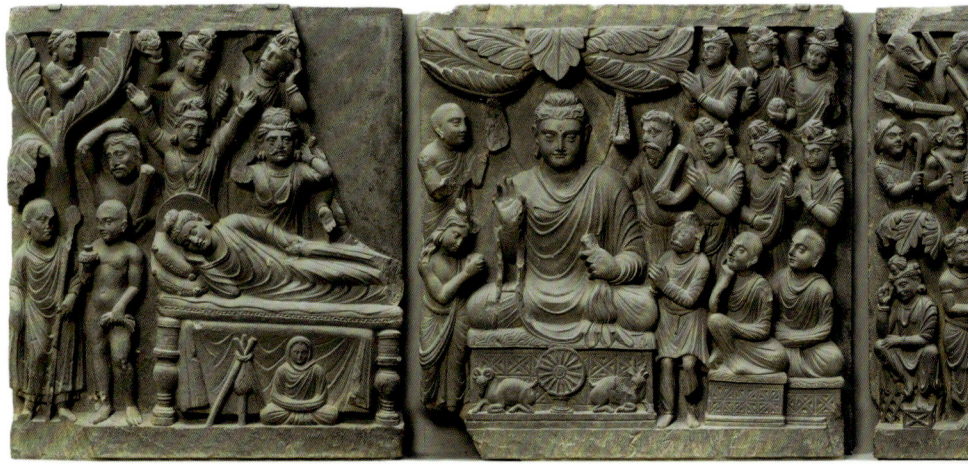

infinite awareness despite the violent efforts of Mara, the god of death and desire. His rowdy army of misshapen demons (including one with a goiter and several with animal heads) offset the Buddha's stately calm. The Buddha lowers his right hand in the earth-touching gesture to prove his spiritual accomplishment to his enemies.

In the third panel, the Buddha raises one hand in a gesture of reassurance as he offers his first sermon to ascetics and deities. The wheel and animals on his throne represent, respectively, his teachings and the sermon's location in the deer park at Sarnath. His wavy hair and naturalistically draped robes are adapted from Greco-Roman art.

At the age of eighty, the Buddha lay down between two trees and abandoned his physical body. Only one tree is visible here; the second was depicted on the now-missing right-hand section. By showing the Buddha lying on his side, artists distinguished his blissful entry into final nirvana, such as the one depicted on page 63, from that of an ordinary death.

DD

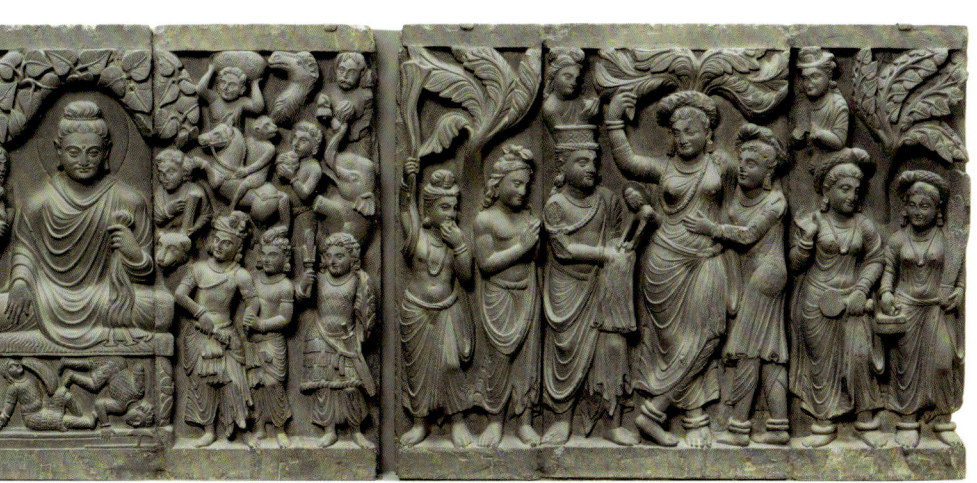

Stele with the Thousand-Buddha motif
China, probably Shanxi Province, Northern Wei dynasty,
ca. 515–25, probably 521
Sandstone with traces of four layers or more of polychrome pigment
195.5 × 76.2 × 38.1 cm
Gift of Marietta Lutze Sackler, Arthur M. Sackler Gallery, S1991.157

The Buddha Shakyamuni, flanked by bodhisattvas, appears in a dragon-topped niche near the base of the two main faces of this stele, or stone monument. Directly above him on both sides, Maitreya, represented as a bodhisattva, sits in a slightly smaller niche. A multitude of small buddha images on all four sides of the stele completes the imagery. A long, partially missing inscription along the bottom edge of the monument expresses the donors' wish for peace and provides a date that probably corresponds to 521, but erosion has made it difficult to read.

Known as the Thousand Buddhas, the small images represent buddhas of all ages and universes, who simultaneously inhabit innumerable realms of the cosmos. Mahayana Buddhist practitioners, who believe all beings have the potential to attain buddhahood, used the motif to visualize buddhahood's omnipresence. They also recited the buddhas' names as a tool for achieving enlightenment. Buddhist believers might have encountered this stele at a well-traveled crossroads or in a temple compound. The pigments on its surface, now dulled and mostly lost, would have attracted attention.

The format of the stele, defined as a large carved or inscribed stone slab erected for a commemorative purpose, has a long history in China that predates and extends beyond Buddhism. The stele was appropriated as an expression of Buddhist devotion for a relatively brief interlude, mainly during the sixth century, in north China. In particular, the Northern Wei sovereigns embraced Buddhism's universal ideology and charitable teachings in a strategy to unite the complex, multiethnic society they ruled during this tumultuous time.

JS

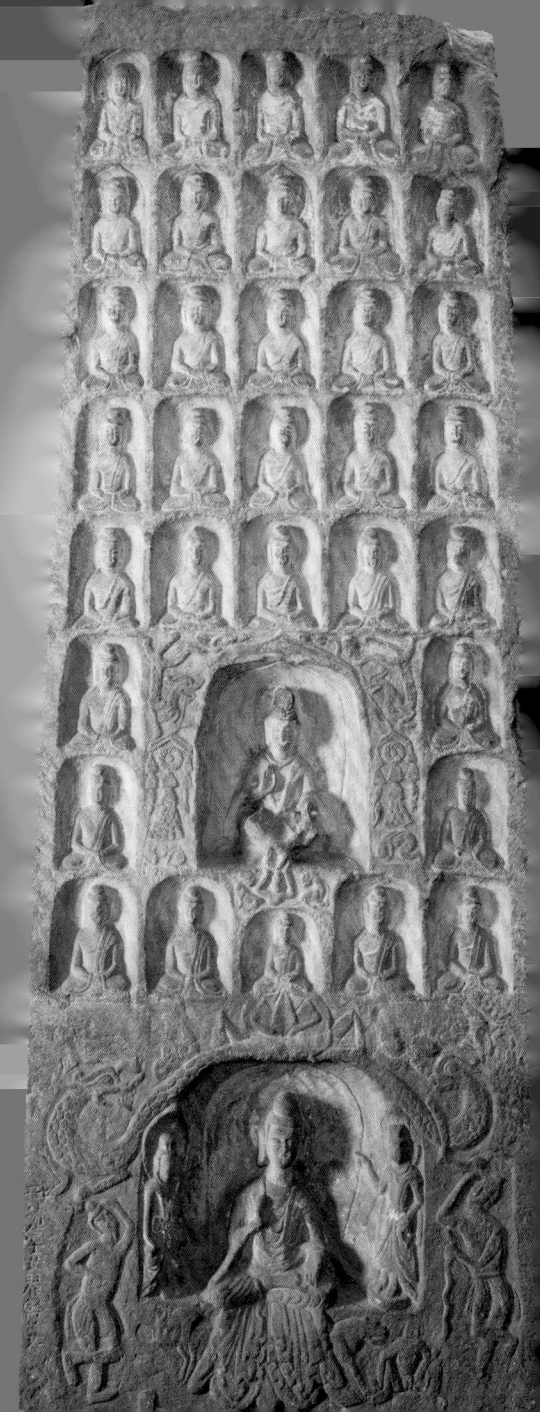

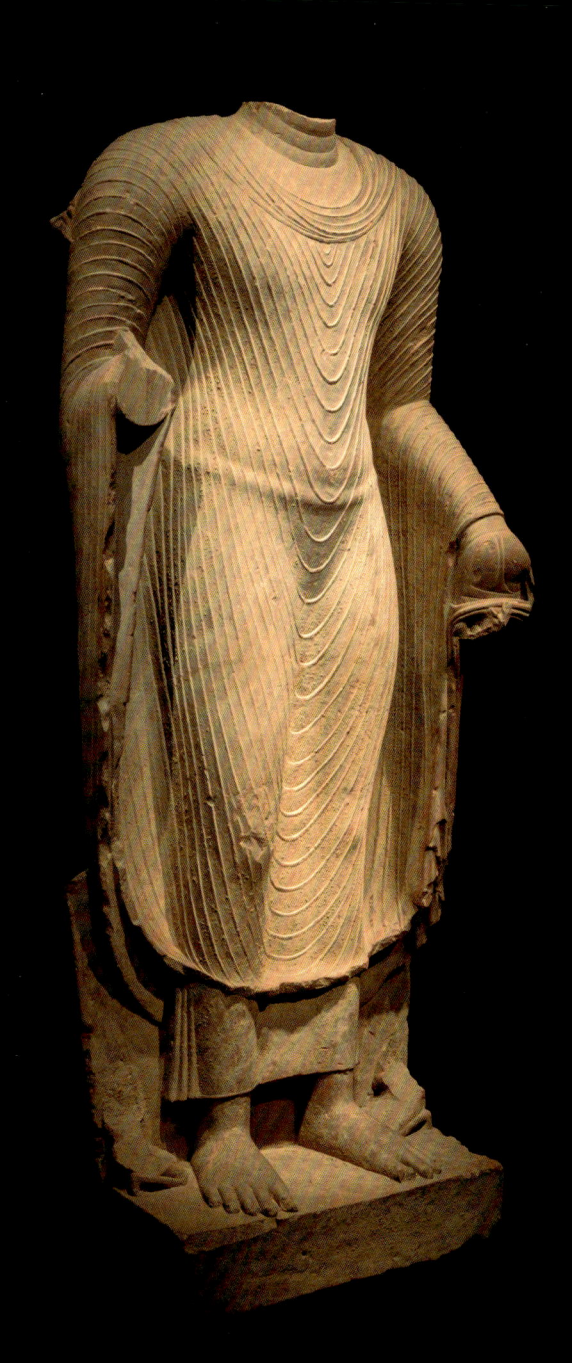

Standing Buddha

India, Mathura, Gupta dynasty, 320–485
Red sikri sandstone
134.6 x 58.4 x 30.4 cm
Purchase, Freer Gallery of Art, F1994.17

Made in the city of Mathura, this Buddha wears over both shoulders his monastic robes, which convey that he has renounced the worldly desires that lead inevitably to sorrow. Radiating string folds, an invention of Mathura's sculpture workshops, emphasize the body by contouring its volumes. The whisper-thin fabric of the Buddha's robe makes visible the traditional marks (*lakshana*) of the great sage's spiritual perfection. Attained over countless ethical lifetimes, these marks include his lion-like chest, retracted male organ, and powerful thighs. We also can see the waistband of a monastic undergarment and a slight bend in one knee—a sign that the Buddha always began walking auspicious (right) foot first.

The *Lalitavistara*, a narrative of the life of the Buddha created at about the same time as this sculpture, relates that the great sage visited Mathura, a "prosperous, large, and beneficial [city] where alms are easily obtainable." Fifty miles south of Delhi, Mathura lay at the nexus of trade routes connecting Taxila (Pakistan), the Buddhist heartland in Bihar, and central and southern India. Mathura's wealth, connectivity, and high-quality sandstone made it a center for Buddhist patronage and a source for sculptures that were exported to sites across northern India.

With its pitch-perfect proportions and decorative restraint, the Mathura-style buddha served as a model for the portable bronzes of Bihar and Bengal. These subsequently became archetypes for icons in China (p. 38) and Southeast Asia (p. 52).

DD

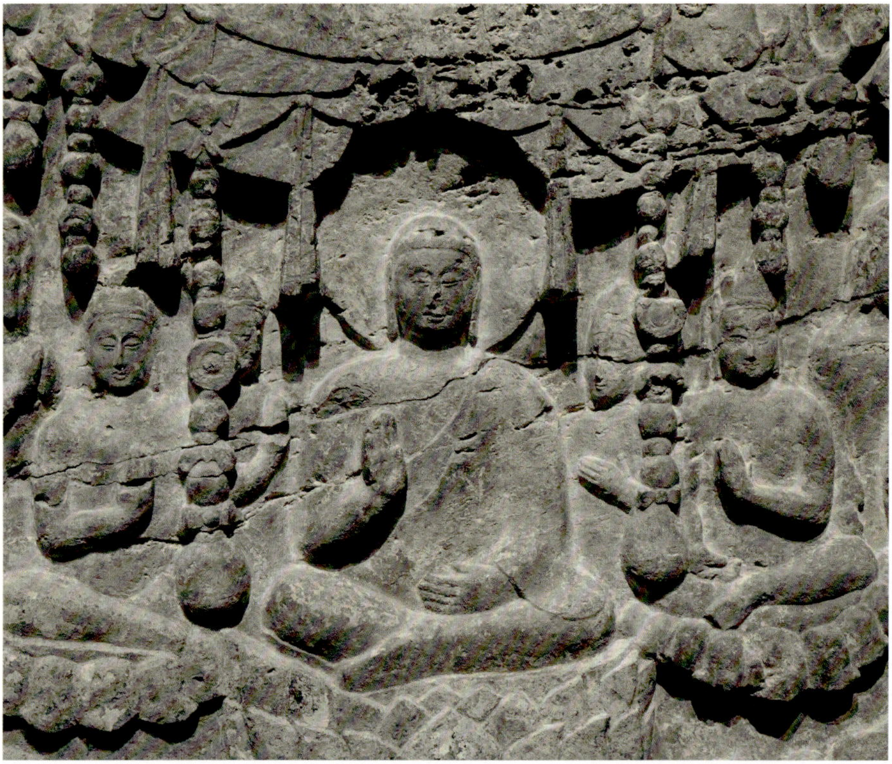

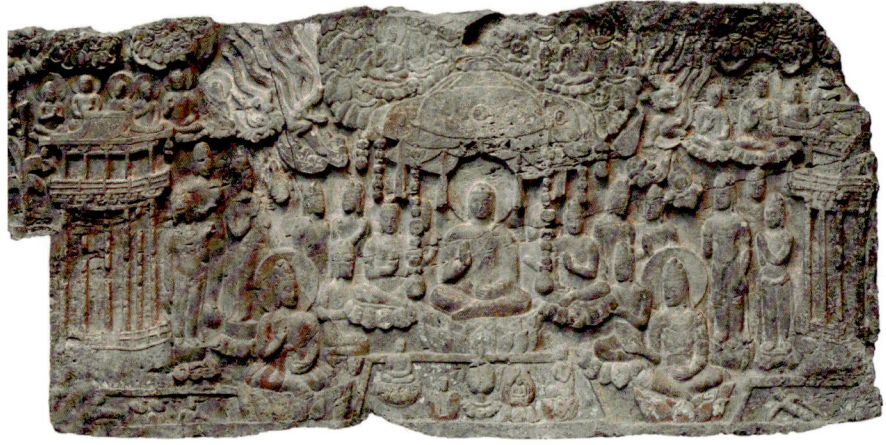

Western Paradise of Buddha Amitabha (Amituo)
China, Hebei Province, Fengfeng, southern Xiangtangshan cave temples, Cave 2
Northern Qi dynasty, 550–77
Limestone with traces of pigment
159.3 × 334.5 cm
Purchase, Freer Gallery of Art, F1921.2

Believed to be one of the earliest surviving depictions of a Buddhist paradise, this sixth-century relief once appeared above the interior entrance to a Chinese Buddhist cave. Originally painted with striking mineral pigments and gold, it would have been the last thing a worshipper saw before leaving the sacred space.

This monumental limestone carving depicts a heavenly realm brimming with Buddhist deities. Framed by towering pagodas, the roughly symmetrical composition emphasizes the central figures—in particular, Buddha Amitabha (in Chinese, Amituo), who raises his right hand in a gesture of reassurance. He sits on a large lotus blossom behind a square pool, alongside which are his two chief attendants, the bodhisattvas Avalokiteshvara (Guanyin) and Mahasthamaprapta (Dashizhi). Based on the prominence of these three figures, we know that the setting is Sukhavati, Amitabha's Western Paradise, or Pure Land. In the pool, lotus blossoms open to reveal the fortunate beings reborn into this heavenly realm.

Devotional worship of Amitabha and hopes of being reborn in his heavenly dwelling grew quickly in sixth-century China. During that period, this relief was carved into the rock wall of a manmade cavern at Xiangtangshan, a Buddhist cave site in Hebei Province. The carving faced the main altar, which featured three pairs of freestanding deities gathered around another depiction of a seated Amitabha. One of those altar figures (p. 74), as well as the relief made for the top of the altar, is also in the Freer and Sackler collections.

KW

Buddha Vairochana (Pilushena) with the Realms of Existence
China, probably Henan Province, Northern Qi dynasty, 550–77
Limestone
151.3 × 62.9 × 31.3 cm
Purchase, Freer Gallery of Art, F1923.15

Narrative scenes carved in low relief cover this larger-than-life standing buddha, suffusing its surface like a magical emanation. Clues to the figure's identity and meaning appear on its front, where six registers show the Buddhist realms of existence. This conceptual map of the Buddhist universe is associated with Vairochana (in Chinese, Pilushena), the cosmic buddha.

The map begins at the upper chest with the realm of devas (divinities). Here, Buddha Shakyamuni preaches to deities in the highest paradise still subject to the suffering of worldly existence. Directly below, just above the waist, is Mount Meru, the center of the universe, depicted as a pillar wrapped with a pair of dragons. Asuras, giant demigods with multiple arms, live at the mountain's base. Descending the sculpture, we see the spheres of humans, animals, and ghosts before reaching the end of the spectrum: the sufferers in Buddhist hells, shown near the feet.

Descriptions of Vairochana are found in the *Avatamsaka Sutra*, known as *Huayan* in Chinese and *Flower Garland* in English. This religious text describes the infinite universe and introduces Vairochana as the force behind all phenomena and the embodiment of enlightenment. In this context, the Historical Buddha, Shakyamuni, is understood to be Vairochana's earthly emanation. This may explain why, on this sculpture, scenes associated with Vairochana are joined by others linked to Shakyamuni.

Images of Vairochana are frequently depicted in large scale. A 180-foot-tall version, dating to the sixth century, stood at Bamiyan, Afghanistan, before it was destroyed by the Taliban in 2001.

KW

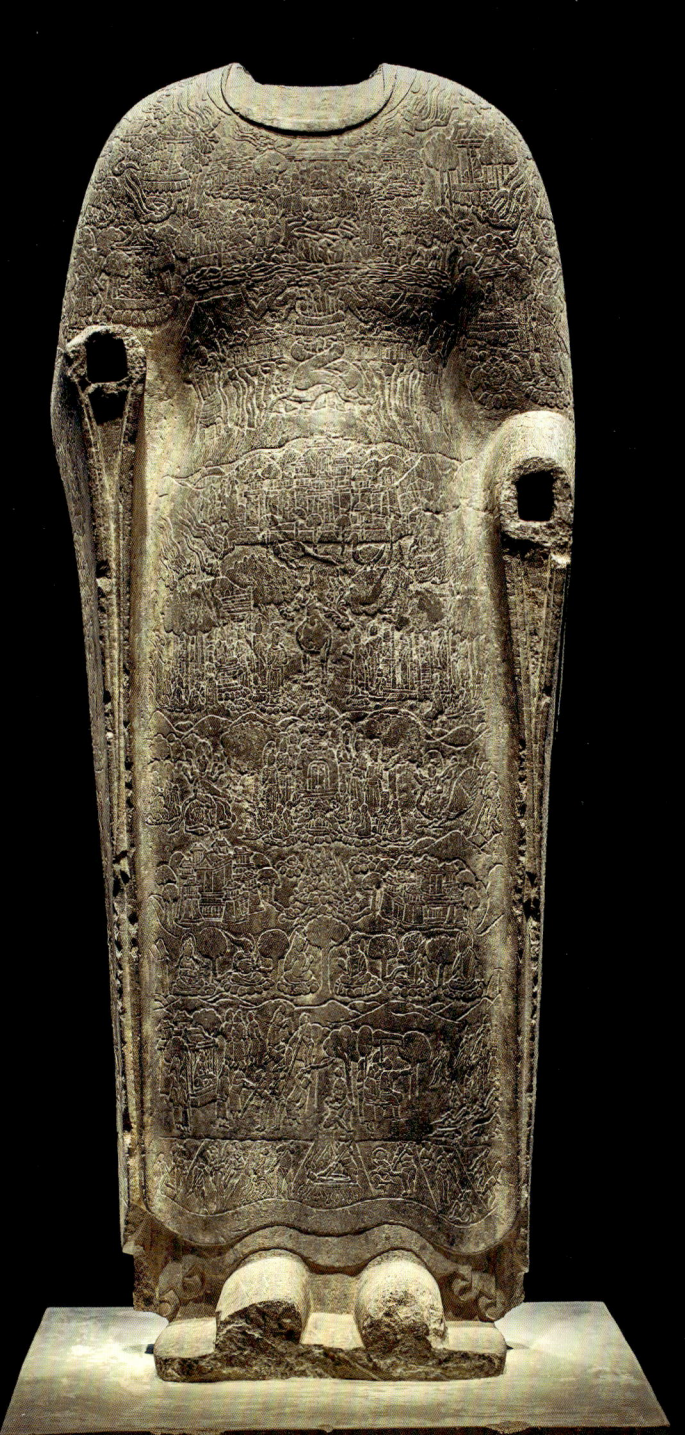

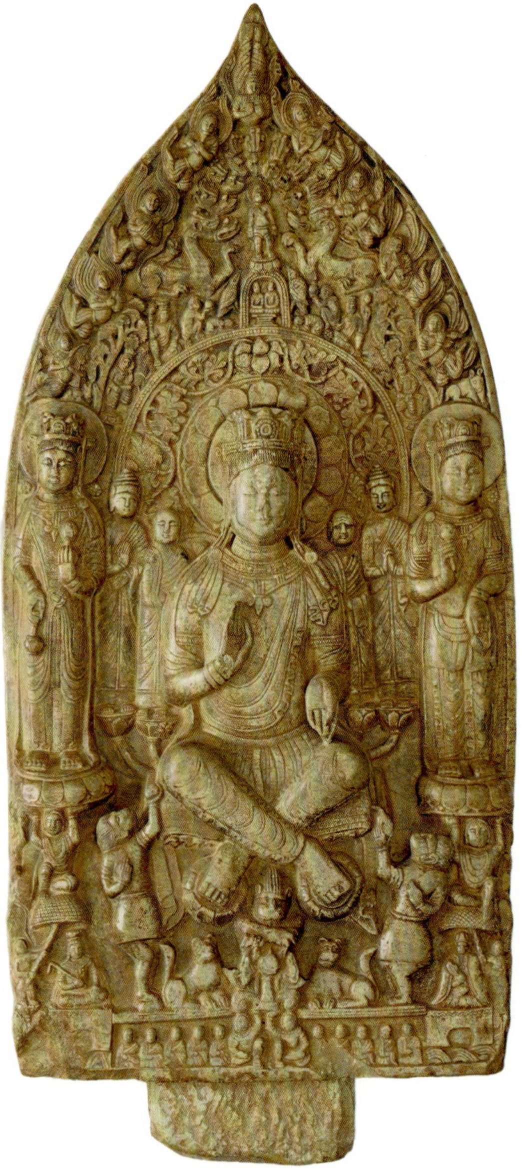

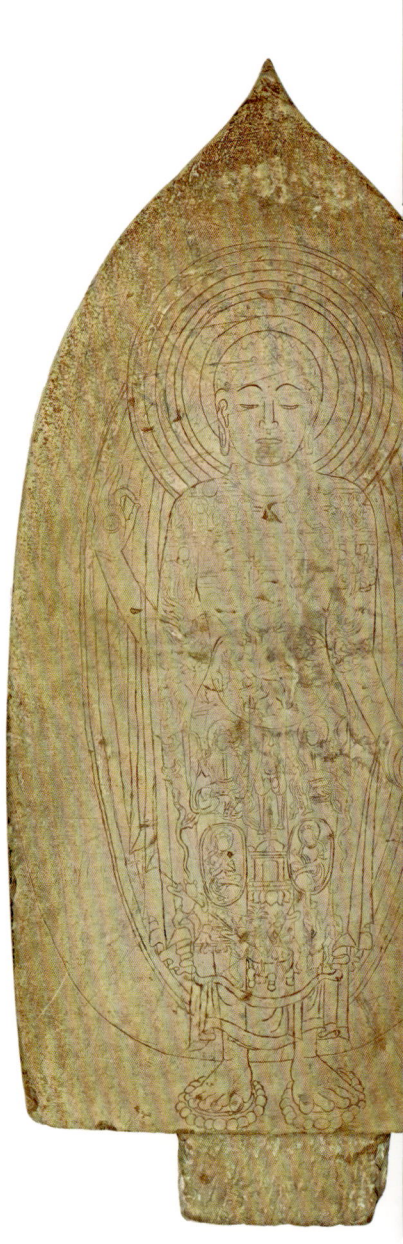

Stele of Future Buddha Maitreya (Mile)
China, probably Shaanxi Province, Northern Zhou dynasty, 557–81
Marble
102.4 × 47.2 × 12.8 cm
Gift of Charles Lang Freer, Freer Gallery of Art, F1911.412

Steles, or freestanding stone slabs such as this one, were designed to be seen from all sides. Instead of residing on sanctuary altars, they were usually set up as independent monuments on the grounds of Chinese temples.

On the front of this sixth-century stele, vignettes illustrating Buddhist scriptures that were popular in China surround the largest figures. They belong to a group centered on the Future Buddha Maitreya (in Chinese, Mile), shown with his legs crossed at the ankles. Still portrayed as a bodhisattva wearing a crown and jewelry, he is joined by figures typically seen with Shakyamuni: Ananda and Mahakashyapa, two of the Historical Buddha's principal disciples, are to Maitreya's immediate left and right, respectively. Two bodhisattvas holding a bottle, fan, and lotus buds stand at the edges of the group. Between them and the monastic figures are deities with hair coiled on top of their heads. Known as pratyekabuddhas, such figures seek their own path to enlightenment and are rarely seen in Buddhist art after the sixth century.

Together, these attendants symbolize the three paths to Buddhist enlightenment. On the path of the pratyekabuddha, one achieves enlightenment through one's own efforts. Those following the path of the disciples or the bodhisattva do so through the Buddha's teachings—but only the latter is able to achieve full buddhahood.

The back of the stele features an image of Vairochana, the cosmic buddha. Rendered in thin carved lines that recall a drawing, this standing figure repeats the design of the realms of existence seen on the large Northern Qi standing buddha (p. 38). Clearly, this concept was prevalent across northern China in the sixth century.

KW

Future Buddha Maitreya (Mile)
China, Hebei Province, Quyang
Northern Qi dynasty, 550–77
Marble with traces of pigment
33 × 17.5 × 15.4 cm
Gift of Charles Lang Freer, Freer Gallery of Art, F1911.411

Lost in thought, this solitary bodhisattva rests his right ankle on his left knee and raises two fingers of his right hand to his chin. The unusual pose often is associated with the Future Buddha Maitreya (in Chinese, Mile). The subject of many religious texts, this bodhisattva patiently and pensively waits in Tushita Heaven for his final rebirth on earth, which will occur once all Buddhist teachings have been forgotten. As with all buddhas connected to our world, Maitreya's job then will be to reestablish Buddhist doctrine before he passes into final nirvana.

For sixth-century Chinese Buddhists, the promise of this coming buddha must have offered comfort in a chaotic time marked by constant warfare and civil disorder. Many associated these times with *mofa*, an age of moral decay when humans' capacity to comprehend Buddhism would diminish. Many devotees of Maitreya hoped to be reborn in the time of his teaching, when the ability to understand Buddhism and achieve enlightenment would be restored to humankind.

Here, Maitreya meditates beneath intertwined trees that resemble the ginkgo, a Chinese native. Now damaged, the tree branches frame the double lotus halo behind the deity's head. The sculpture's white marble, which was originally painted, can be traced to Quyang, Hebei Province, and its large quarry and image-making workshops. In 1953, more than two thousand marble sculptures were excavated in Quyang. Similar to those unearthed pieces, this sculpture may have been buried or lost during the anti-Buddhist persecutions of the eighth and ninth centuries. Like many of the Quyang marble sculptures, this example is relatively small, suggesting it was made to target lay believers who were not aristocrats.

KW

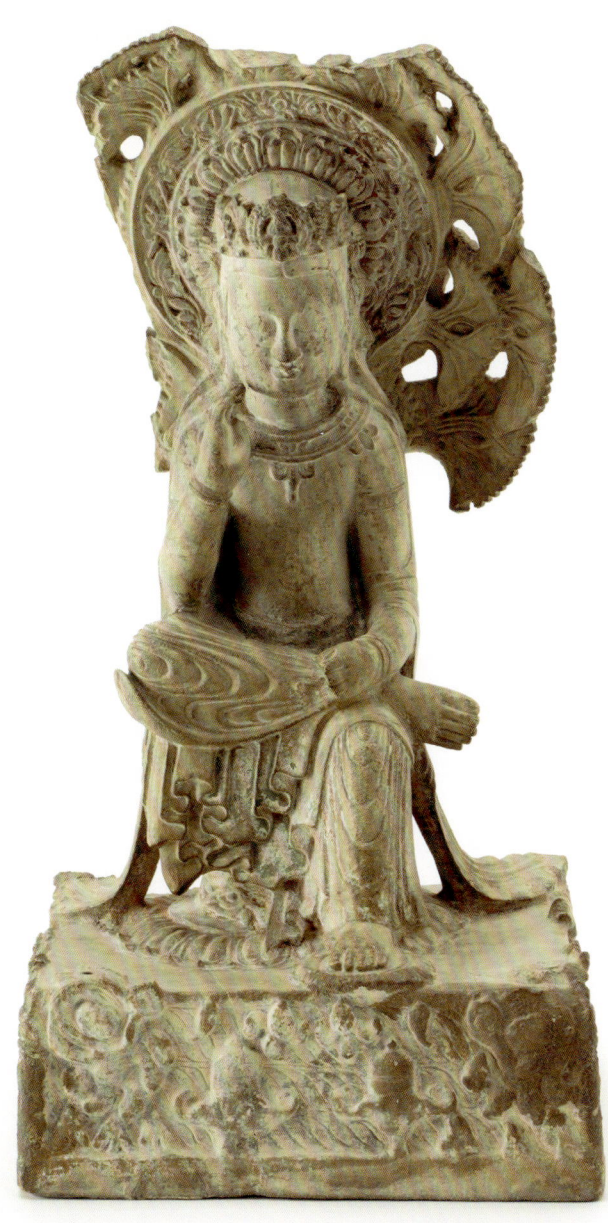

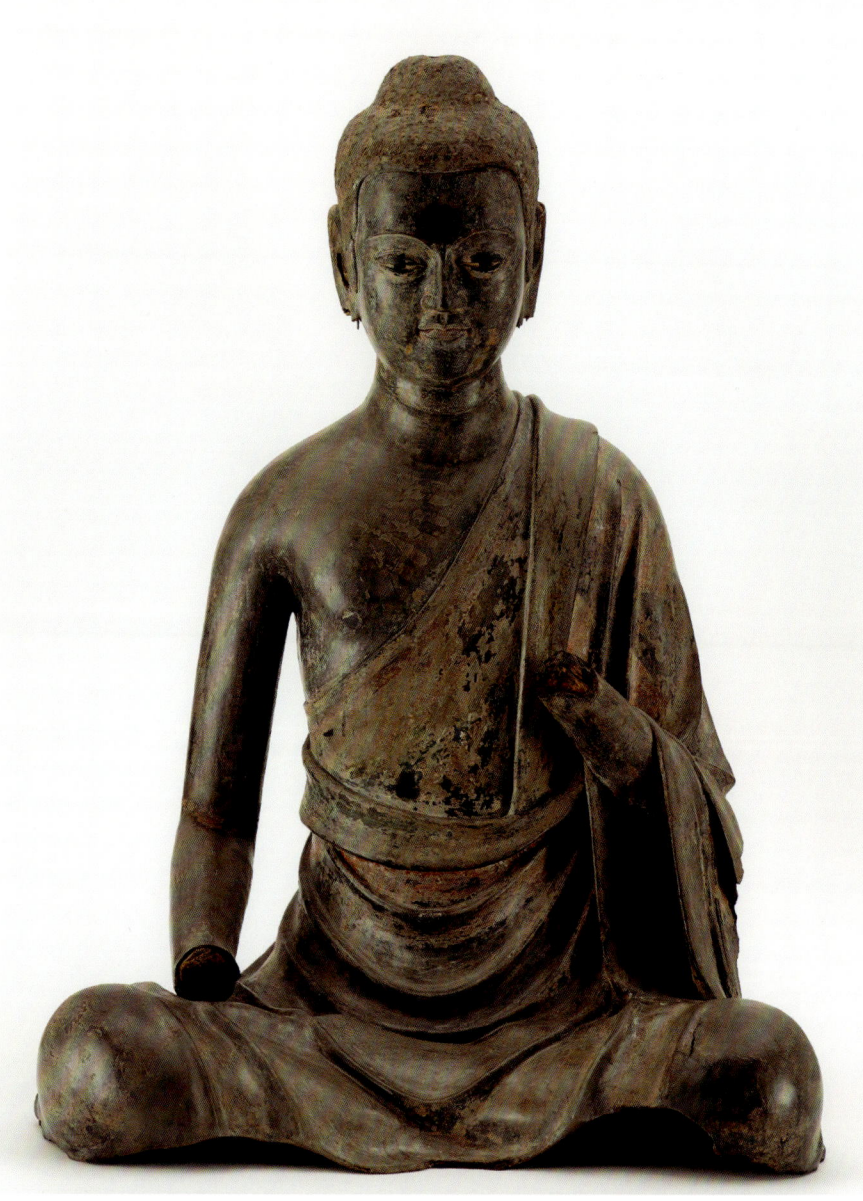

Seated Buddha
China, Sui dynasty or early Tang dynasty, late 6th–early 7th century
Fabric, lacquer, wood, iron wire, and glass (or stone?)
with traces of pigment and gilding
99.5 × 72.5 × 56.7 cm
Purchase—Charles Lang Freer Endowment, Freer Gallery of Art,
F1944.46

This softly modeled statue of the Buddha, leaning slightly forward, projects a serene, introspective mood. His aloof grace transcends the fragmentary condition of the sculpture, which is missing its long earlobes, hands, and part of the legs, folded in the lotus pose. The back of the head has a tenon that supported a now-lost halo. The lean proportions are typical of sixth-century Chinese sculpture, but the naturalistic drapery and hints of anatomical modeling suggest a date closer to the seventh century.

Surprisingly lightweight for its size, the hollow statue was constructed using the demanding "dry lacquer" process, of which few examples are extant. Conservators, scientists, and scholars recently studied this example. With X-rays and a CT scan, they discovered that the makers began by fashioning a clay core and covering it with layers of fabric strips. Wet lacquer, a resin from a tree species native to north Asia, coated the fabric. Extra clay was added between the layers to depict the deep folds of the Buddha's monastic garment.

After achieving a basic form, the makers applied at least four layers of lacquer. Each was thickened with slightly different bulking materials, including oils and partially burned bone. After the lacquer fully hardened—each layer had to dry for a day in air of at least sixty percent humidity—the clay core was removed. The makers then added finishing touches, which are now mostly missing. The Buddha's skin was painted pink beneath a layer of glimmering gold leaf. Traces of bright blue around the hairline indicate the original color of the hair, and the lips retain hints of red. The outer robe was painted with red squares to represent a monk's patchwork robe, and the inner robe preserves traces of a decorative border.

JS (with conservator Donna Strahan)

Altarpiece
Northern China, Sui dynasty, dated 597
Gilt bronze
32.1 × 14.1 cm
Gift of Charles Lang Freer, Freer Gallery of Art, F1914.21a–h

According to an inscription around the base, sixteen women, several with prominent court connections, commissioned this altarpiece in 597. It comprises eight removable components: figures, haloes, and bases. The Buddha stands on a lotus flower pedestal, flanked by bodhisattvas on leafy tendrils. Gesturing "fear not" and "bestowal," he wears a simple monastic robe. The bodhisattvas sport ribboned headdresses, jewelry, and scarves draped across their graceful bodies. Together, the figures share a subtle connection that projects a sense of welcome and reassurance—the hope of Buddhist salvation.

Compared to its partner, the right-hand bodhisattva has a less prominent nose, tinier waist, simpler headdress, and less jewelry. These differences have raised questions about whether the bodhisattvas were created at the same time. However, an analysis of the metal alloy has indicated that all of the sculpture's components are very similar. In addition, a microscopic examination of the surface corrosion has confirmed that all eight pieces were buried for a long time, although we cannot confirm they were in the same place.

How should we interpret the bodhisattvas' variations? Perhaps they signify a tolerance in sixth- and early seventh-century China for minor differences that resulted when art was made in a workshop. Perhaps the bodhisattva on the right was lost or damaged in antiquity and replaced with a slightly earlier figure from the same workshop. Or, perhaps the altarpiece was buried with a large cache of objects from a single temple and, when excavated, some of the sculptures' components were mixed up. In the end, the three figures relate with such natural grace that most viewers do not notice the differences and only feel the sublime power of the work.

JS

BUDDHAS

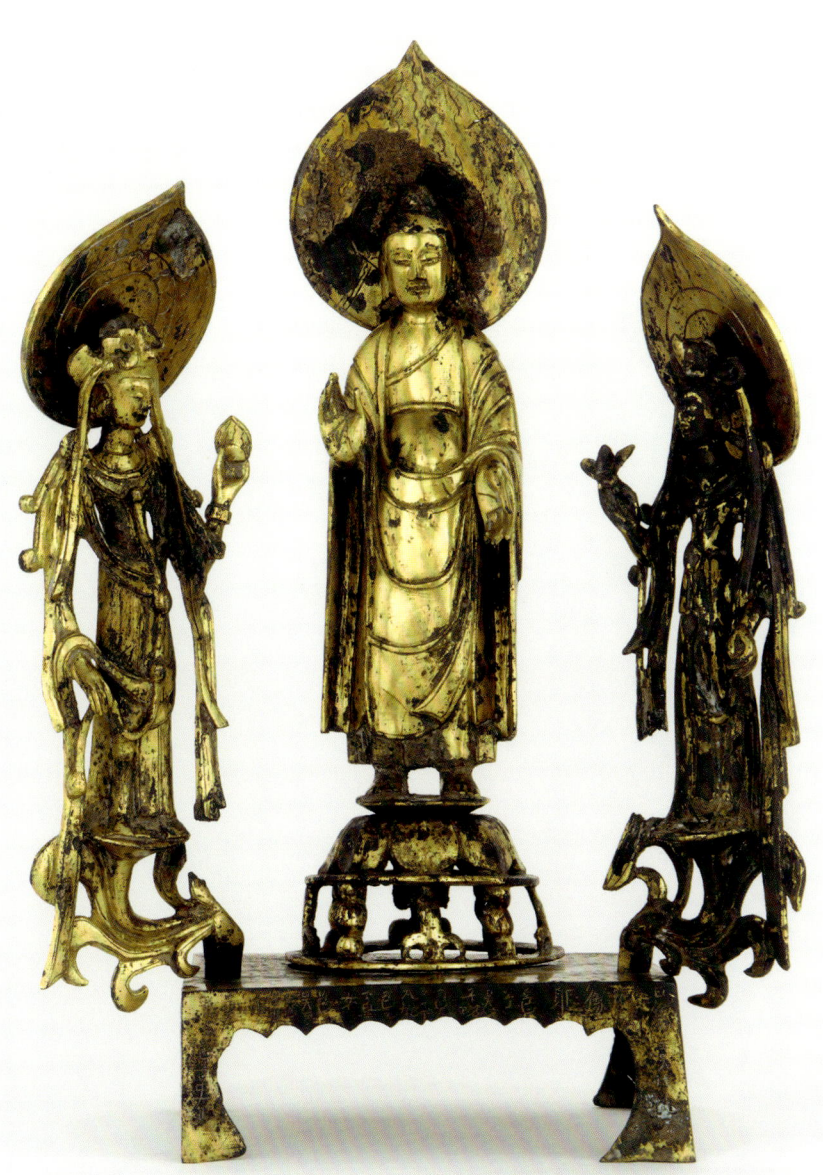

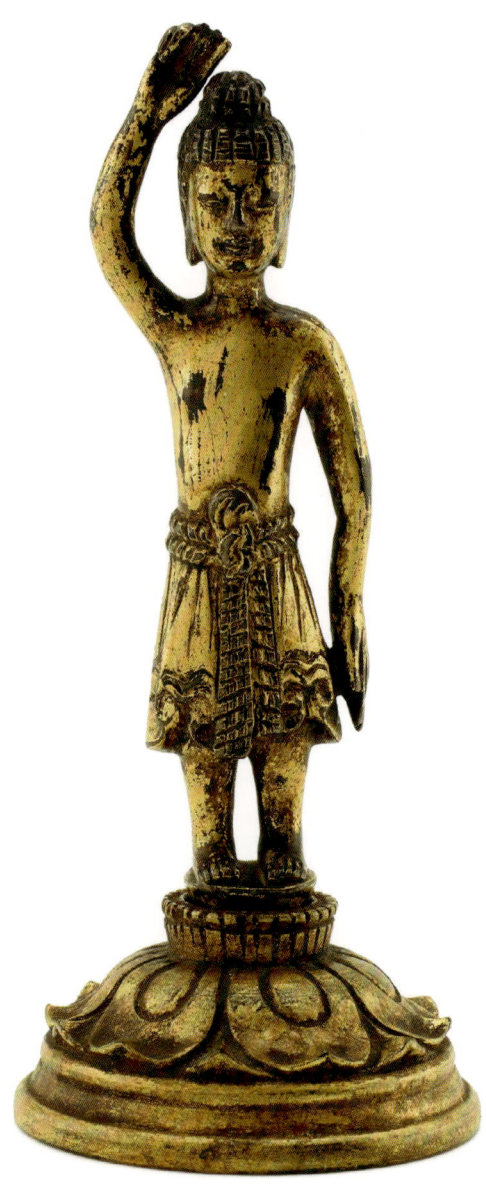

Buddha Shakyamuni (Shaka Nyorai) at Birth
Japan, Asuka period, 7th century
Gilt bronze
11.7 × 5.2 cm
Gift of Sylvan Barnet and William Burto in honor of Takashi Yanagi
Freer Gallery of Art, F2005.9a–b

Narratives recorded in sutras recount the miraculous events of the birth of Shakyamuni (in Japanese, Shaka Nyorai), the Historical Buddha. The infant passed from his mother's body without causing her any pain. He then took seven steps and pointed toward heaven and earth, declaring himself lord of the cosmos and savior of all sentient beings.

This small Japanese representation of the Buddha at birth (*tanjobutsu*) is a rare example of the gilt bronze images produced soon after Buddhism came to Japan in the mid-sixth century. The infant stands on a lotus-form pedestal that replaces a lost original. Pedestals are typical features of *tanjobutsu* images, which were used for lustration rites to celebrate the Buddha's birthday. Standing in a basin, the image was bathed in perfumed water or fragrant tea. According to the *Nihon shoki* (Chronicles of Japan), such ceremonies were held in Japanese temples as early as 606.

Although images of the Buddha at birth began to appear in India around the second or third century (see p. 30), this sculpture draws on East Asian models. The elongated facial features and the stylized folds of the garment, tied around the waist with a double cord, closely resemble the earliest known Japanese image of the Buddha at birth, a registered Important Cultural Property in the temple Shogenji, Aichi Prefecture. In turn, these figures reflect in miniature the refined style of the Tori school of Buddhist sculptors. A prime example of the school's work is a bronze Shakyamuni attended by two bodhisattvas. Dated to 623, this registered Japanese National Treasure is enshrined in the Golden Hall of Horyuji, a temple in Nara.

AY

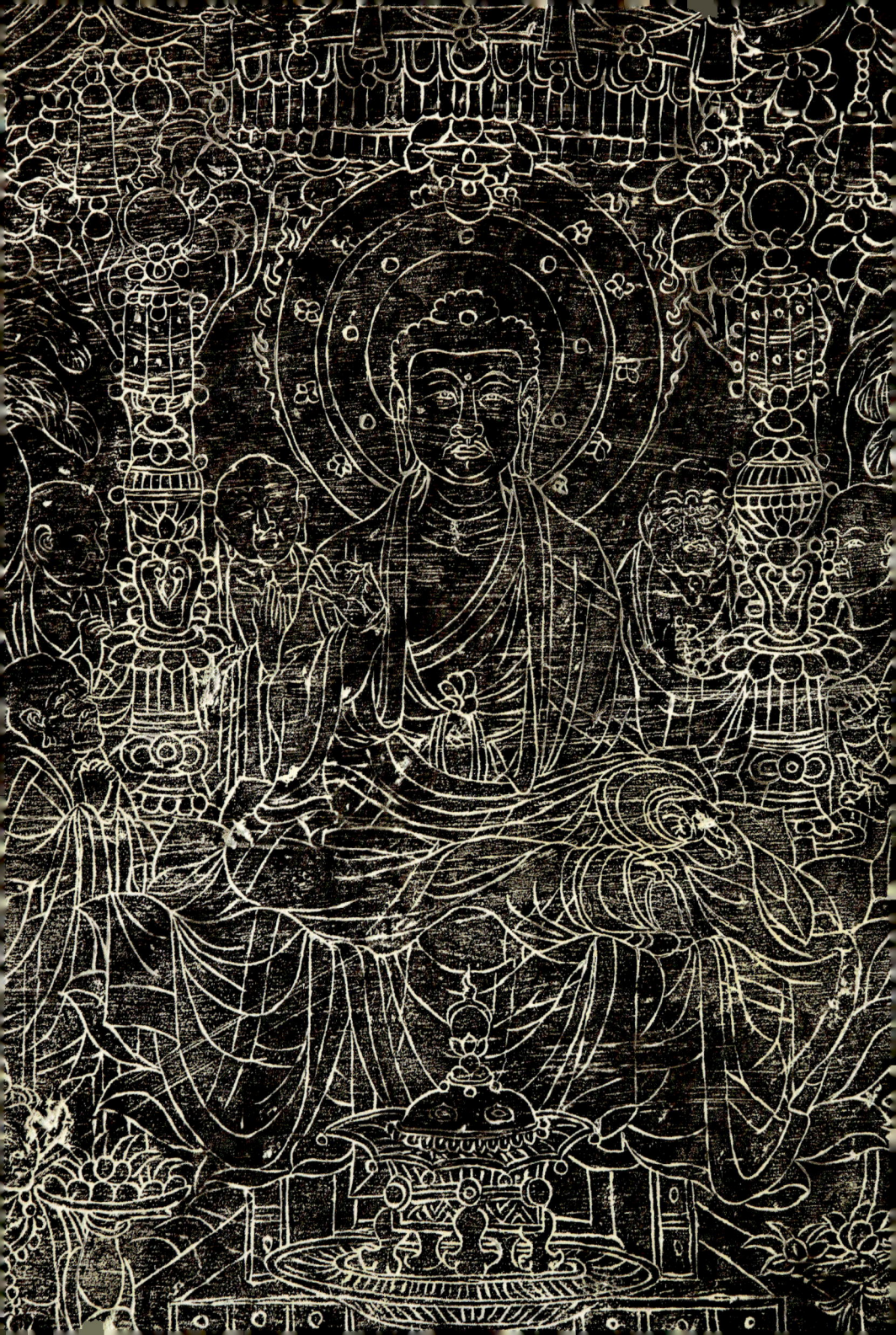

Western Paradise of the Buddha Amitabha (Amituo)
China, Shaanxi Province, probably Chang'an (Xi'an)
Tang dynasty, 8th century
Marble
86.6 × 146.2 × 17 cm
Gift of Charles Lang Freer, Freer Gallery of Art, F1913.137

In 1977, museum staff added a pigmented paste to the thin, elegant lines of this crowded scene, making the design somewhat easier to see. A buddha sits at the center of a lush garden, surrounded by figures arranged in symmetrical pairs. Bodhisattvas and pratyekabuddhas are identified by halos; they are joined by less-exalted figures, including disciples or monks and lay devotees. Two armored guardians, also with halos, frame the scene.

Decorated only on one side, this arched slab of marble was intended to be mounted above the door of a masonry pagoda or temple hall. Some scholars believe that it represents the heavenly paradise of Sukhavati. If that is accurate, the large central buddha seated beneath a jeweled canopy is Amitabha (in Chinese, Amituo), and the two attendants looking toward him on either side are the bodhisattvas Avalokiteshvara (Guanyin) and Mahasthamaprapta (Dashizhi).

Unlike the vision of Sukhavati created for the Xiangtangshan caves (p. 37), however, this design lacks the distinctive pool filled with beings reborn in lotus blooms. Consequently, this assembly deserves further study. Details of the iconography —specifically, the pratyekabuddhas—reflect an earlier model, suggesting that this may be a reproduction made to look like a lost original.

KW

Medicine Buddha Bhaishajyaguru
Indonesia, Java, 8th–9th century
High tin bronze
31.1 × 18 × 18.2 cm
Gift of Ann and Gilbert Kinney, Arthur M. Sackler Gallery, S2015.25

The goal of the Buddhist path is to escape all worldly suffering by attaining nirvana. Devotees of Bhaishajyaguru, the medicine buddha, however, worship him to alleviate physical discomfort and illness in the here and now. The veneration of Bhaishajyaguru first emerged in northern India during the early centuries of the Common Era and subsequently spread to Tibet, China, and Japan. Examples of his presence in Southeast Asia, such as this bronze, are extremely rare.

We don't know exactly how or when the worship of Bhaishajyaguru in Java began. By the eighth and ninth centuries, when this bronze was made, Buddhist ideas and goods flowed in abundance between Java and the Buddhist heartland of northern India. Javanese monks visited famous pilgrimage sites in northern India and studied at the great Buddhist university of Nalanda. They brought back new teachings and portable devotional images, which is likely how Bhaishajyaguru entered Java's religious and artistic world.

Images from India had a considerable impact on Javanese religious art. This sculpture has several northern Indian stylistic elements: the lotus throne on a rectangular base, the single row of pearls encircling the top of the throne, and the curly flames adorning the circular back slab, to name a few. Only the stylized features of Bhaishajyaguru's serene face reveal the bronze's Indonesian origin.

JE

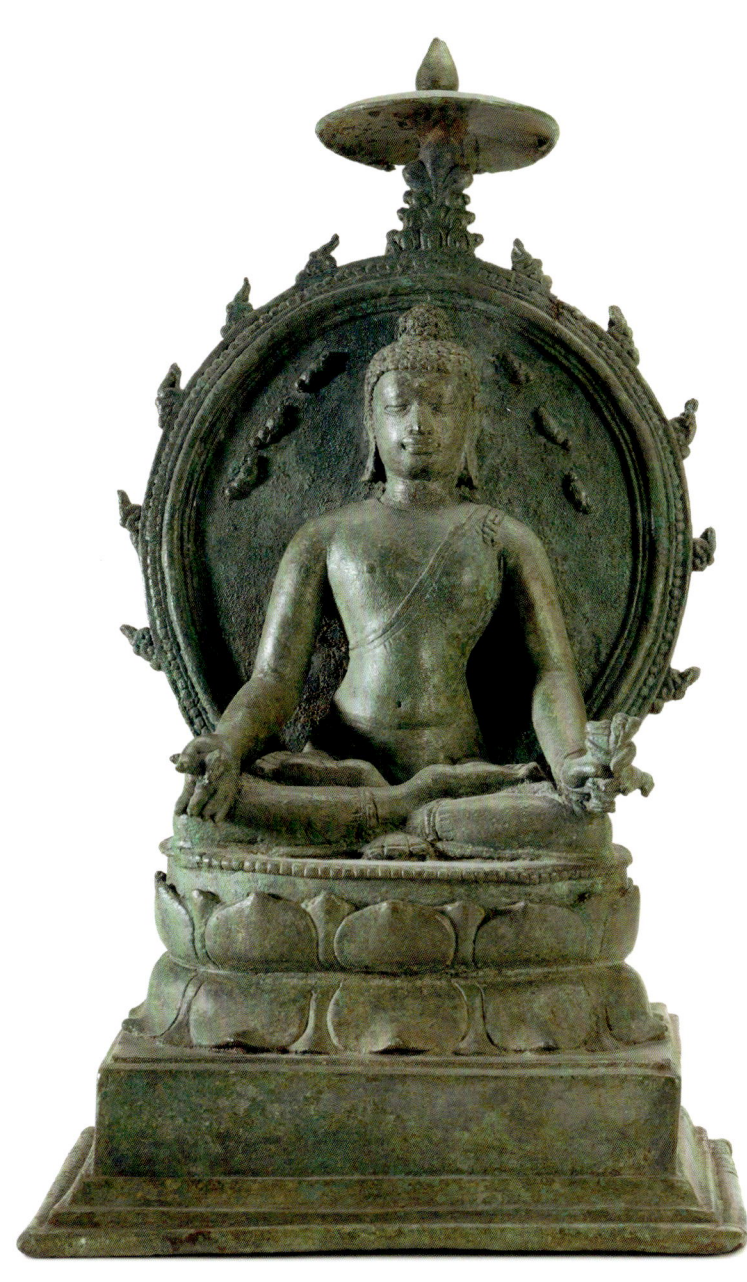

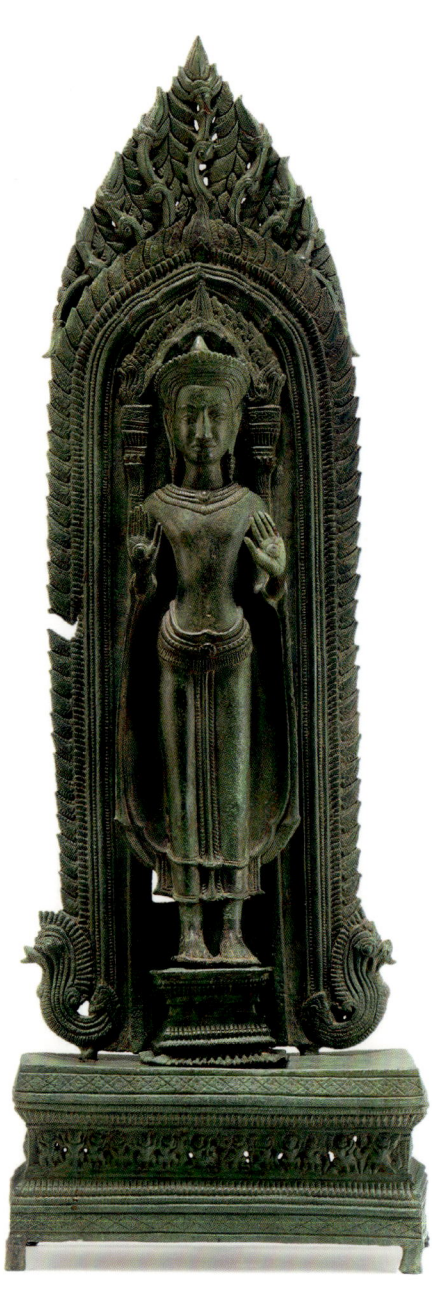

Standing Buddha
Thailand, 12th–13th century
Bronze
49 × 17.6 × 11.5 cm
Purchase—Charles Lang Freer Endowment, Freer Gallery of Art,
F1976.11a–e

To evoke the compassion that the Buddha experiences after his awakening, artists often depict him raising his right hand in the "fear not" gesture (*abhayamudra*). In the Thai tradition, images of the Buddha often have both hands raised in *abhayamudra*, as this one does. His open palms are marked with the wheel of the law (*dharmachakra*), representing his teachings. This Buddhist symbol is one of the thirty-two major marks of a great being that identify a buddha.

References to the Buddha's awakening and teachings suggest this statue represents Shakyamuni, the Historical Buddha. Buddhas are conventionally depicted in simple monk's robes. This is especially true for Shakyamuni, who gave up his royal life to become an ascetic. Here, however, the Buddha wears elaborate jewelry, an ornate girdle, and a crown. These features sometimes are seen in Buddhist art of northeast India and Southeast Asia, especially in northern Thailand.

Several explanations for this statue's regal accessories are possible. They might relate to the story of Jambupati, which was popular in Southeast Asia. According to this tale, the Buddha adorned himself with splendid regalia to convert Jambupati, an arrogant king. Humbled, Jambupati atoned for his arrogance and took the five vows of a Buddhist layman. Another interpretation is that the Buddha's royal attire refers to an astrologer's prediction at Shakyamuni's birth: the young prince would either become a world ruler or a great holy man. Shakyamuni became the latter, but the crown and jewelry might symbolize how his teachings conquered the world as a king would.

JE

Buddha Shakyamuni Emerging from the Mountains
Traditionally attributed to Hu Zhifu (13th century)
China, Southern Song dynasty, mid-1250s
Hanging scroll mounted on panel; ink on paper
92 × 31.7 cm
Purchase—Charles Lang Freer Endowment, Freer Gallery of Art, F1965.9

Startled by the morning star, an emaciated Shakyamuni descends from the mountain where he has practiced physical austerities for six years in a fruitless quest for enlightenment. His downcast eyes express deep introspection. Raising clasped hands below his robes, he realizes that he has fallen short and abandons strict asceticism as the means to spiritual awakening. Chinese practitioners of Chan Buddhism understood this event as a key point in the process that led to Shakyamuni's buddhahood. Depictions of this scene were particularly popular among Chan painters during the thirteenth and fourteenth centuries.

This unsigned portrait is traditionally attributed to a little-known artist named Hu Zhifu, though his actual contribution to the work is unknown. The painter combined two distinct styles: Certain features are rendered in crisp, dark lines, such as Shakyamuni's coiled hair, wispy eyebrows, stubbly beard, and claw-like toenails. Other aspects, such as the figure's billowing robes, are in light-gray ink and reflect a looser, more abbreviated manner.

The Chan abbot Xiyan Liaohui (1198–1262) inscribed a poem at the top of the painting:
At midnight, he spied the morning star,
In the mountains, he made cold remarks,
Before his feet had left the mountains,
Those remarks went out into the world:
When I behold all the living creatures,
Becoming Buddha happens all the time,
There's only you, this poor old fellow,
Who still lacks awareness of what is.

SDA (entry and translation)

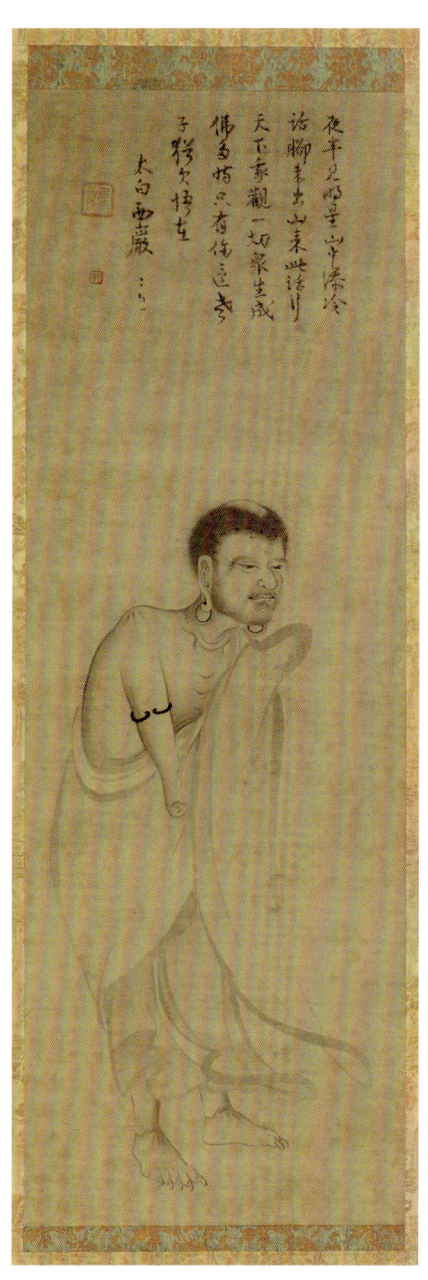

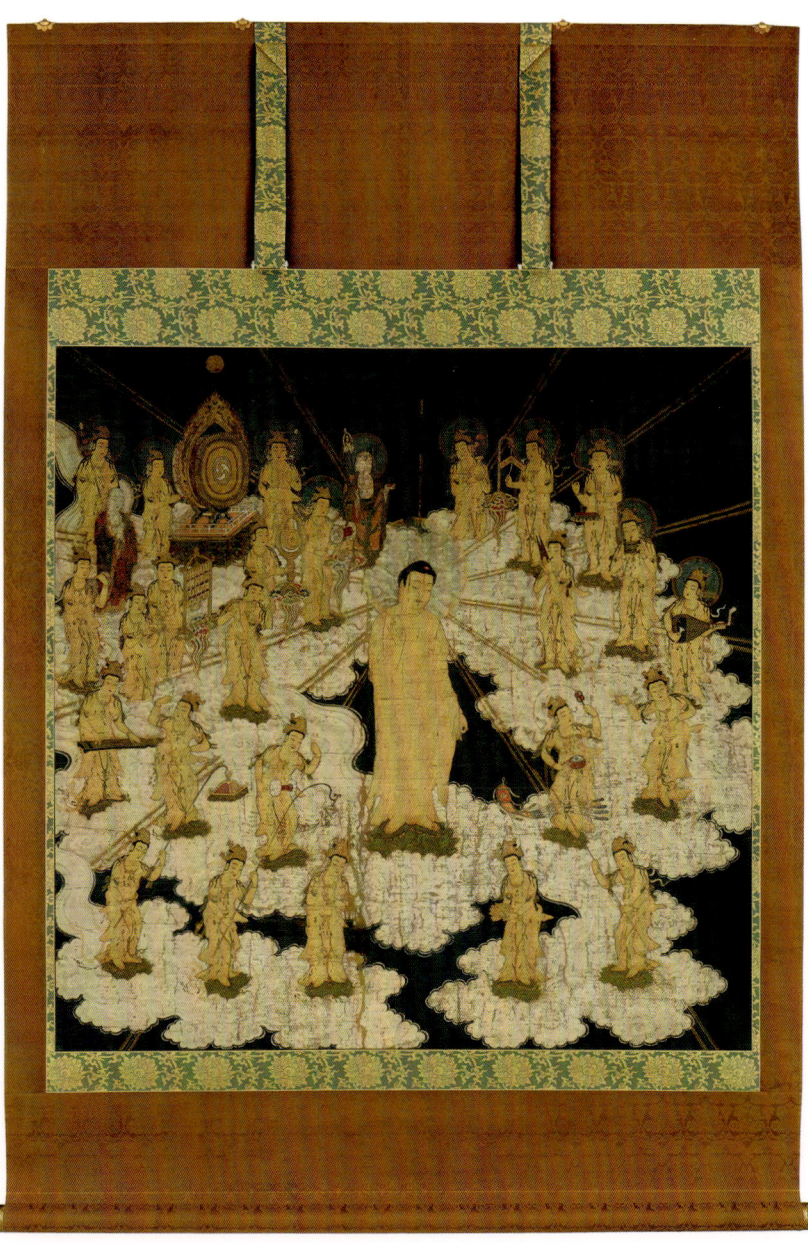

Buddha Amitabha welcoming souls to the Western Paradise
Japan, Kamakura period (1185–1333)
Hanging scroll; ink, color, and gold on silk
273 × 186.2 cm
Gift of Charles Lang Freer, Freer Gallery of Art, F1911.475

The Buddha Amitabha (in Japanese, Amida) and a retinue of celestial beings, including a contingent of bodhisattvas, descend from the Western Paradise. Their mission is to greet and guide the spirit of a deceased believer back to Amitabha's heavenly realm.

Paintings such as this one were produced extensively in Japan from the eleventh thorough the fourteenth century. During this tumultuous time, Japanese Buddhists increasingly relied on powerful imagery that suggested the possibility of rescue from life's suffering and an inhospitable world. Such iconography was created under the broad auspices of the Pure Land Buddhist sect, which flourished during the period.

The asymmetrical composition in this painting of heavenly descent effectively conveys a dynamic rescue. Details of the deities' costumes are richly embellished with linear designs executed by cutting and applying gold leaf, a technique known in Japanese as *kirikane*. A painting this large would have belonged to a temple; priests would have carried smaller versions, in the form of scrolls or folding screens, to the bedside of a dying believer to offer reassurance of salvation.

JU

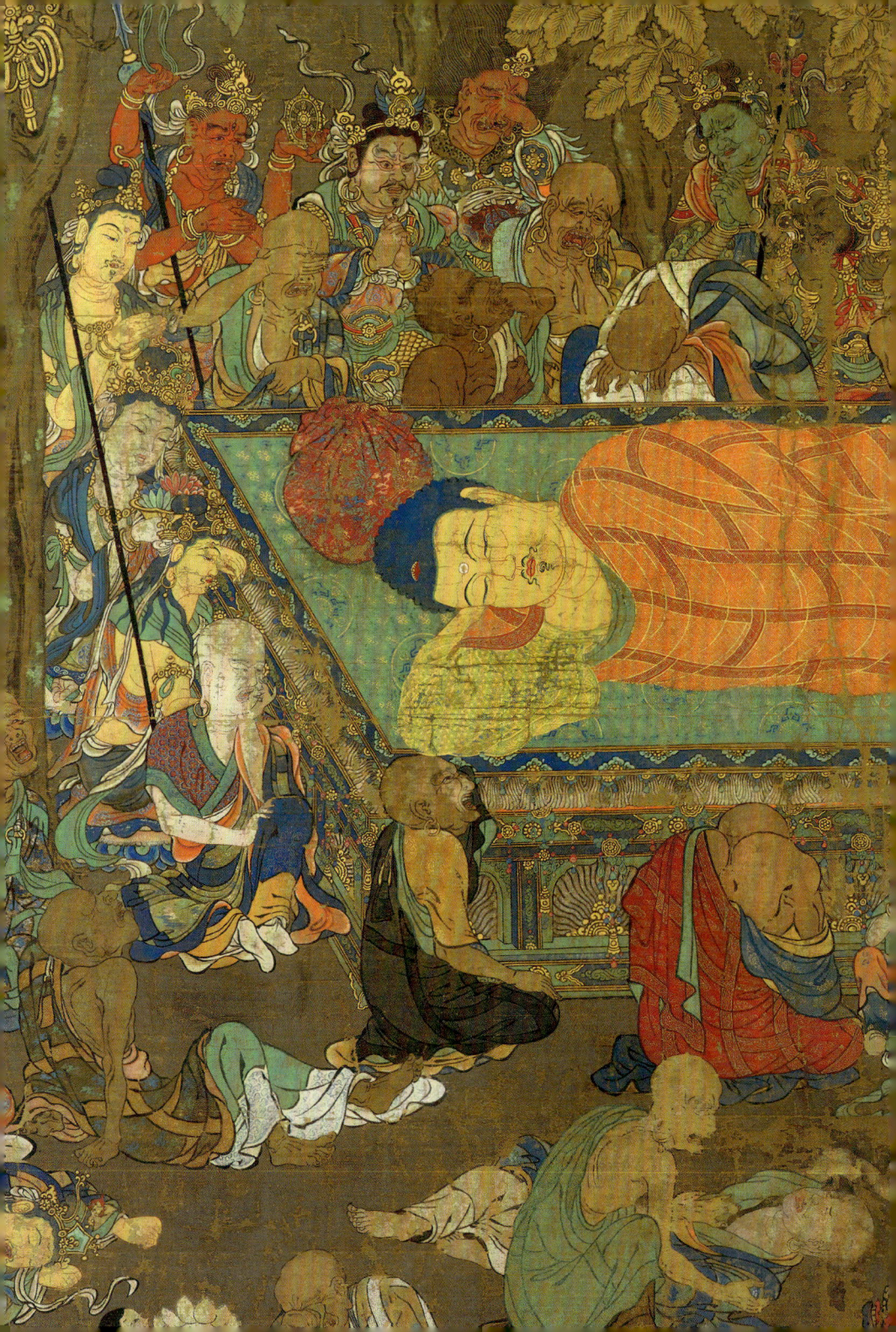

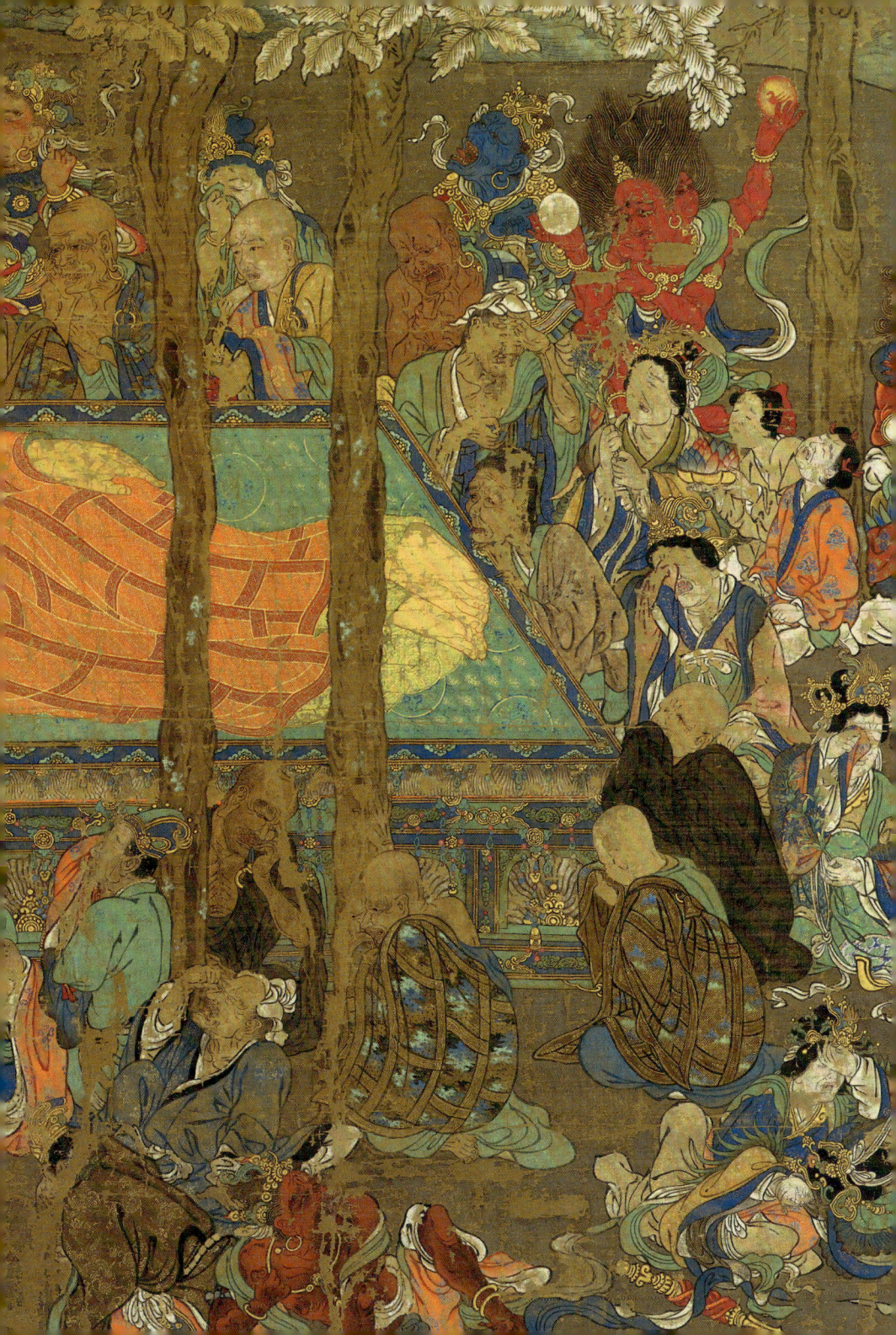

Final Nirvana of Buddha Shakyamuni
Japan, Kamakura period, early 14th century
Hanging scroll; ink, color, gold, and silver on silk
195.8 × 189.1 cm
Purchase, Freer Gallery of Art, F1970.30

Buddha Shakyamuni lies between two trees as he enters final nirvana (*parinirvana*). Surrounding him is essentially a universe in mourning: bodhisattvas, disciples, and, most charmingly, representatives of the world of animals. In the upper right, Maya, Buddha's mother, descends on a cloud to pay homage to her son.

The variety of mourners represents the universal power of Buddha's teachings. These figures grieve because they do not fully grasp that nirvana is a liberation and transcendence from earthly bonds. Shakyamuni's composed, peaceful figure emphasizes this transformation rather than the loss of his human form.

The final rebirth of Buddha Shakyamuni concludes a series of key episodes in Shakyamuni's life that were, over the centuries, painted and sculpted in standardized forms. Beginning in the eighth century in Japan, the subject of Buddha entering nirvana became so popular that such images were reproduced by woodblock printing.

Late eleventh-century Japanese interpretations of this scene depict the Buddha lying on his back with his face up and arms extended. Starting in the early fourteenth century, when this painting was made, the Buddha is placed on a bedlike platform with his right arm bent to form a pillow for his head. Here, careful attention to detail in color and patterning suggests that artists had fully adapted a Chinese model to Japanese taste. Though this painting was usually rolled up in storage, each year it was suspended from the altar of a Japanese temple for a ceremony celebrating the Buddha's entry into nirvana.

JU

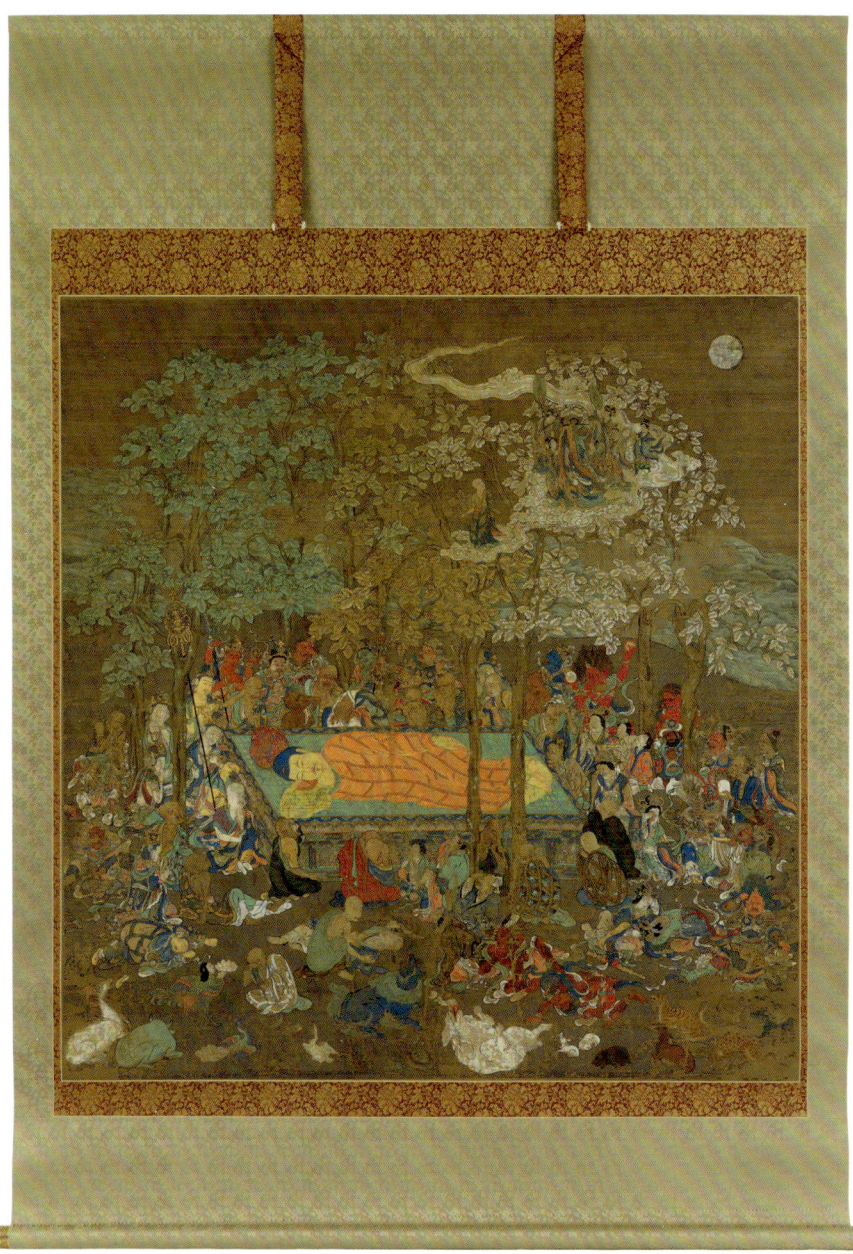

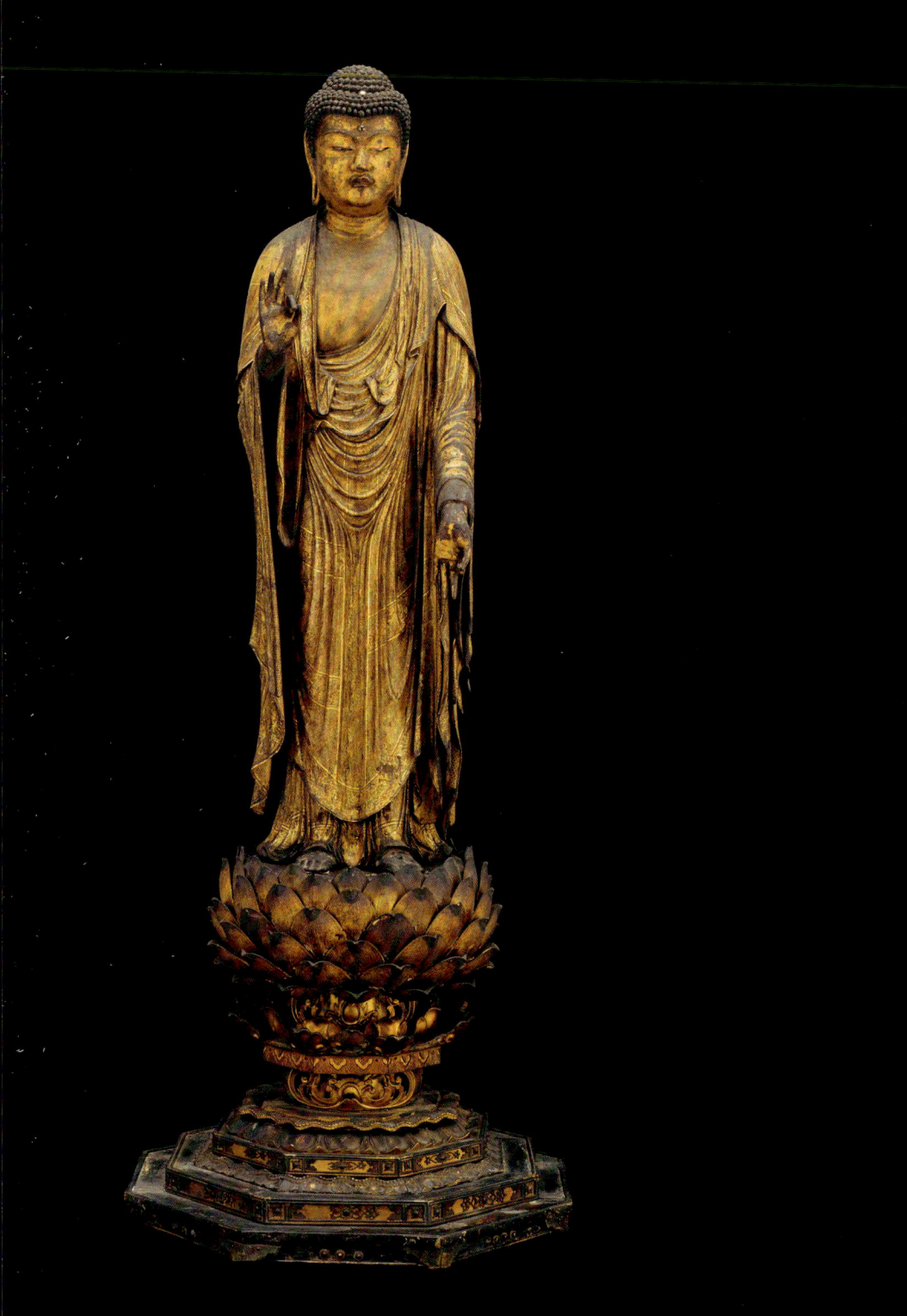

Buddha Amitabha (Amida)
Japan, Kamakura period, early 14th century
Wood with gold leaf, crystal, linen, and lacquer
112.6 × 45.5 × 44.1 cm
Purchase—The Harold P. Stern Memorial Fund and museum funds in appreciation of Nancy Fessenden and Richard Danziger and their exemplary service to the Galleries as leaders of the Board of Trustees, Freer Gallery of Art, F2002.9a–f

Buddha Amitabha (in Japanese, Amida), lord of the Western Paradise, tilts forward on his lotus blossom pedestal. He is descending to greet deceased beings before carrying them to his heavenly realm. The sculpture once stood among several divine forms designed to assure believers that, at death, they would be whisked off to a beneficial rebirth, merely one lifetime away from enlightenment.

Sculptural technique flourished in late 1200s Japan. Craftsmen fashioned intricate faces, feet, and garment folds and then assembled the parts. Detailed with paint, gold leaf, and glass or crystal eyes, the completed figures were lifelike and seamless.

A Buddhist sutra fragment dated to 741 was discovered inside this sculpture. Perhaps it was intended to invoke the spirit of eighth-century Japan, a comparatively stable era.

JU

Buddha Amitabha (Amita) and the Eight Great Bodhisattvas
Korea, Goryeo period, mid- to late 14th century
Hanging scroll mounted as a panel; ink, color, and gold on silk
160.3 × 86 cm
Gift of Charles Lang Freer, Freer Gallery of Art, F1906.269

Chinese monks introduced Buddhism to the Korean peninsula in the late fourth century CE. Within two hundred years, the faith was flourishing under court patronage that lasted nearly a millennium. This elite support led to remarkable products. Of those, religious paintings such as this one, rendered in saturated mineral pigments and gold on tightly woven silk, were among the best. Though they were inspired by subjects and compositions that originated in China, these religious icons illustrate a distinctly Korean achievement.

Like most of these Goryeo-dynasty Buddhist paintings, this image represents a Pure Land subject. Shown with his arm raised in the gesture of teaching, the central deity is Amitabha (in Korean, Amita), the compassionate buddha who preaches in his Western Paradise, Sukhavati. The two foremost bodhisattvas, encased in transparent veils, are his spiritual companions Mahasthamaprapta (Taeseji), whose crown holds a vessel of spiritually refreshing liquid, and Avalokiteshvara (Gwaneum), who bears a tiny representation of Amitabha. Together, these three deities assist believers in their quest for rebirth in Amitabha's heavenly Pure Land. Those reborn in hell can be redeemed by Kshitigarbha (Jijang), seen here standing beneath the buddha's right knee, wearing a blue hooded garment and carrying a transparent "wish-granting jewel."

Instead of grand temple halls, in which monumental murals were painted on the walls, finely detailed images such as this one were intended for closer viewing in more intimate settings. Scholars believe that these paintings were produced both to aid private meditation and to symbolically guide mortal beings to paradise at death.

KW

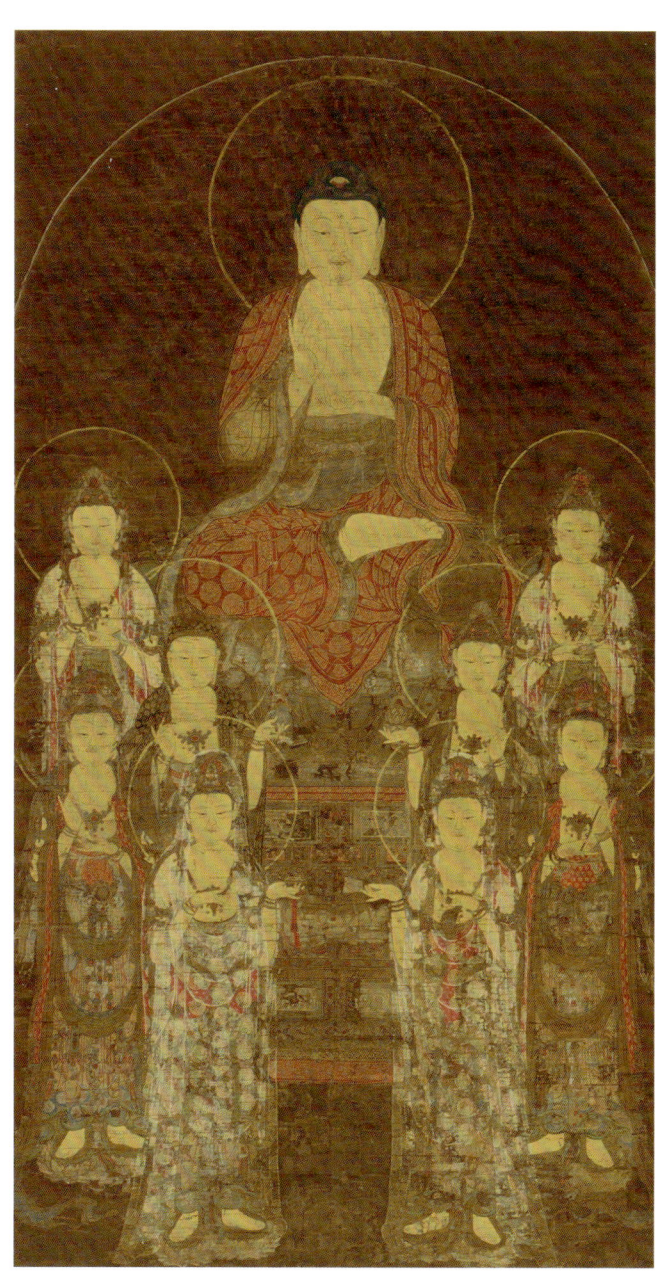

Buddha Amitabha
Central Tibet, second half of 15th century
Gilt copper repoussé, traces of pigments on hair and face
75 × 53.3 × 38.8 cm
The Alice S. Kandell Collection, Arthur M. Sackler Gallery,
S2014.20

Amitabha is one of the most widely worshipped buddhas in the Mahayana tradition. In this large Tibetan altarpiece, he appears characteristically with his legs crossed in the meditation posture (*dhyanasana*) and his right hand resting on the palm of the left in the meditation gesture (*dhyanamudra*).

With broad shoulders and an hourglass waist, this Amitabha is both majestic and energetic. His forehead mark and cranial bump signify a profound spiritual attainment gained over thousands of virtuous lifetimes. His long ears, devoid of jewelry, and his patched monk's robe indicate that he relinquished material comforts in his final life.

Beginning with the auspicious syllable *om*, an inscription on the pedestal's lowest rim tells us that a group of government officials commissioned this "victorious buddha body made of the finest gilded copper." The sculpture's precious materials signal not only the luminous perfection of Amitabha (in Sanskrit, "Infinite Light") but also the donors' generosity. Their goals—to hasten the enlightenment of all beings and protect their kingdom's borders—are a typical combination of spiritual and practical, eternal and immediate.

The inscription also praises the image's makers, "seven jewel-holding" artists from Nepal. Their skill is evident in the sculpture's lively volumes as well as its details. Delicate patterns border the robe's "patches," and the incised floral pattern of the robe's lining is visible beneath Amitabha's right arm. And at the point where the garment's hems drape onto the pedestal, the pleats are arranged with a particularly graceful flourish.

DD

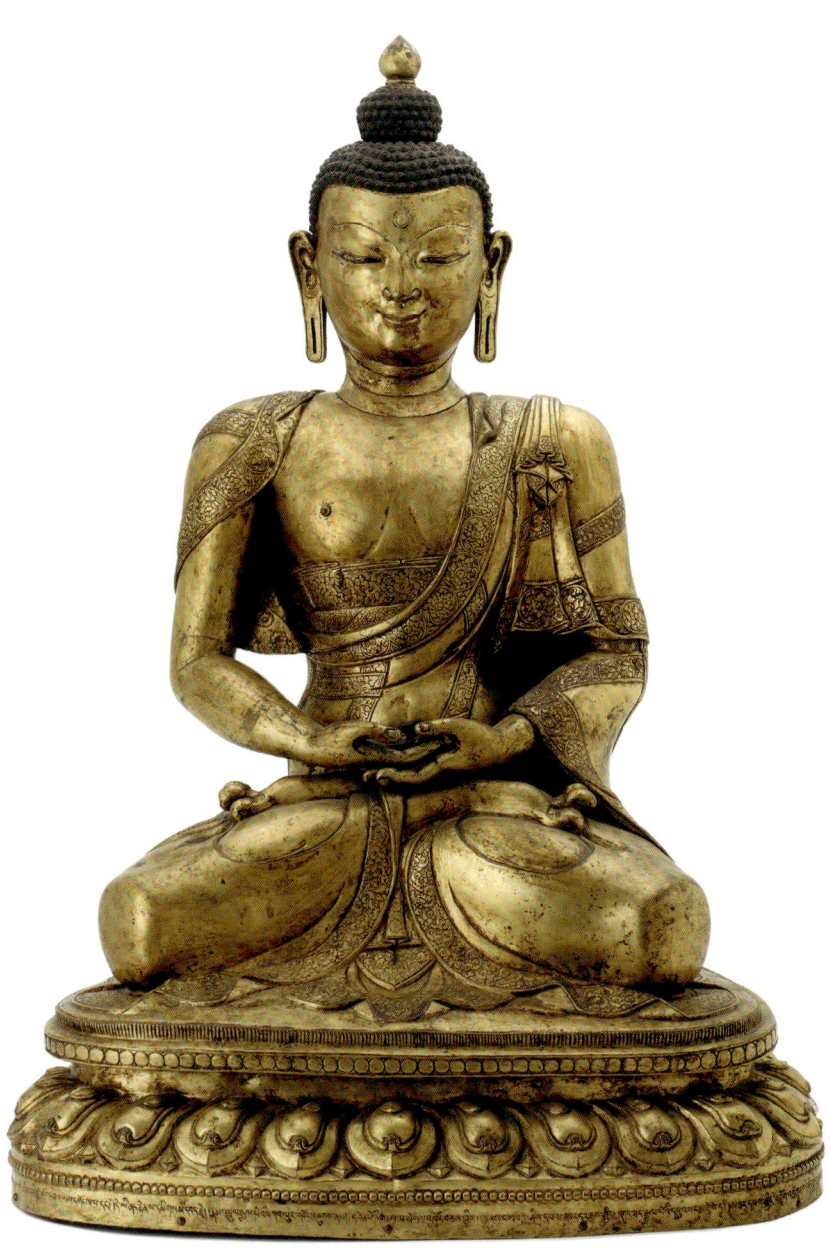

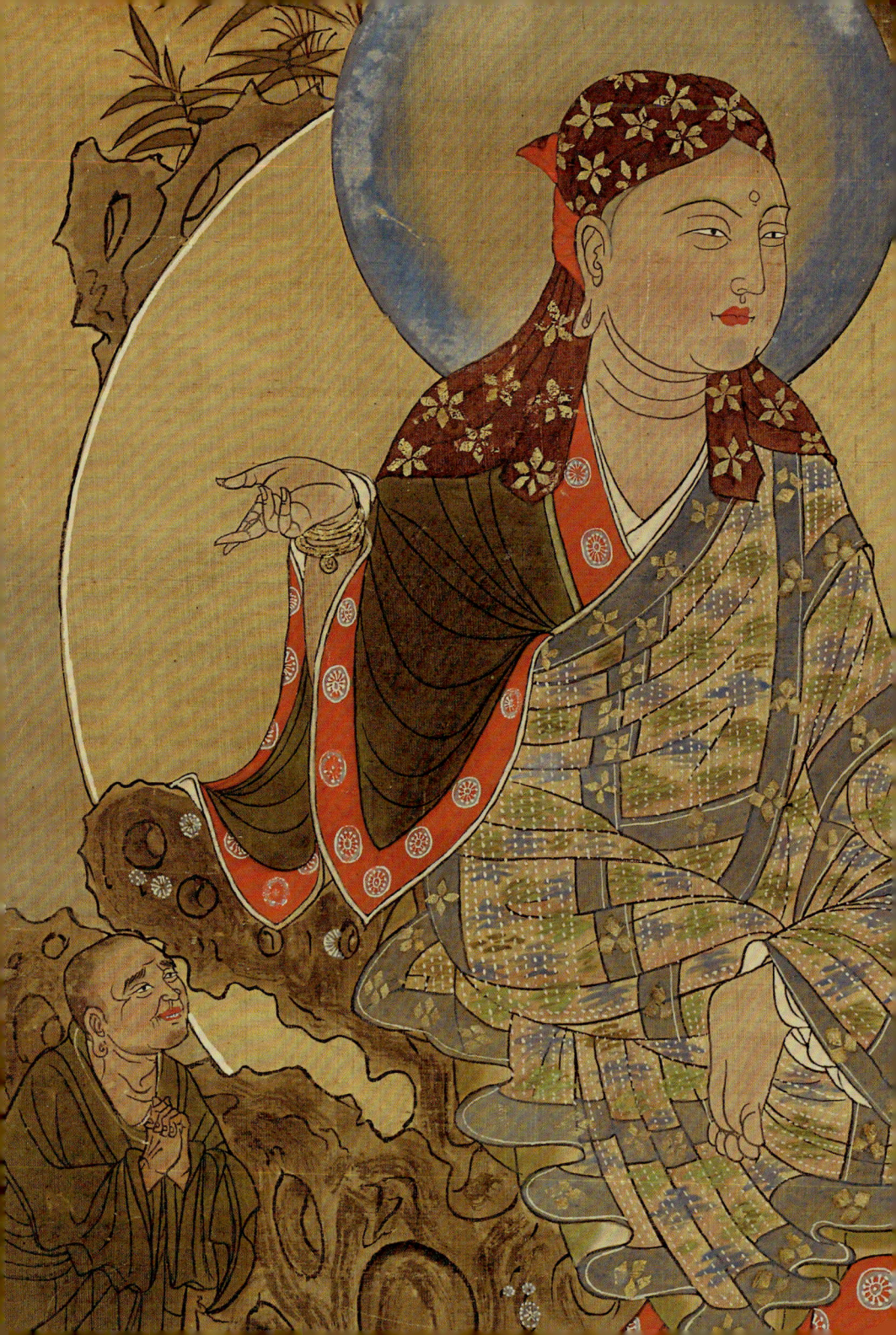

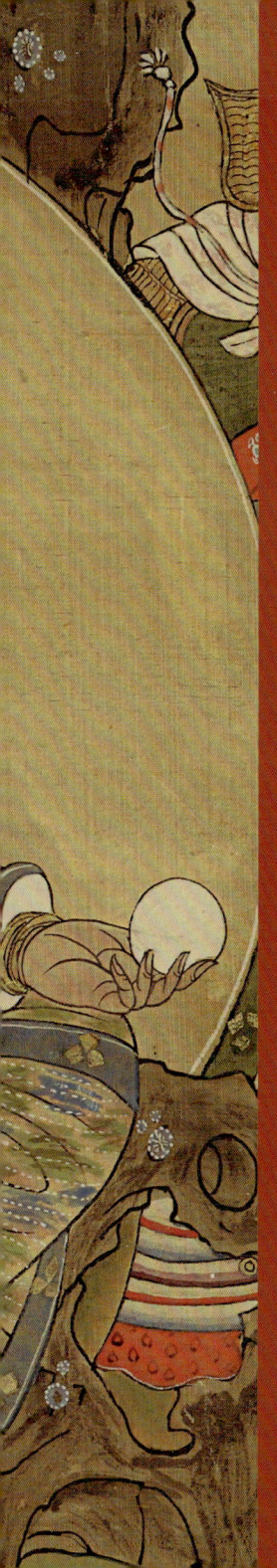

Bodhisattvas

The path to becoming a buddha is long and arduous. By most accounts, it takes countless virtuous lifetimes to achieve. The process usually begins with a sincere vow in which a practitioner proclaims buddhahood as the ultimate goal. Those walking the path to buddhahood are called bodhisattvas, individuals whose being (sattva) is dedicated to attaining enlightenment (bodhi) in order to help other beings.

Such exalted beings can assist others—and they have the generosity and patience to do so willingly. Bodhisattvas are generally depicted as beautiful, richly adorned figures, reflecting their inner virtues and the good karma their benevolence has garnered. Notable bodhisattvas include Avalokiteshvara (associated with compassion), Manjushri (associated with insight), Samantabhadra (associated with meditation), and Kshitigarbha, who is known for protecting children and easing the suffering of those in hell.

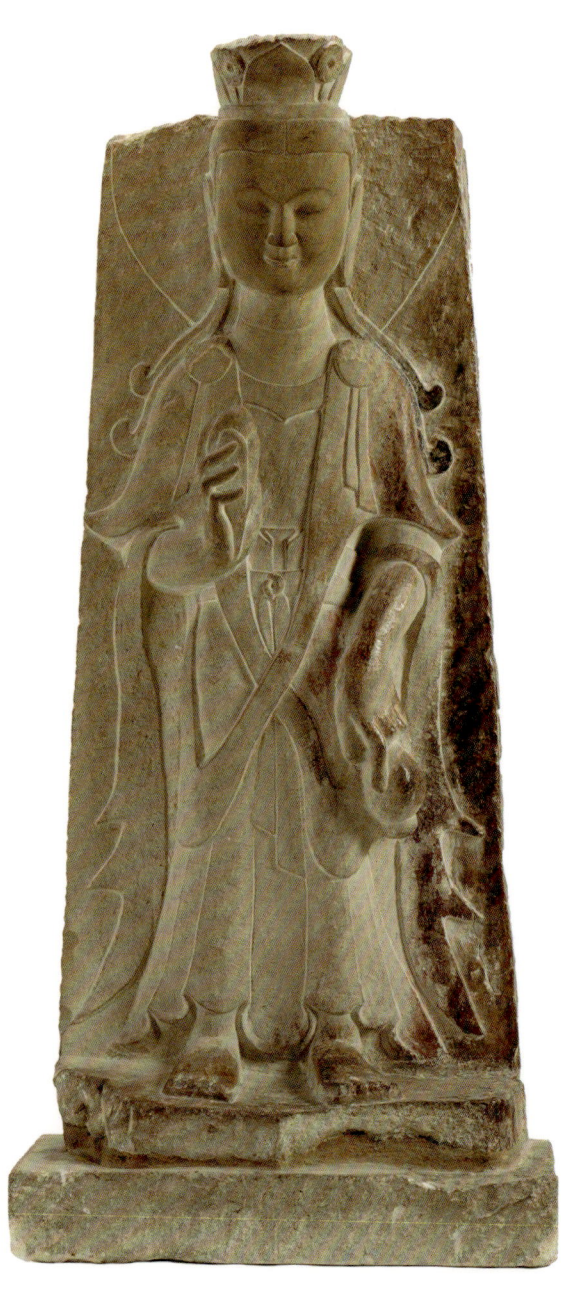

Bodhisattva, probably Avalokiteshvara (Guanyin)
China, Henan Province, Luoyang, Gongxian cave temples, Cave 1
Late Northern Wei dynasty, ca. 523
Sandstone with traces of pigment
104.1 × 47.4 × 27.2 cm
Purchase, Freer Gallery of Art, F1952.15

Seeking shelter during the rainy season, India's wandering holy men stayed in caves. Thus began the Buddhist practice of cutting caverns into hillsides. The tradition accompanied Buddhism to northern China, where many cave temples still survive. Only rulers, aristocrats, and other wealthy patrons could afford to have caverns sliced into the earth, a complex and costly act of devotion.

The most important caves, created between the fourth and eighth centuries, held sculptural groups of deities in niches along the walls and in the central altar. Typically, these images came as pairs flanking a central buddha.

Recent research proves that this sculpture once inhabited Cave 1 at Gongxian, located near Luoyang, where the capital was moved in 494. Made of sandstone, the bodhisattva was one of two that stood beside a seated buddha in a large wall niche. This one must have been removed before 1914, when it was documented as part of a collection in Berlin. The lotus in the deity's right hand suggests that this is Avalokiteshvara (in Chinese, Guanyin). Created in the sixth century, the bodhisattva's flattened form and angularly pleated robes seem rigid and abstract compared to later sculptures.

KW

Bodhisattva, possibly Avalokiteshvara (Guanyin)
China, Hebei Province, Fengfeng, southern Xiangtangshan
cave temples, Cave 2
Northern Qi dynasty, 550–77
Limestone with traces of pigment
172.5 × 51.8 × 42.9 cm
Gift of Eugene and Agnes E. Meyer, Freer Gallery of Art, F1968.45

The rulers of China's brief Northern Qi dynasty (550–77) sponsored three large Buddhist cave chapels at a site called Xiangtangshan ("Mountain of Echoing Halls") near their capital. Inspired, courtiers developed a related set of seven caves about nine miles farther south. Although smaller in scale, the southern caves featured some of the most beautiful devotional stone sculpture ever created in China, including this piece.

Many scholars believe that this sculpture originally stood on the main altar of Cave 2 at southern Xiangtangshan. Unlike our bodhisattva from the Gongxian Cave Temples (p. 73), carved some thirty years earlier directly into the rock wall, this figure is freestanding, cut from quarried stone, and designed for the altar. A stone extension beneath its feet would have fit into a socket cut into the cave floor. Although the back is relatively plain, sharply cut details on the front and sides define a figure with a swelling bare chest, a skirt tied at the waist, a long wrap and scarves, and relatively modest jewelry. In each respect, this representation is more naturalistic than the Gongxian bodhisattva, illustrating the rapid pace of stylistic change in sixth-century Chinese Buddhist sculpture.

When Cave 2 was first surveyed and photographed in 1922, a seated buddha and two flanking monastic figures were still in place; they had been cut into the cave itself. Two additional pairs of freestanding attendants were missing, however, as indicated by empty sockets in the floor. Since this cave also contained the monumental depiction of the Western Paradise of Buddha Amitabha (p. 37), the main altar image was probably Amitabha flanked by his bodhisattvas Avalokiteshvara (in Chinese, Guanyin) and Mahasthamaprapta (Dashizhi).

KW

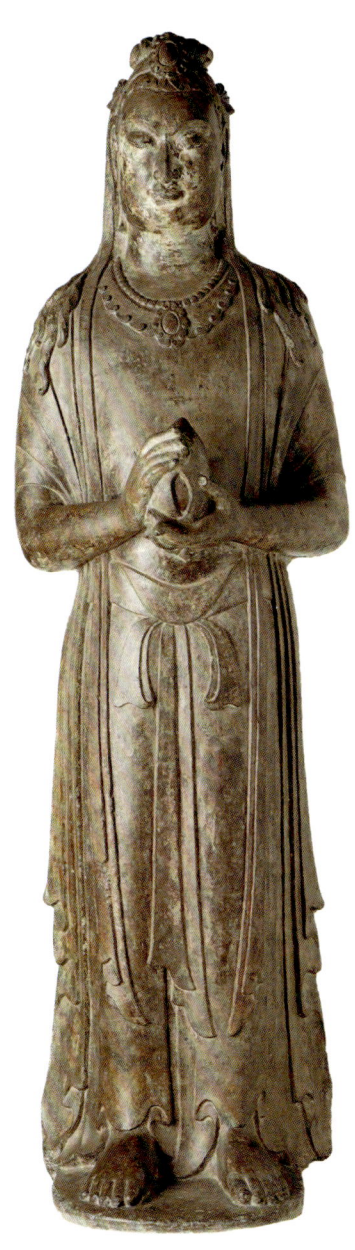

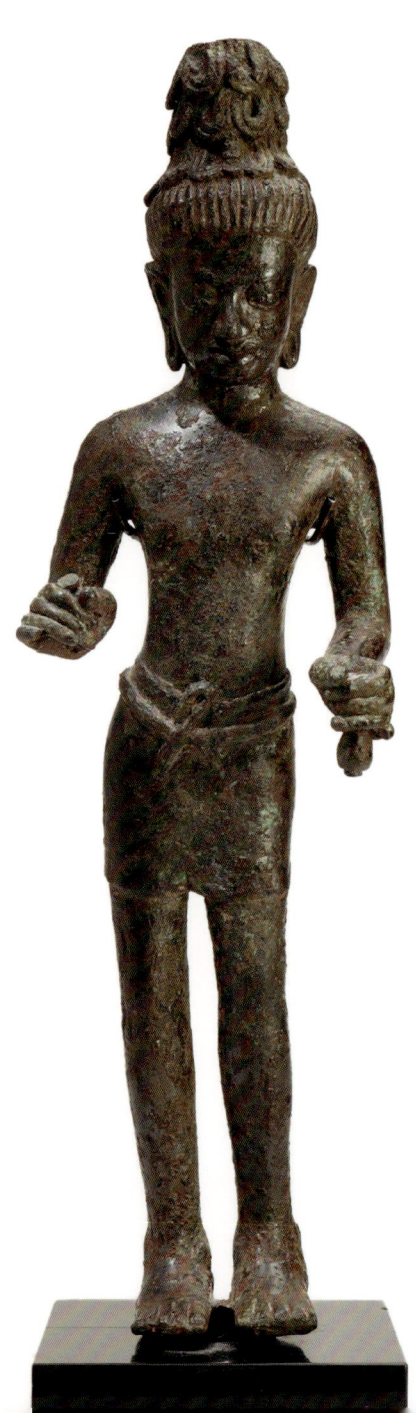

Maitreya or Avalokiteshvara
Northeastern Thailand, 7th century
High tin bronze
35 × 9.8 × 7 cm
Gift of Ann and Gilbert Kinney, Arthur M. Sackler Gallery, S2015.24

In 1964, villagers in northeast Thailand discovered an underground chamber while exploring a derelict temple. Inside, they found more than thirty Buddhist bronzes of considerable quality. Ranging in date from the late seventh to the early ninth century, most of these images depict Maitreya and Avalokiteshvara.

What immediately sets this group of bodhisattvas apart from similar works is their lack of lavish clothes and jewelry. Instead, each bears characteristics of an ascetic: matted hair tied up in a high, conical topknot (*jatamukuta*) and a simple loincloth. Many images from the group, including this sculpture, hold a water vessel. Most of the bodhisattvas can be identified by an attribute on the topknot: Avalokiteshvara has a seated buddha, and Maitreya has a small stupa.

We don't know why this hoard of bronzes was hidden away. It may have been related to a period of religious instability. Traces of cloth wrapping indicate that the sculptures were buried with care and respect. Unfortunately, this protection did not prevent the attribute in this bodhisattva's topknot from weathering beyond recognition. It is now impossible to determine if it depicts a buddha or a stupa. Is this Avalokiteshvara or Maitreya? The identity of this bodhisattva remains a mystery.

JE

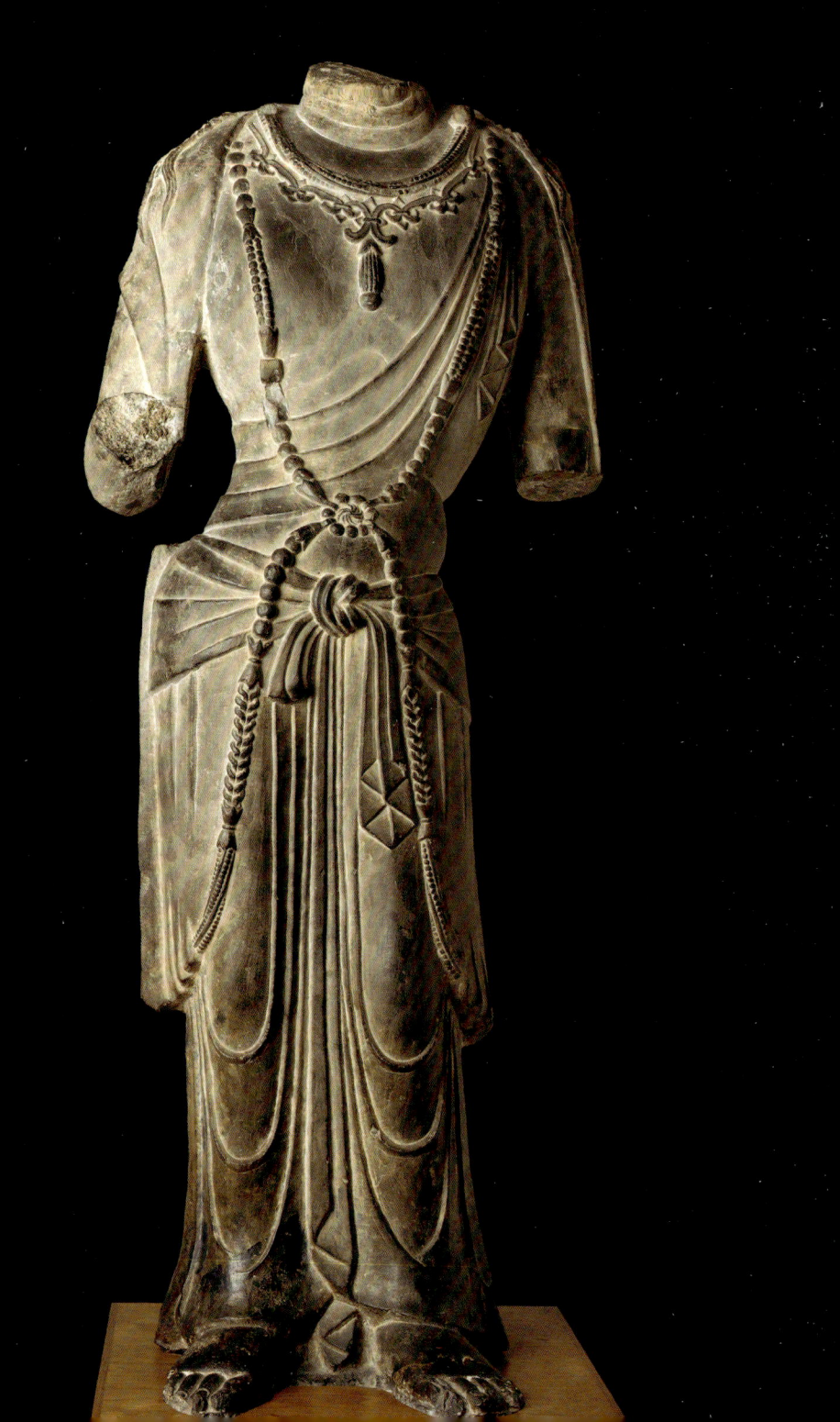

Bodhisattva

China, Shaanxi Province, probably Chang'an (modern Xi'an)
Tang dynasty, early 8th century
Limestone with traces of pigment and gesso
101.7 × 40.9 × 26.7 cm
Gift of Charles Lang Freer, Freer Gallery of Art, F1916.365

With its sensuous nature, this bodhisattva manifests the sculptural style characteristic in China during the Tang dynasty (618–907), when Indian precedents were heavily influential. Travelers and pilgrims—notably the monk Xuanzang, who returned to China in 645 after a sixteen-year journey to India—introduced a stunning new sensibility for Buddhist art in the capital city of Chang'an. The Chinese court welcomed the hybrid style, which was followed widely throughout the Tang dynasty.

Here, Indian sculpture inspired the tiny waist, soft folds of the abdomen, and thrusted hip as the figure takes an incipient step. Such features would become more striking later in the eighth century. The palpable fleshiness and sense of movement contrast with earlier Chinese statues, fashioned with flat bodies in static poses. The clinging skirt, jeweled chains, and tendrils of hair cascading onto the shoulders (now somewhat difficult to visualize without the figure's head) are also familiar in Indian statuary, but they have been modified by Chinese taste. The linear flow of the sash across the sculpture's chest and of the drapery folds are reminiscent of earlier Chinese models.

The sculpture is missing its head, arms, and double-lotus pedestal, making it more difficult to enjoy the sublimely balanced proportion—a high point of early eighth-century masterpieces. Comparing this torso with complete sculptures in situ almost certainly confirms it was made in Chang'an under imperial patronage. We don't know when the figure was damaged, but many sculptures incurred such losses when they were removed from China around the fall of the Qing dynasty in 1911.

JS

Avalokiteshvara (Guanyin) with Eleven Heads
China, Shaanxi Province, Chang'an (Xi'an), Guangzhai Temple,
Qibaotai Pagoda
Tang dynasty, 703
Limestone
77.8 × 31.5 × 18.8 cm; 108.8 × 31.7 × 15.3 cm
Gift of Charles Lang Freer, Freer Gallery of Art,
F1914.55 and F1909.98

Avalokiteshvara (in Chinese, Guanyin) sometimes is shown in a superhuman mode with eleven heads. This subject can be traced to a story in which, overwhelmed by the immense suffering of all the beings in the universe, the bodhisattva's head split into eleven pieces. Buddha Amitabha refashioned the fragments as eleven heads so that Avalokiteshvara could better see, hear, and tend to the needs of sentient beings.

Such multiheaded and, often, multilimbed images were created for tantric Buddhism. Characterized by symbolic rituals and magic spells or incantations (dharanis and mantras), tantric Buddhism began gaining popularity in China in the early seventh century. An increasingly sensuous style of sculpture, distinguished by fleshy and more naturalistic figures, also marked this period.

These two sculptures belong to a set that once decorated the Tower of Seven Treasures, a pagoda commissioned by Wu Zetian (624–705), the only female to rule China using the title "emperor." In 696, a nomadic group from Mongolia overran the Tang armies. To safeguard the state, Wu Zetian, a devout Buddhist, ordered protective dharanis to be chanted at an eleven-headed Avalokiteshvara altar in Chang'an, the Tang capital. Shortly thereafter, the invaders were defeated, and the pagoda was built to celebrate Avalokiteshvara's role as a national protector. Although it no longer exists, the structure is thought to have occupied a central location in the Guangzhai Monastery in Chang'an.

KW

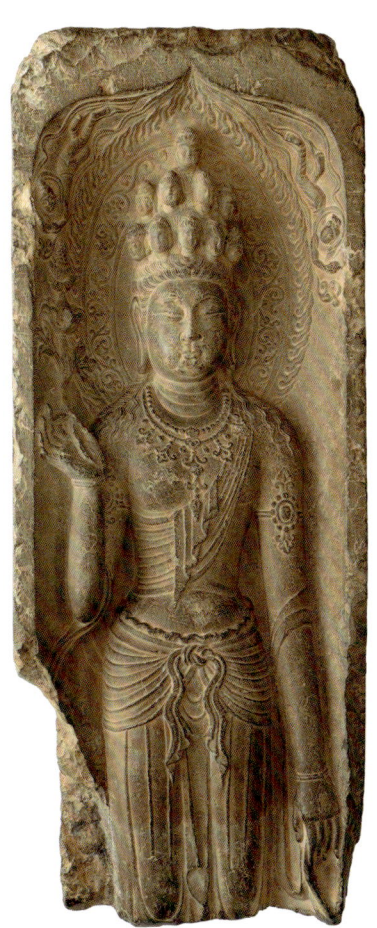
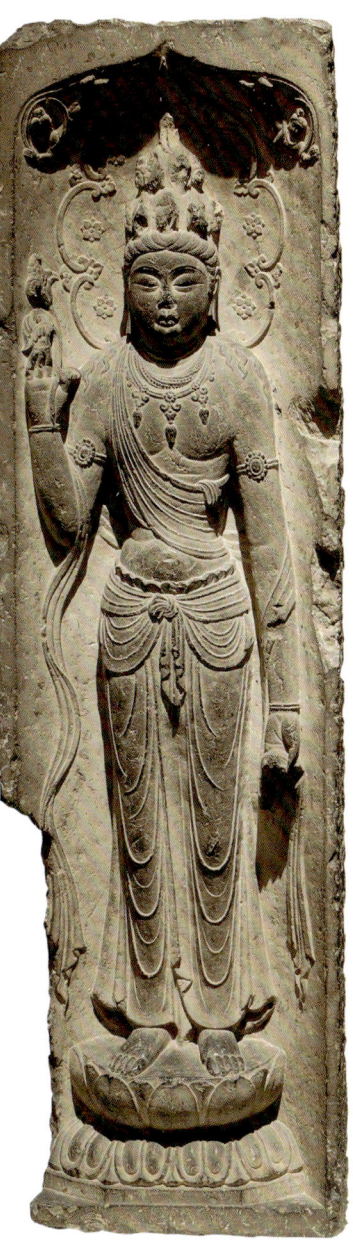

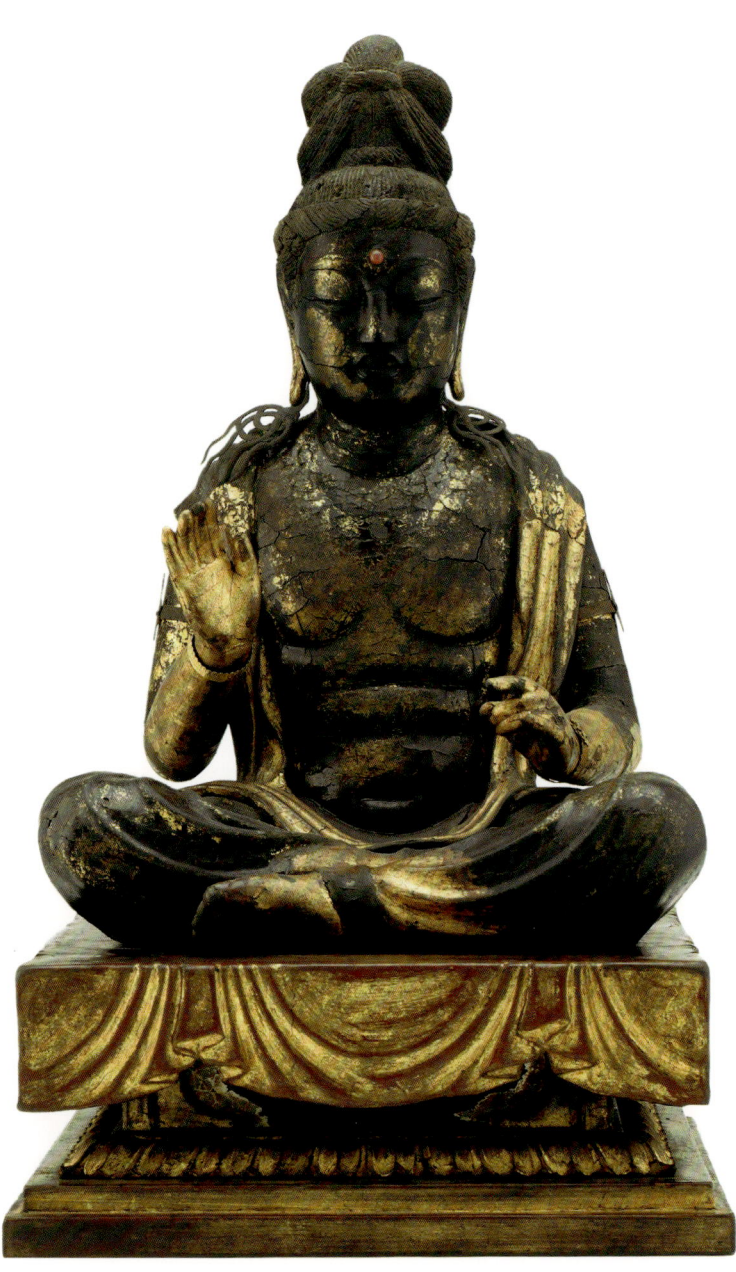

Avalokiteshvara (Kannon)
Japan, Heian period, late 9th–early 10th century
Wood, lacquer, gold, and agate
59.8 × 35.4 × 32.3 cm
Gift of Charles Lang Freer, Freer Gallery of Art, F1909.344a–i

Golden skin is one of the distinctive features of buddhas and enlightened bodhisattvas. Whether created for temples or smaller private shrines, sculptures of buddhas and bodhisattvas often were embellished with gold pigment or gold leaf. Light seemed to emanate from their gilded forms on altars, where they were worshipped and given offerings of food and flowers. Only traces of gilding remain on this seated bodhisattva, but we can imagine its original splendor. The figure also once wore a gilt metal crown and jewelry, and it may have held a lotus in its left hand.

Serenely seated in meditation, the figure conveys the compassion of the bodhisattva Avalokiteshvara, known in Japan as Kannon (and in Chinese, Guanyin). Wood and a thick layer of lacquer and other materials lend the body and face a fleshy, lifelike appearance. This sculptural technique, known as wood-core dry lacquer, was replaced during the Heian period (794–1185). Carved wood became the principal material for Japanese Buddhist images destined for temple altars.

The Japanese Buddhist preference for using wood to sculpt sacred images drew on older beliefs that spirits dwelled in trees and other natural features. Japanese stories about the founding of Buddhist temples often describe the main icons as carved from sacred trees that emanate light.

AY

Fragment of a temple wall painting
China, Henan Province, Wen Xian, Cisheng Temple
Five Dynasties period, Northern Zhou, ca. 952
Ink and colors on primed mud-wall construction
175.6 × 85.5 cm
Gift of Arthur M. Sackler, Arthur M. Sackler Gallery, S1987.224

Large interior paintings were a special feature of many northern Chinese temples. Artists worked on primed mud or stucco-like surfaces, using ink, pigments, and gold to render grand Buddhist paradises. Illustrating Buddhist teachings, such images offered believers a tool for visualization and meditation practices.

In 1923, monks attempting to raise funds to repair their temple sold pieces of a large wall painting to the dealer C. T. Loo. This fragment was among those he brought to America. The others are dispersed among museums in Boston, Chicago, Honolulu, Kansas City, Minneapolis, Princeton, St. Louis, and Toledo, as well as in Paris, Loo's original overseas base.

Wai-kam Ho, a great twentieth-century Buddhist art authority, studied a fragment in the Nelson-Atkins Museum of Art in Kansas City and found content that applies to the whole group. He discovered the original wall painting was in a temple named Cisheng, in Henan near its border with Shanxi Province. An inscription dates it to 952 and indicates the painting was completed to initiate a wish. Buddhists commonly commissioned works to make wishes for peace and for the salvation of the recently deceased.

The fragment in the Freer|Sackler pictures two haloed, bejeweled figures, who probably were part of a procession toward the painting's central buddha. The standing bodhisattva holds an offering in a translucent bowl, which conjures an image of luxury and exotica: through at least the tenth century, China's finest glass was imported. The fragment retains the beauty of the painting's lines, as well some of its elegant coloring, such as the green tones. Other colors, including the skin of the seated figure, have darkened.

JS

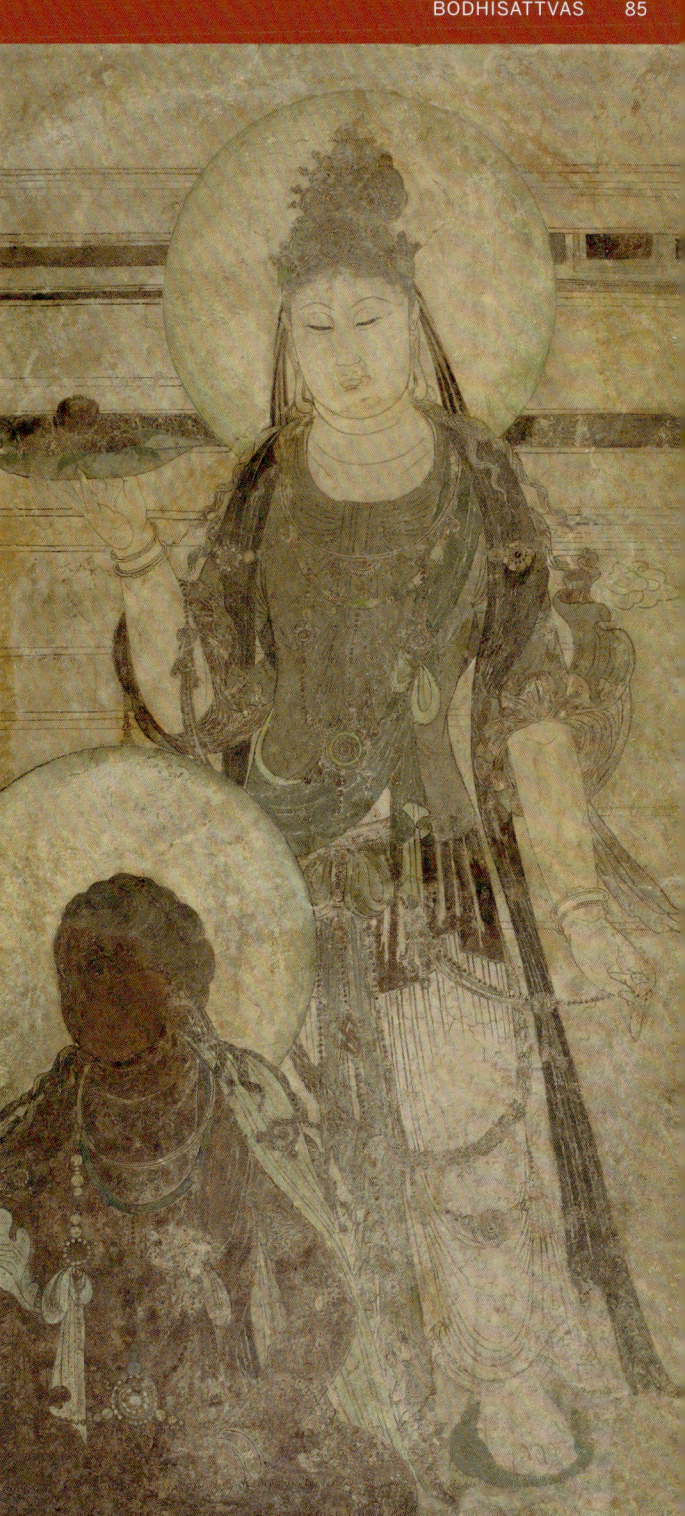

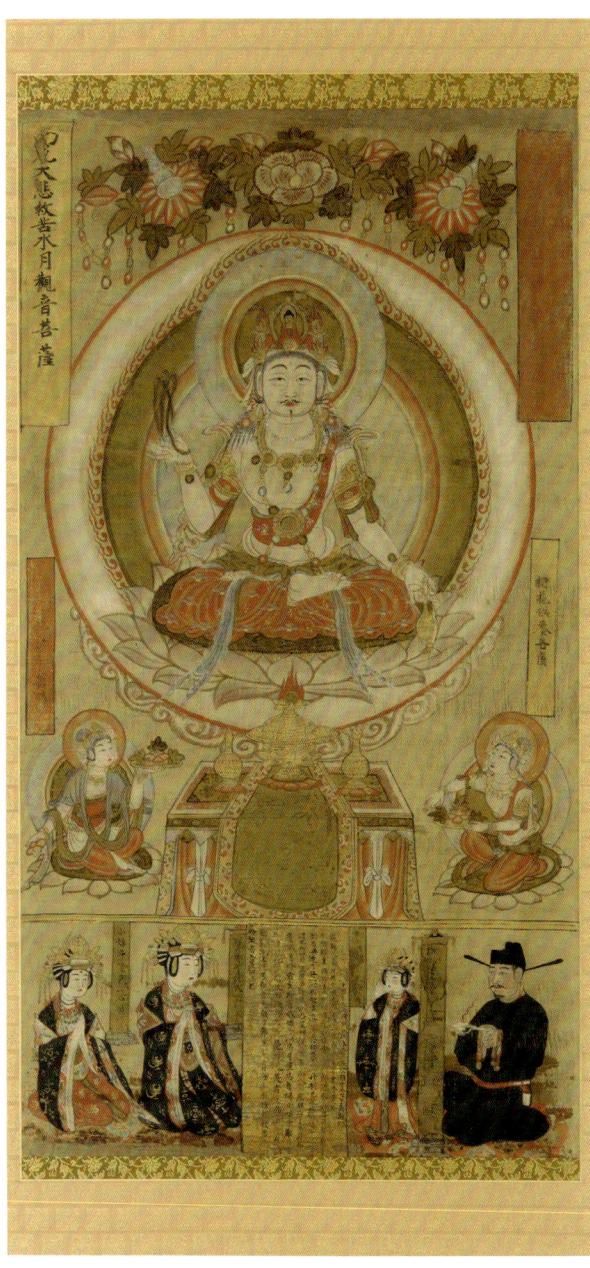

Water Moon Avalokiteshvara (Guanyin)
Anonymous painter
China, Gansu Province, Dunhuang, Northern Song dynasty, 968
Hanging scroll mounted on panel; ink and color on silk
106.8 × 58.9 cm
Purchase—Charles Lang Freer Endowment, Freer Gallery of Art, F1930.36

In 1900, this scroll and one of Kshitigarbha (p. 88) were discovered in a sealed chamber at the Mogao Caves, a Buddhist temple complex located outside the Chinese town of Dunhuang. Beneath a canopy of flowers strung with jewels, a majestic figure sits cross-legged on a mat supported by a white lotus. Softly curving lines define his broad oval face; a mustache and goatee set off his full lips. Two multicolor halos pulsate from his head and body, encompassed by a large lunar disc. His gaze is fixed directly on the viewer. The yellow box at upper left reads: "Homage to the Compassionate Deliverer from Suffering, Bodhisattva Guanyin of the Water Moon," identifying this figure as Avalokiteshvara (in Chinese, Guanyin), one of the most potent and popular of Buddha's followers and the embodiment of compassion.

Originally an Indian prince, Avalokiteshvara wears the jewelry customary to his noble station: a tall crown; heavy earrings; a crystal necklace; bracelets on his wrists, arms, and ankles; and a harness of gold and precious stones that culminates in two scarves. Light blue-and-peach designs decorate his orange-red skirt.

At the bottom, the artist depicted the four donors of the painting: a man in somber black robes and matching official hat, and three robed women with gold phoenix headdresses. Two figures kneel on either side of the central inscription, which invokes the blessings of Avalokiteshvara. Next to each figure is a green box inscribed with his or her name; two of the boxes are damaged, one too extensively to read. Fortunately, an early owner recorded the names when he received the scroll in 1904. Evidently, the male was a high-ranking prince of Dunhuang's ruling family, and the others were the chief women of his household.

SDA

Kshitigarbha (Dizang)
Anonymous painter
China, Gansu Province, Dunhuang, Northern Song dynasty, ca. 1002
Hanging scroll mounted on panel; ink, color, and gold on silk
106.6 × 58.1 cm
Purchase—Charles Lang Freer Endowment, Freer Gallery of Art, F1935.11

Resting on a stone pocked with holes and lichen, the bodhisattva Kshitigarbha (in Chinese, Dizang) wears a spangled purple head scarf and the patchwork robe of a Chan monk. As if about to issue instructions, he gestures with his right hand to his follower Monk Daoming and a white lion-dog below. In his left hand, he holds a glowing "wish-granting jewel." Armed with sword and bow, a warrior identified as General of the Five Ways attends him, reverently holding the bodhisattva's long-handled staff.

Kshitigarbha is sworn to rescue suffering souls from hell. Appropriately, texts on this painting indicate that it was created for the third anniversary of the death of Princess Li, wife of Cao Yanlu, who ruled Dunhuang from 976 to 1002. After three years, her deceased soul had completed its sojourn in hell and was ready for rebirth—with Kshitigarbha's benevolent intercession—in paradise.

The princess appears on the bottom right. Kneeling on a red carpet and holding up a flower and incense burner, she wears a splendid gown and a spectacular golden phoenix headdress. Behind her are two young female attendants, one bearing a large fan with bird motifs and the other a bundle that may contain a musical instrument.

SDA

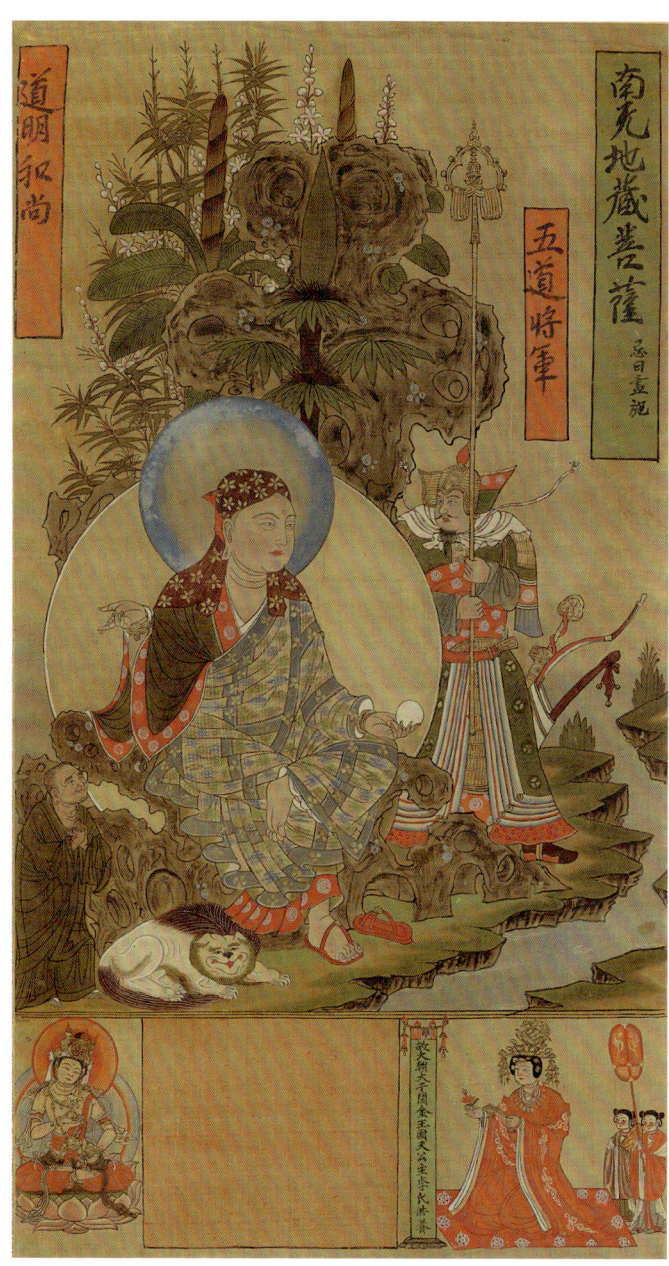

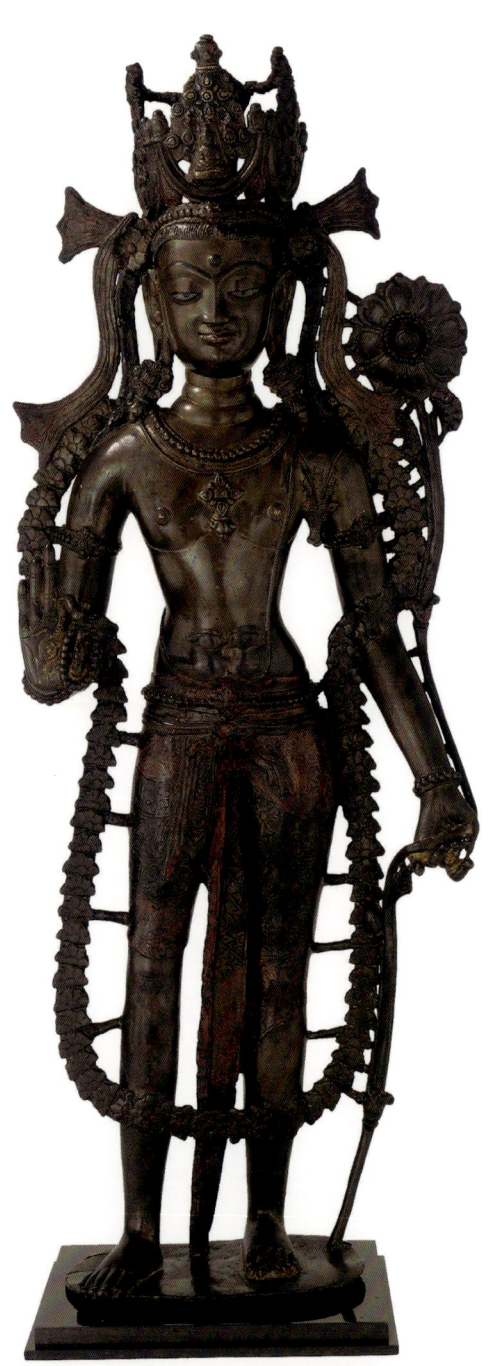

Avalokiteshvara
Western Tibet, Guge, 1000–1050
Brass alloy with copper and tin inlay, colored wax, traces of gilding and pigment
82.3 × 32.1 × 21.6 cm
Purchase—Charles Lang Freer Endowment, Freer Gallery of Art, F2001.2a–d

Following the ninth-century collapse of the Tibetan empire, descendants of royal and noble families established small kingdoms encompassing the western Himalayas. Seeking to revive Buddhism among their subjects, the new rulers looked to neighboring Kashmir, one of ancient India's great centers of Buddhist artistic and intellectual production. Kashmir became the young kingdoms' primary source for expert teachers to educate new monks, skilled artisans to build new monasteries, and elite artists to populate new shrines with images such as this one. Kashmir's masters of art and religion brought with them cultural and intellectual innovations that became integral to the development of Buddhism and Buddhist art in the western Himalayas.

This sculpture of Avalokiteshvara, made by a master Kashmiri artist (or his Tibetan student) in western Tibet, highlights Kashmir's significant impact on and collaboration with the region's blossoming culture. A long flower garland frames the bodhisattva's triangular torso, voluminous chest, and gently curving posture. Traces of gilding can be seen on his palms, while remnants of red pigment still decorate the delicately embellished dhoti around his waist and the scarves unfurling from his three-pointed crown. Inlaid, heavy-lidded eyes and colored, full lips punctuate Avalokiteshvara's peaceful countenance. A blossom is tucked behind each ear. These distinctive attributes place the sculpture among the remarkable small and monumental images made by Kashmiri artists and their students in northern India and western Tibet during the tenth and eleventh centuries.

RB

Avalokiteshvara (Guanyin)
China, Yunnan Province, historic Dali kingdom
12th century
Arsenical copper with gilding
49.4 × 11.4 cm
Purchase, Freer Gallery of Art, F1946.10a–b

This statue of Avalokiteshvara (in Chinese, Guanyin), the bodhisattva of compassion, was cast in the Dali kingdom, an independent realm that ruled over an area in southern China from 937 to 1253. Buddhism was the state religion, and a special cult was devoted to Avalokiteshvara. Located at the crossroads of Southeast Asia, Tibet, and China, the kingdom was characterized by an eclectic style of transnational Buddhist imagery.

A small group of figures similar to this one is dispersed among several museums. One in the San Diego Art Museum is especially important as a rare example with a dated inscription, which corresponds to between 1147 and 1172. The inscription links the sculpture to the patronage of Emperor Duan Zhengxing, who wished for the prosperity and longevity of the Dali kingdom's royal family.

All of the related statues feature the same slender, flat body and serene face, as well as the same kind of jewelry, including heavy earrings. All are dressed in a light, transparent skirt tied at the waist in the same elaborate manner. And all have a tall chignon embellished with a small image of a seated Amitabha. Long braids bind the topknot and cascade onto the shoulders. Furthermore, all of the images' hands make the same mudras: exposition (*vitarka*) and wish granting (*varada*). Originally, a gilded metal nimbus, or body halo, was attached behind each sculpture to represent the radiant light of the bodhisattva's spirituality.

The Freer|Sackler's Department of Conservation and Scientific Research discovered charcoal inside this figure—the remains of relics and texts used to consecrate the image. The relics burned when the surface of the statue was gilded using high heat.

JS

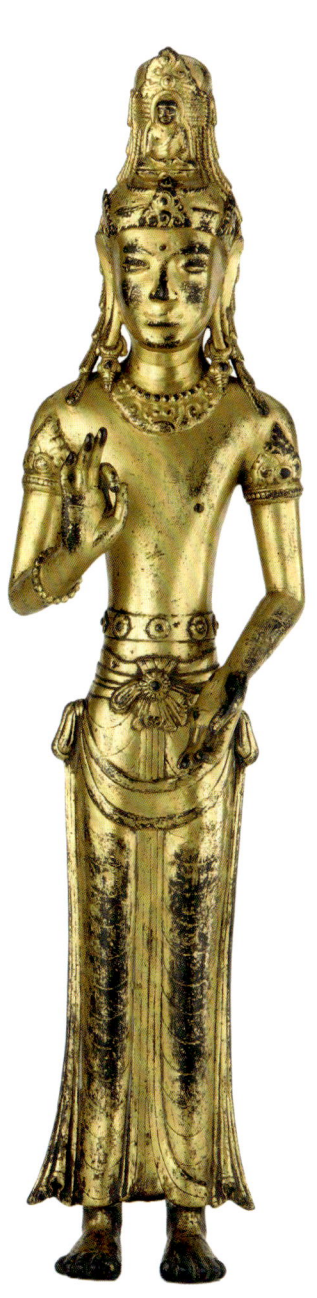

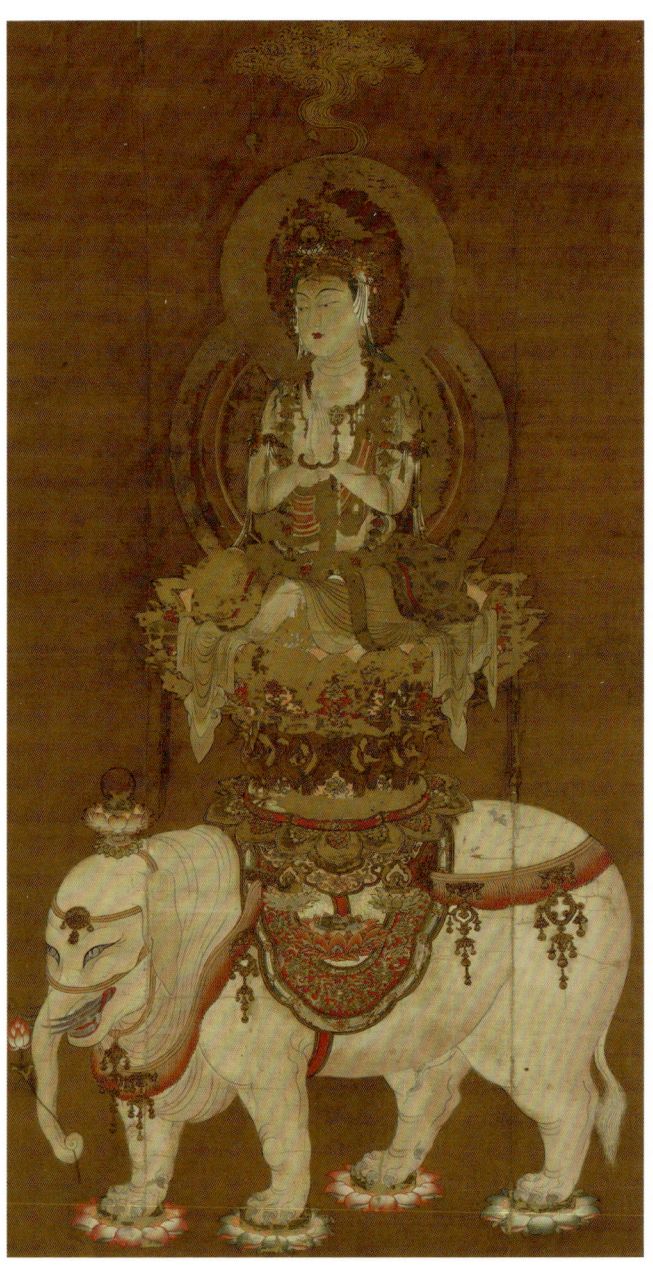

Samantabhadra (Fugen)
Japan, Heian period, 12th century
Hanging scroll mounted on panel; ink, color, gold, and silver on silk
155.9 × 83.3 cm
Purchase—Charles Lang Freer Endowment, Freer Gallery of Art, F1963.6

Worship of the bodhisattva Samantabhadra (in Japanese, Fugen) flourished in Japan from the twelfth through the fourteenth century. Japanese Buddhists believed that this time of disorder and suffering would continue until the next buddha appeared. The *Lotus Sutra* (Hokkekyo), with its promise of salvation to those who read and recited it, became a rich source of solace, hope, and imagery for Buddhist art.

Samantabhadra, whose name means "Universal Worthy," is the focus of the *Lotus Sutra*'s final chapter. Often followed by a closing text (see p. 170), this chapter promises that the bodhisattva will ride in on a six-tusked white elephant to teach, bless, and protect those who recite the sutra. Samantabhadra is described as arriving from the east atop his elephant, which bears lotuses in its trunk and beneath its feet as it strides across the sky. This is the largest-known Japanese painting of Samantabhadra from its time.

Samantabhadra often is paired with the bodhisattva Manjushri (in Japanese, Monju; see p. 99) as a fellow attendant to Shakyamuni. In Japan, however, Samantabhadra often was worshipped independently, especially by members of the Tendai school, which focused on the *Lotus Sutra*. This painting can be traced to the temple Daiganji, according to a record of its repair in 1743. Using complex techniques, including painting on both sides of the thin silk, the artist created an image of imposing authority.

AY

Bodhisattva
Kaikei (act. ca. 1185–1220)
Japan, Kamakura period, early 13th century
Wood with lacquer, gold, copper, and crystal
62.8 × 43.2 × 36 cm
Gift of Charles Lang Freer, Freer Gallery of Art, F1909.345a–h

In the waning years of the twelfth century, Japan was convulsed by a civil war that essentially deposed the imperial court and established the first of a long line of military governments ruled by shoguns. Massive destruction left temples and monasteries, along with their iconography, in ruins. When political stability returned, artisans received substantial commissions to produce new works.

Dating to the early thirteenth century, this gentle figure of an unidentified bodhisattva comprises several parts, a technical innovation that evolved most prominently in this period. Notably, the hollow torso fits onto the figure's lap. Glass or rock-crystal insets enhance the realism of the eyes, a new technique at the time that later became commonplace. Realistic and sensitive modeling distinguishes this style, which was largely an adaptation of Chinese Buddhist iconography techniques from the Song dynasty. Recent scholarship and the authentication of a signature mark inside this sculpture confirm it is by Kaikei (active circa 1185–1220), a master sculptor whose innovations were central to the flowering of a sculptural style during the Kamakura period (1185–1333).

JU

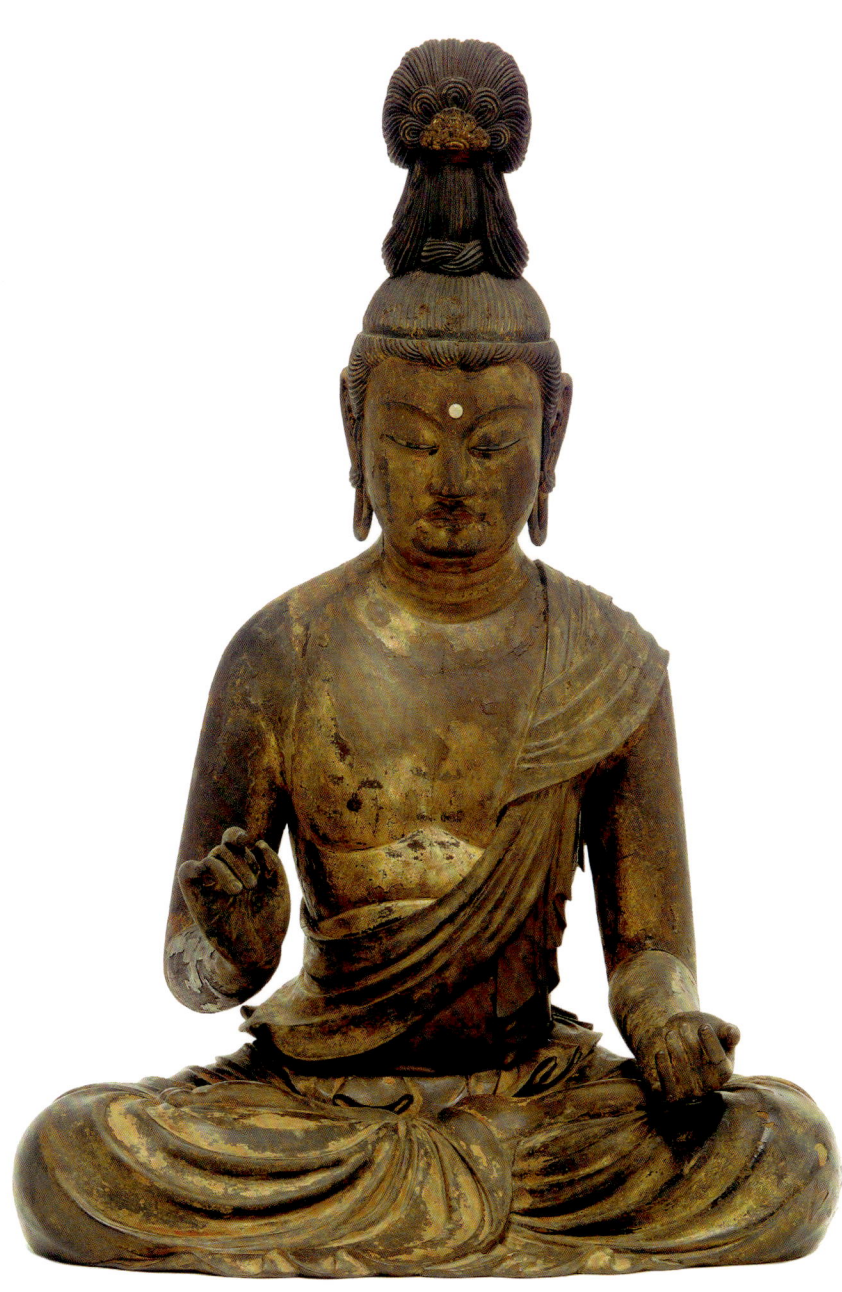

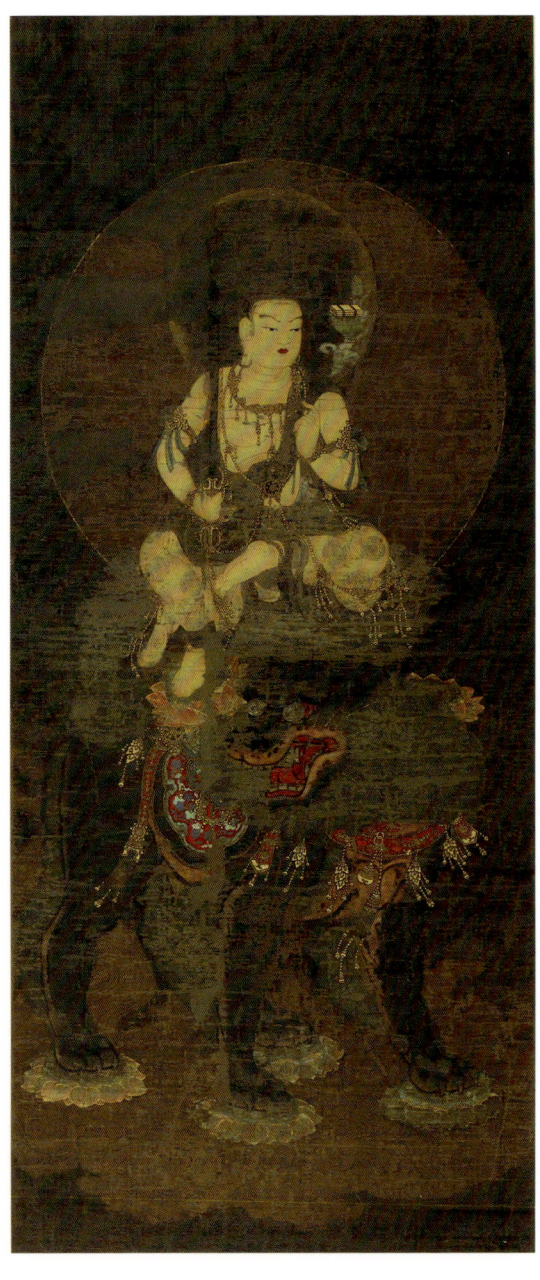

Manjushri (Monju)
Japan, Kamakura period (1185–1333)
Hanging scroll; ink, color, and gold on silk
129.6 × 56.7 cm
Gift of Charles Lang Freer, Freer Gallery of Art, F1905.292

The bodhisattva Manjushri (in Japanese, Monju) represents *prajna* (insight) and wisdom. He often is paired with the bodhisattva Samantabhadra (Fugen) as an attendant to Shakyamuni; like Samantabhadra, however, Manjushri came to be worshipped independently. He is traditionally depicted riding a blue lion, a visual metaphor for the power of wisdom to tame the mind. In this painting, the bodhisattva holds in his left hand a lotus surmounted by a sutra. In his right hand, he holds a *vajra*, a weapon that dispels ignorance and illusion.

Manjushri is said to live in a heavenly realm known as the eastern Pure Land. Here, he rides his lion as it approaches through the clouds. Standing on lotuses, the lion bears the deity in a lotus-form seat, much like Samantabhadra's elephant (p. 95).

The painting's large scale—it is more than four feet tall—and rich decoration indicate that it was an important work. An inscription on its storage box indicates that the painting once was held in Seijoshin'in, a temple at the great monastic center at Mount Koya (Koyasan), headquarters of the Shingon school.

AY

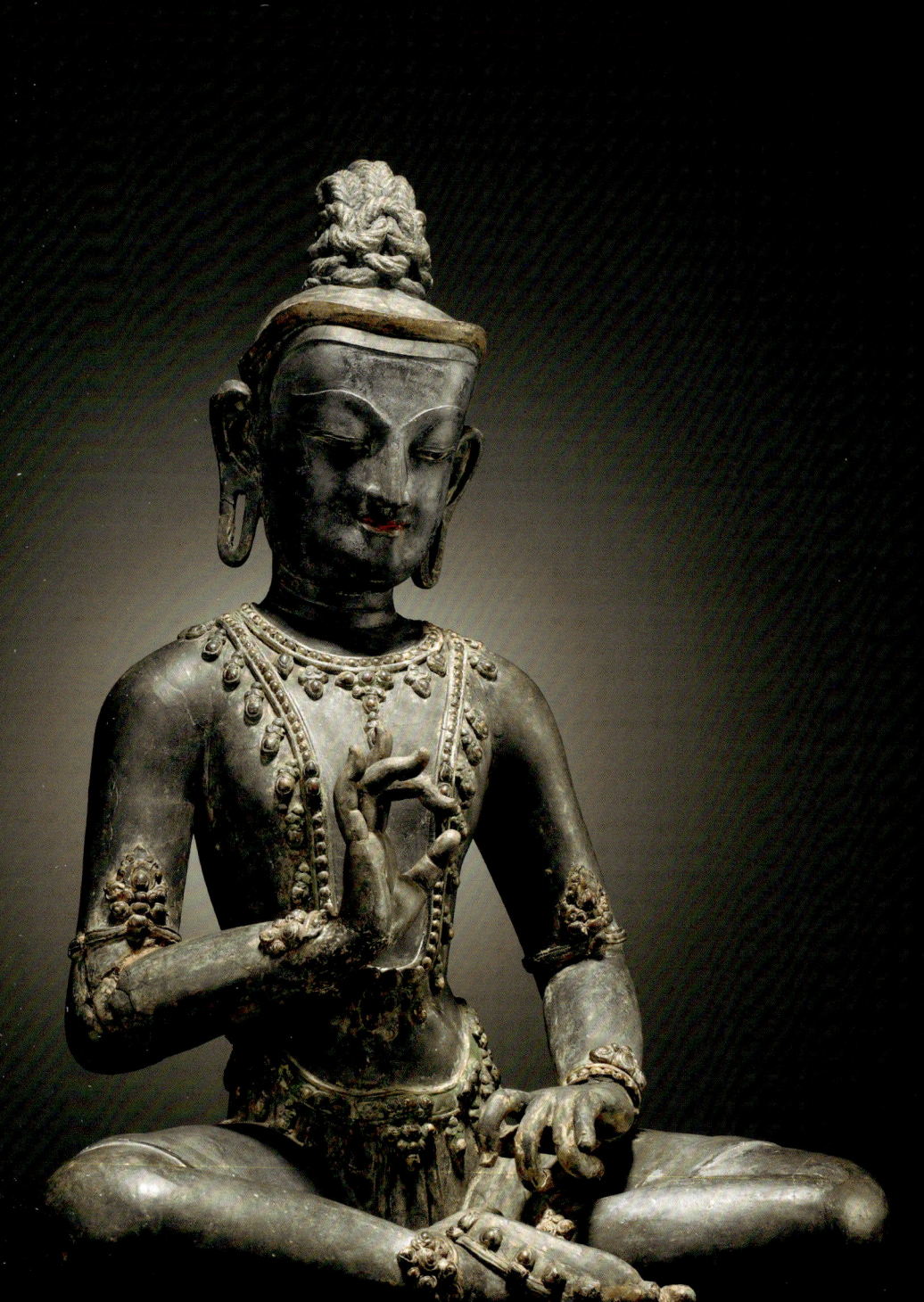

Bodhisattva
Attributed to the workshop of Anige (1244/45–1306)
China, Yuan dynasty, mid- to late 13th century
Lacquer over cloth, with traces of color and gilt
58.5 x 43.3 x 29.5 cm; Purchase, Freer Gallery of Art, F1945.4

This lacquer sculpture attests to the cosmopolitanism and artistic synthesis that characterized the rule of Qubilai Khan, ruler of the Mongol Empire from 1260–94. During his reign, Qubilai founded a dynasty in China known as the Yuan. The dynasty's capital in Daidu (modern Beijing) was home to a workshop directed by the brilliant Nepalese artist Anige, which created this bodhisattva image.

As a youth, Anige had distinguished himself outside of his homeland by heading a group of artists in central Tibet. The monastery they constructed caught the eye of a Tibetan lama named Phagspa, who brought Anige to the Yuan court in 1265. The khan and his court greatly admired Anige for his rare ability to instill objects and monuments with the Buddha's potent presence.

In 1273, Anige was appointed director of all artisan classes. Five years later, he became the controller of imperial factories. He was given architectural commissions and asked to produce sculpture and even gold jewelry at his workshop in Daidu. Anige's workforce likely included more than a thousand artists of Chinese, Nepalese, and Tibetan heritage, who produced works in a traditional Chinese style, with Indo-Himalayan imagery, or both.

This graceful image is a perfect example of the sophisticated multiculturalism that characterized Yuan-dynasty art. Its hollow, lightweight form is made in the exclusively East Asian method known as dry lacquer (see p. 45). Yet the style seen in the anatomical modeling of a thinly clad, supply swayed body and the high topknot is characteristically Nepalese (see p. 112). Given the rarity of dry lacquer images, the museum sought to confirm the sculpture's date. Scientific analysis supports the art historical judgment that the work was created in the thirteenth century.

JS and DD

In the late twelfth century, the bodhisattva Kshitigarbha (in Japanese, Jizo) emerged from a second-tier role among Japanese Buddhist deities to become a beloved cult figure. In Japan, Kshitigarbha is considered especially attentive to the needs of women, children, and the unborn.

This graceful figure is an assembly of parts: its hands and head were carved separately. A layer of gold leaf suggests the sculpture was commissioned by a high-level patron. Perhaps the sculpture was used as a private devotional figure or in a temple of consequence.

Kshitigarbha is most often found throughout Japan in the form of small stone figures in temples or roadside shrines. The deity generally is portrayed as a handsome young Buddhist monk. Sometimes, he is depicted with his right hand forming the wish-granting mudra, as seen in this sculpture. At other times, his right hand holds a *shakujo*, or monk's staff, a sacred implement associated with Kshitigarbha.

Examples of the monk's staff appeared in Japan as early as the eighth century. The form comprises an ornamental head, or finial, attached to a long pole of iron or wood. This finial's design centers on a stupa, a major symbol of the Buddha, between two disc shapes atop stylized clouds. The discs represent the sun and moon, signifying the complete universe in the Buddha's embrace.

The six metal rings at top represent the six Buddhist perfections and the six realms of the cosmos, from heaven to hell, that Kshitigarbha traversed as he brought relief to suffering beings. These rings would jangle to announce the approach of monks, who were required to observe silence, as they collected daily alms in villages. Reverberation from the staff beating the ground would warn tiny creatures to get out from underfoot.

JU

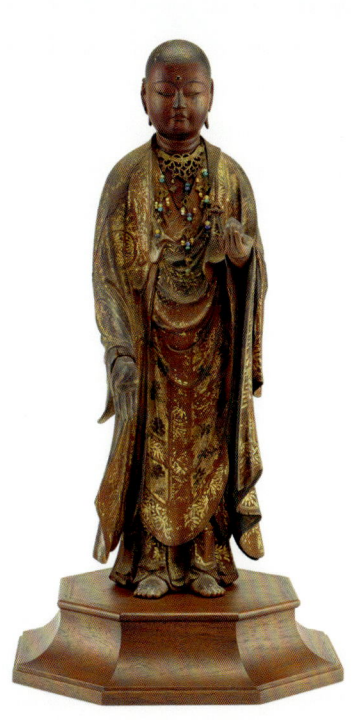
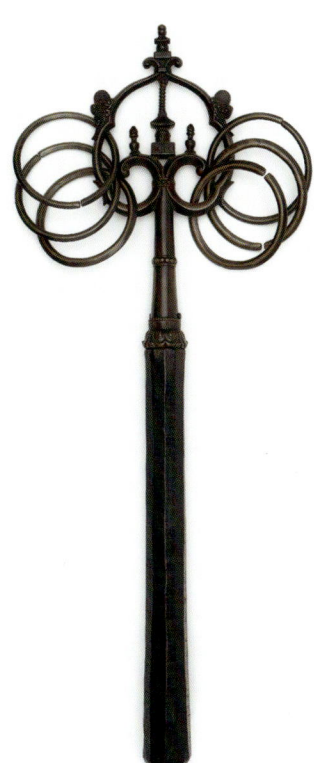

Kshitigarbha (Jizo)
Japan, Kamakura period, 1185–1333
Wood with applied gold
35.5 × 12 × 10.5 cm
Purchase
Freer Gallery of Art
F1965.19a–h

Finial of a Buddhist monk's staff
Japan, Kamakura period, 1185–1333
Bronze, wood
45.4 cm
Purchase—Charles Lang Freer Endowment
Freer Gallery of Art
F1974.15

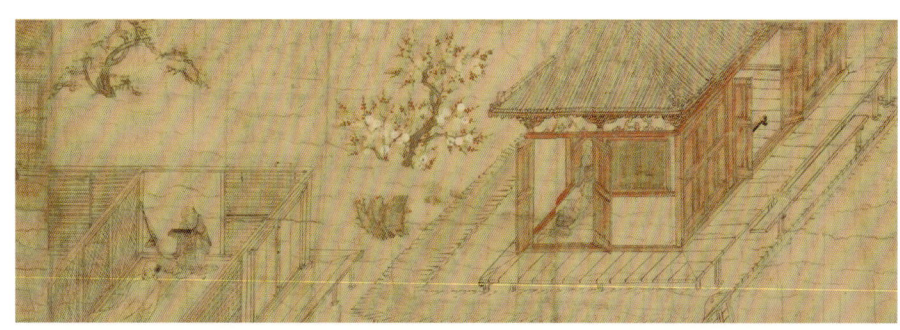

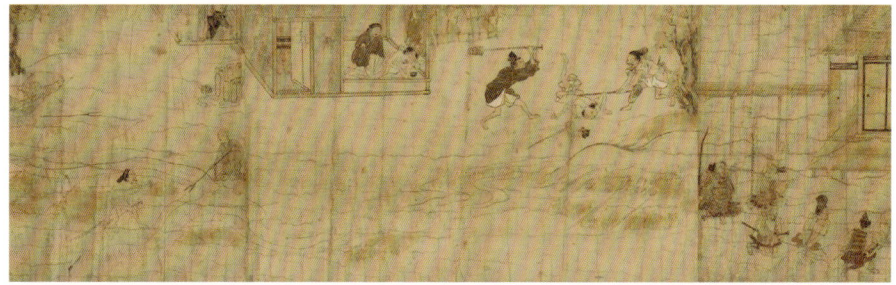

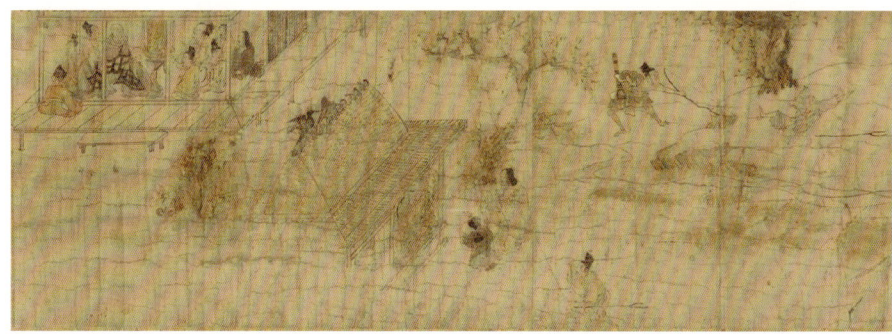

Miraculous Interventions of Kshitigarbha (Jizo)
Japan, Kamakura period, 13th century
Handscroll; ink and color on paper
30.5 × 1431.9 cm
Gift of Charles Lang Freer, Freer Gallery of Art, F1907.375a

This handscroll is one of the earliest Japanese depictions of the miraculous interventions of the bodhisattva Kshitigarbha (in Japanese, Jizo) into the daily lives of both the prominent and the humble. It is testimony to the diverse and intense devotion to this gentle figure that emerged in thirteenth-century Japan.

Within the five distinct episodes recounted in this scroll, the only common link is Kshitigarbha's miraculous intervention, sometimes to announce his presence and at other times to relieve suffering. In one episode, he appears in the dream of a noted Buddhist monk and demands that a ceremonial dance be performed. In another scene, a farmer's rice crop needs water, but he is unable to irrigate his fields from a neighboring plot. A monk-like figure appears and begins to dig a trench to divert water to the afflicted farmer's field. Neighbors intervene, and one shoots the monk with an arrow. The monk disappears, but the field becomes perpetually abundant. Returning to his hut, the farmer notices that the feet of his small Kshitigarbha sculpture are covered with mud.

Strong hints within the scroll suggest it was created to assert that Kasuga myojin, a centrally worshipped Shinto spirit, was a manifestation of Kshitigarbha. The scroll might have been part of a Japanese Buddhist proselytizing strategy called *honji-suijaku*, which gently proposed that local spirits were surrogates of principal Buddhist deities. A wide range of iconographic innovations emerged to depict these double presences, including narrative approaches such as this one.

JU

White-Robed Avalokiteshvara (Kannon)
Mokuan Rei'en (act. 1326–45)
Japan, Muromachi period, mid-14th century
Hanging scroll; ink on silk
103.3 x 41.3 cm
Purchase—Charles Lang Freer Endowment
Freer Gallery of Art, F1968.61

Japanese Zen monks painted images unlike the ornate, colorful works hung for ceremonies in temples of other Buddhist schools. The distinctions are most noticeable in images of bodhisattvas. Typically using only monochromatic ink, Zen (in Chinese, Chan) artists depicted bodhisattvas sitting in earthly settings, wearing simple monks' robes rather than elaborate, princely garments.

Paintings in this monochrome style entered Japan with Japanese monks who had traveled to China to study, as well as with Chinese Chan masters who came to teach and establish new lineages. The imported works served as models for Zen monks, some of whom became professional painters of religious subjects.

Mokuan Rei'en, a Zen monk and painter, traveled to China to study with the master Liaoan Qingyu (1288–1363). In this work, Mokuan painted Avalokiteshvara (in Japanese, Kannon) relaxing on a rock overhanging the sea, surrounded by a luminous halo. Only a small crown remains of the traditional iconography associated with the bodhisattva, who represents the Buddha's infinite compassion. The setting refers to the mythical Mount Potalaka. Buddhist texts say this mountain rises from the sea south of India, but East Asian Buddhists believed that the true location was off the coast of Ningpo, China.

AY

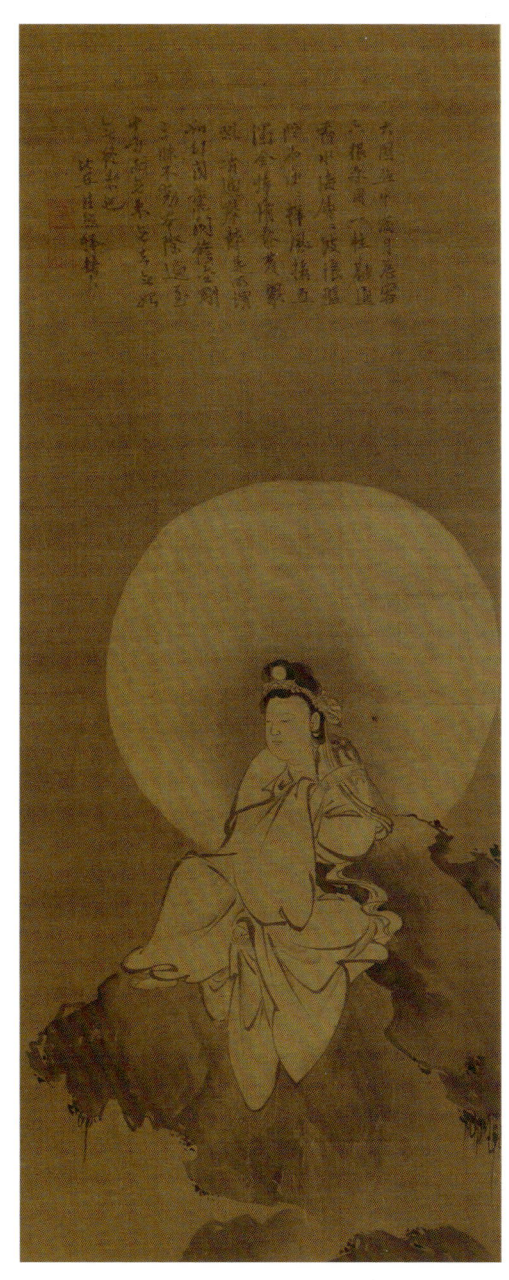

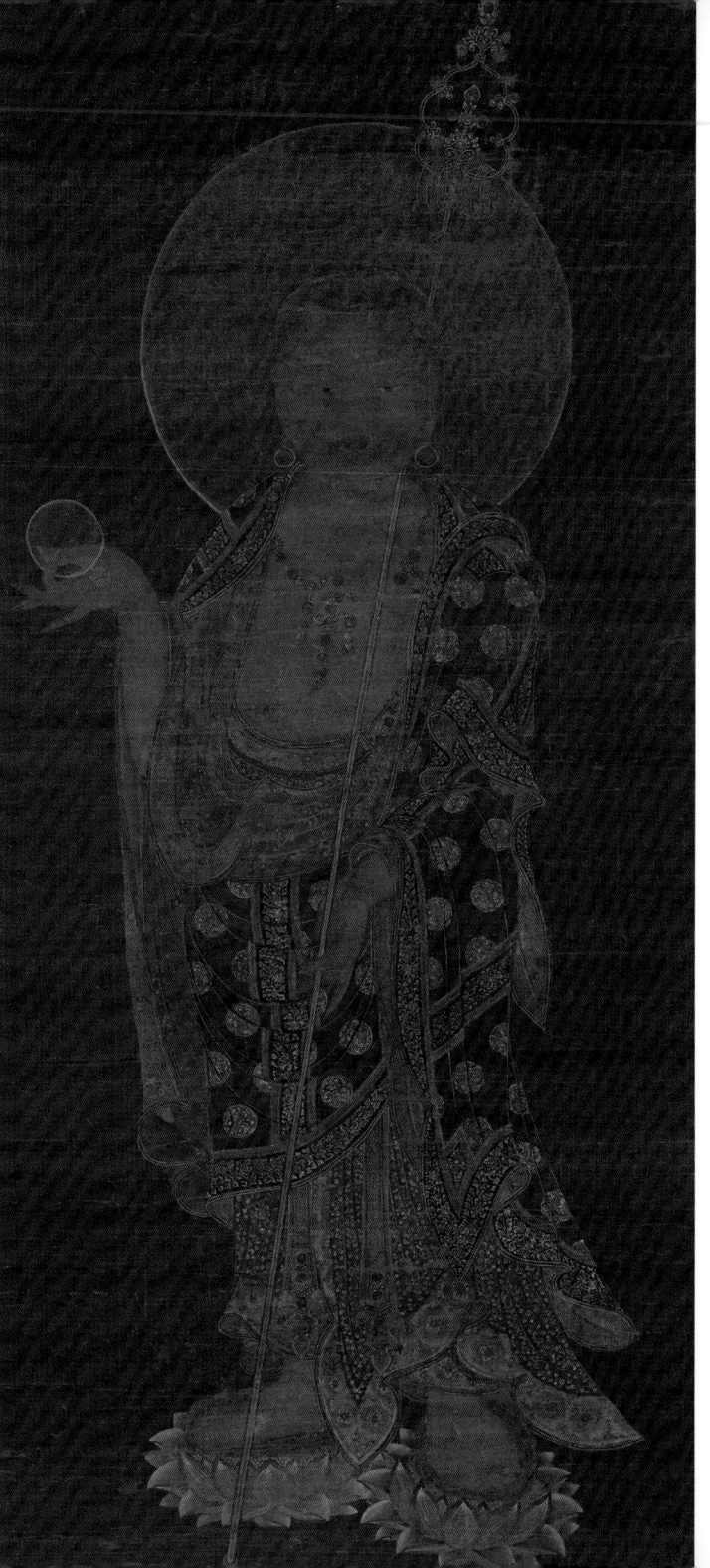

Kshitigarbha (Jijang)
Korea, Goryeo period, late 13th or early 14th century
Hanging scroll; ink, color, and gold on silk
107.6 × 49.4 cm
Anonymous gift, Arthur M. Sackler Gallery, S1992.11

The bodhisattva Kshitigarbha is the primary subject of a sutra, or Buddhist scripture, bearing his name. This text first appeared in the late seventh century in Chinese; since no Sanskrit version has been found, some scholars believe that the text and deity were Chinese creations. The narrative describes how Kshitigarbha (in Korean, Jijang) became a bodhisattva after vowing to rescue those reborn in Buddhist hells due to their past deeds. Along with the horrors of the underworld and the basics of karmic retribution, the text describes the promise of redemption through devotion to Kshitigarbha, who pledges not to achieve buddhahood himself until all of the hells are empty.

In this depiction, the bodhisattva is isolated against a blank background and dressed in rich garments patterned in gold. Several iconographic details identify the deity, chiefly the transparent "wish-granting jewel" (*chintamani*) in his right hand and the jingle staff in his left. His exposed skin is rendered in a rosy flesh color, achieved by applying pigments to both the front and back of the painting surface.

Most Korean depictions of Kshitigarbha from this time are incredibly similar in composition, style, and even garment patterns. This suggests that the paintings were part of a highly standardized ritual context. The prevalence of Pure Land deities such as Kshitigarbha also indicates that the images played an important role in salvation rites of the sect, which was extremely attractive to aristocratic patrons in the late Goryeo period. From an art historical point of view, the repetition suggests that the images were created in professional painting workshops, whose specialists may have been sharing basic templates.

KW

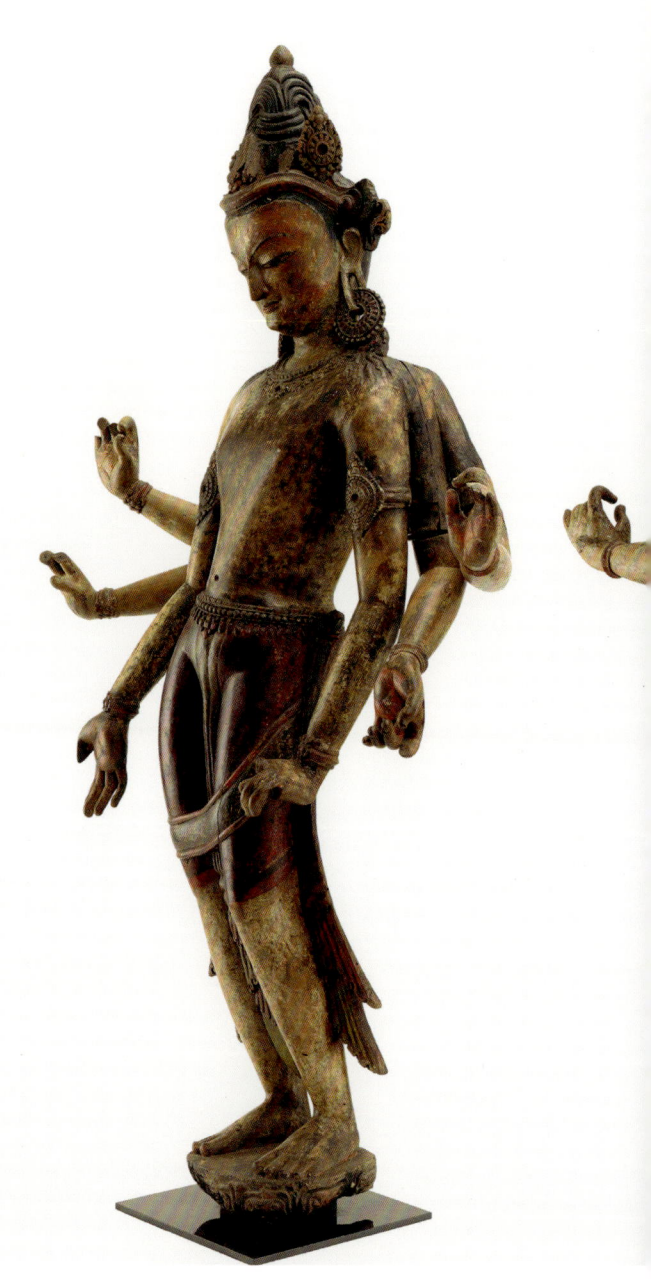

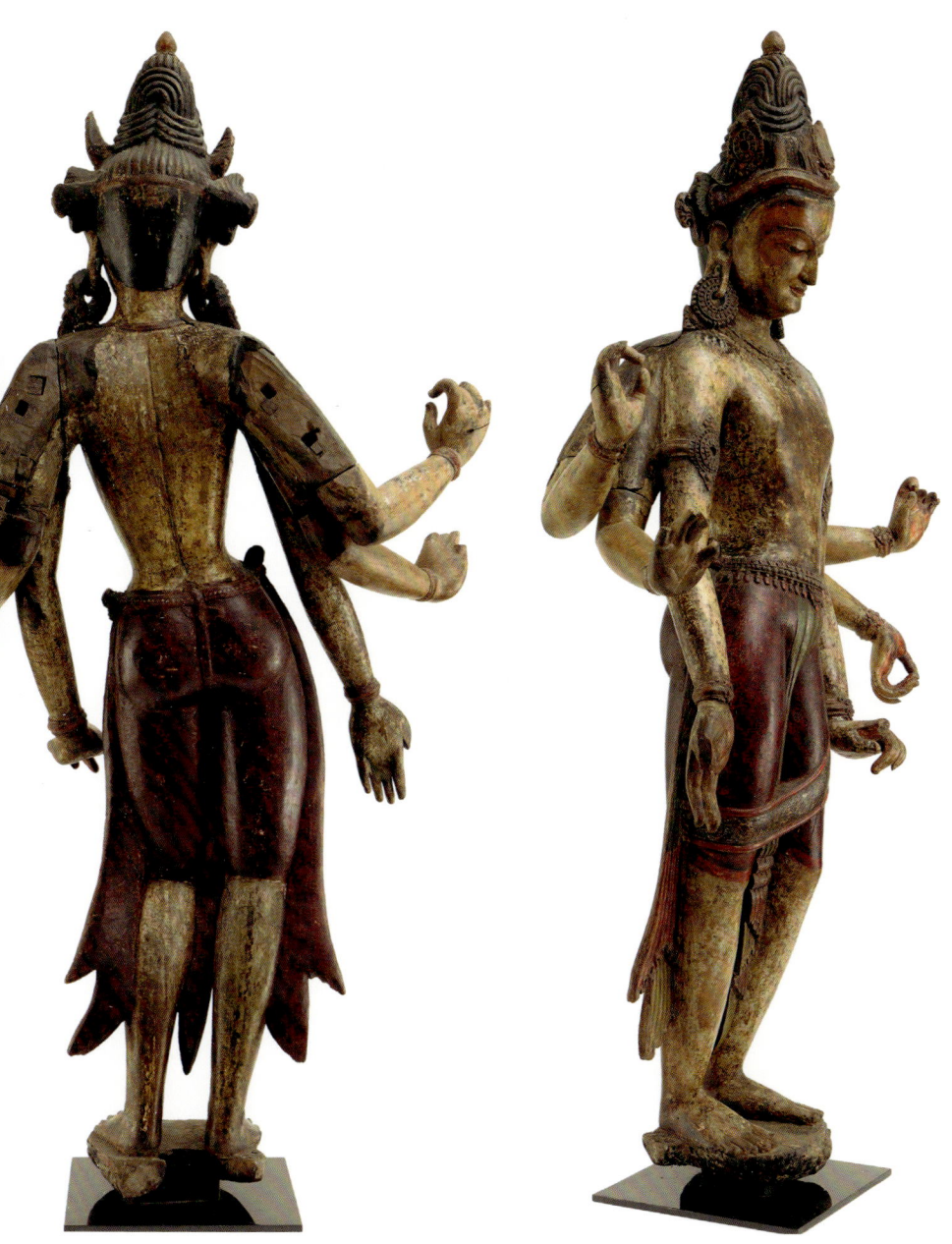

Avalokiteshvara
Nepal, Malla dynasty, 14th century
Polychromed wood
162.5 × 96 × 37 cm
Purchase—Friends of the Freer and Sackler Galleries
and Sigrid and Vinton Cerf, Freer Gallery of Art, F2000.5

In Nepal, sculptors perfected the art of carving monumental wooden figures that artists then painted and adorned with gemstones. Today, such sculptures are little known. Few of the freestanding figures have left Nepal. Even in the past, they were publicly displayed for only a few days each year, during an annual festival in which the ground floors of Buddhist monasteries were turned into temporary museums of the temples' treasures.

This particular form of Avalokiteshvara is cherished as a guardian of the Kathmandu Valley. With his arms rhythmically poised, head and hips gently tilted in opposite directions, and pleated sashes flaring, Avalokiteshvara sways with vitality. It is a mark of the sculptor's mastery that the head, body, and lotus base were fashioned from a single piece of tropical hardwood. Square wooden pegs attach six separately carved arms (two of the original eight are missing) to the body. X-ray analysis has revealed that a cavity within the torso, at the level of the heart, contains small metal relic boxes. Relics transform sculptures into objects with the power to protect and enlighten.

Renowned for their skill and their connection to the geographically proximate heartland of Buddhism, Nepalese artists were highly sought after in foreign lands. In China, a celebrated Nepalese artist headed the imperial workshop of the Yuan dynasty's first ruler. A bodhisattva produced in that workshop (p. 101) has similarly broad cheekbones and elegant gestures. And the inscription on a Tibetan Amitabha (p. 68) boasts of its Nepalese artists.

DD

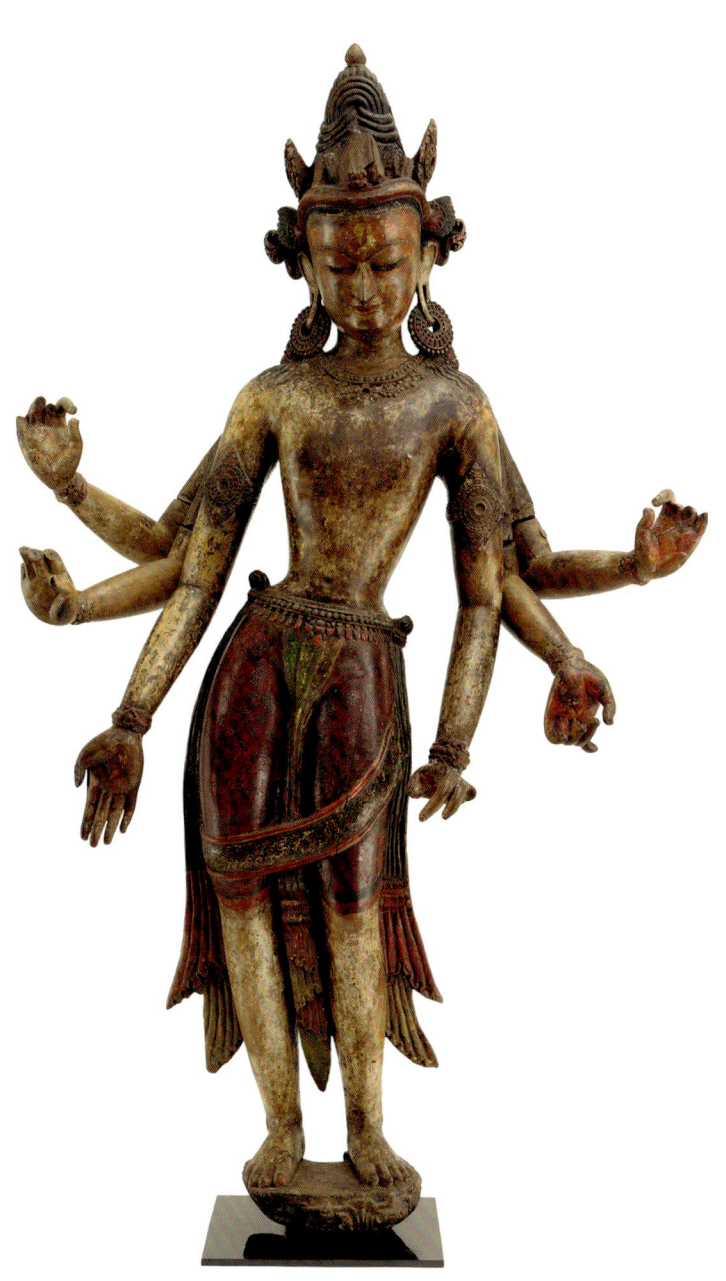

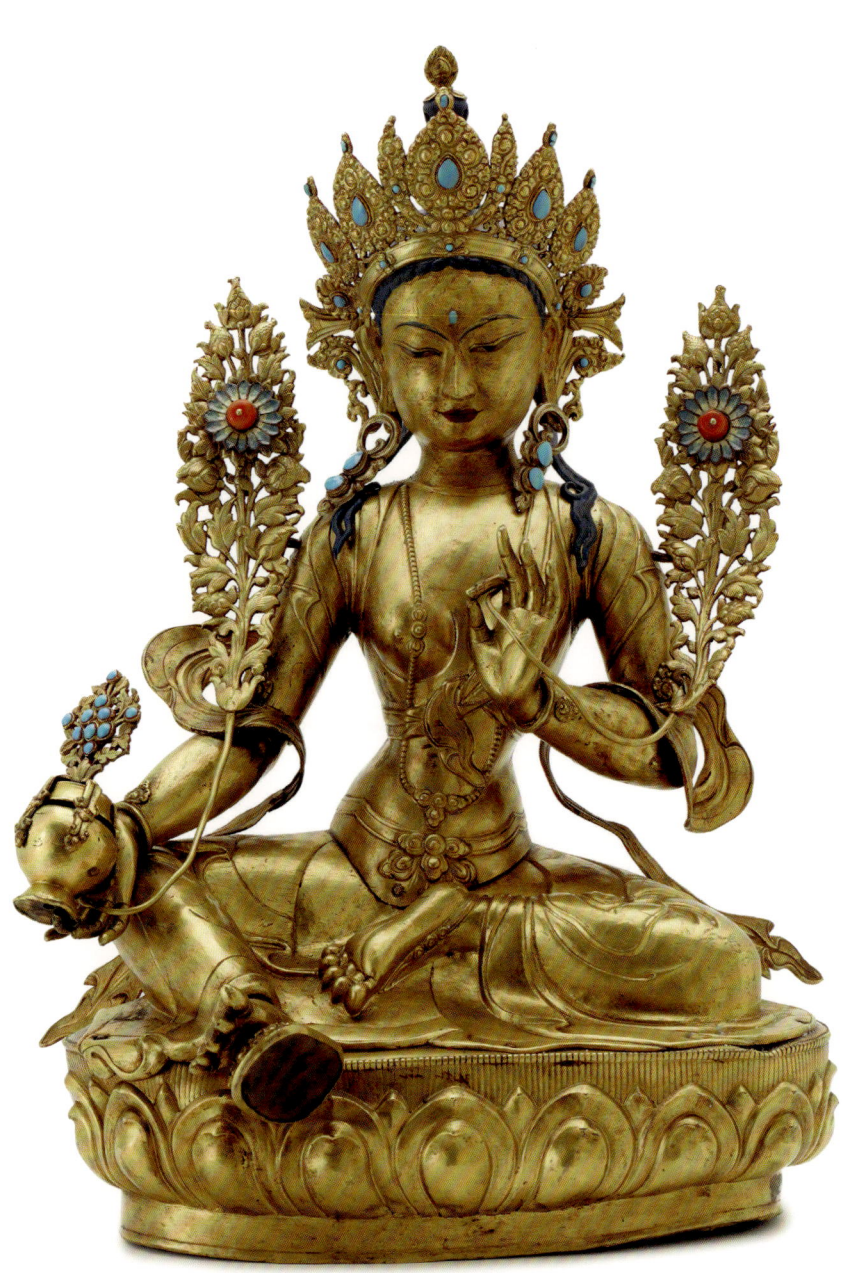

Tara

Central Tibet; second half of 17th century
Gilt copper alloy, turquoise, enamel, and coral
48.3 x 31.8 cm
The Alice S. Kandell Collection, Arthur M. Sackler Gallery,
S2011.12a–c

The protector and helper of all those on the Buddhist path, Tara is the supreme savioress. Revered by laypeople and monastics alike, Tara is worshipped in many ways and engaged in many forms: as bodhisattva, buddha, and meditational deity. Her ability to intercede in matters both spiritual and worldly is apparent in the many emanations Tara takes to fulfill her devotees' diverse needs. When she is colored green, she protects from the eight great fears; white, she heals illness and extends longevity; red, she expedites spiritual accomplishments. She can be peaceful or wrathful, multiarmed and multifaced, alone or in sexual union.

Tara is, however, always a woman, having vowed to remain in a female body, even as a buddha, until all beings attain buddhahood themselves. Although Tara's female form amplifies her nurturing qualities, it is also a lesson in the universal possibility of enlightenment, which transcends gender distinctions.

This sculpture portrays Tara in one of the twenty-one emanations described in an important Tibetan text. All twenty-one Taras share the posture, hand gestures, and attributes that we see in this sculpture. She sits with one leg folded and the other extended, her foot resting on a lotus. Her left hand, gracefully suspended before her chest, holds an *utpala* flower. Her right hand, resting on her knee in a gesture of supreme generosity, holds another *utpala* flower and a vase.

Each of Tara's twenty-one forms is associated with a compassionate activity. Though they are distinguished by color in the text, when a Tara is cast in bronze rather than painted with pigment, her true color can only be imagined.

RB

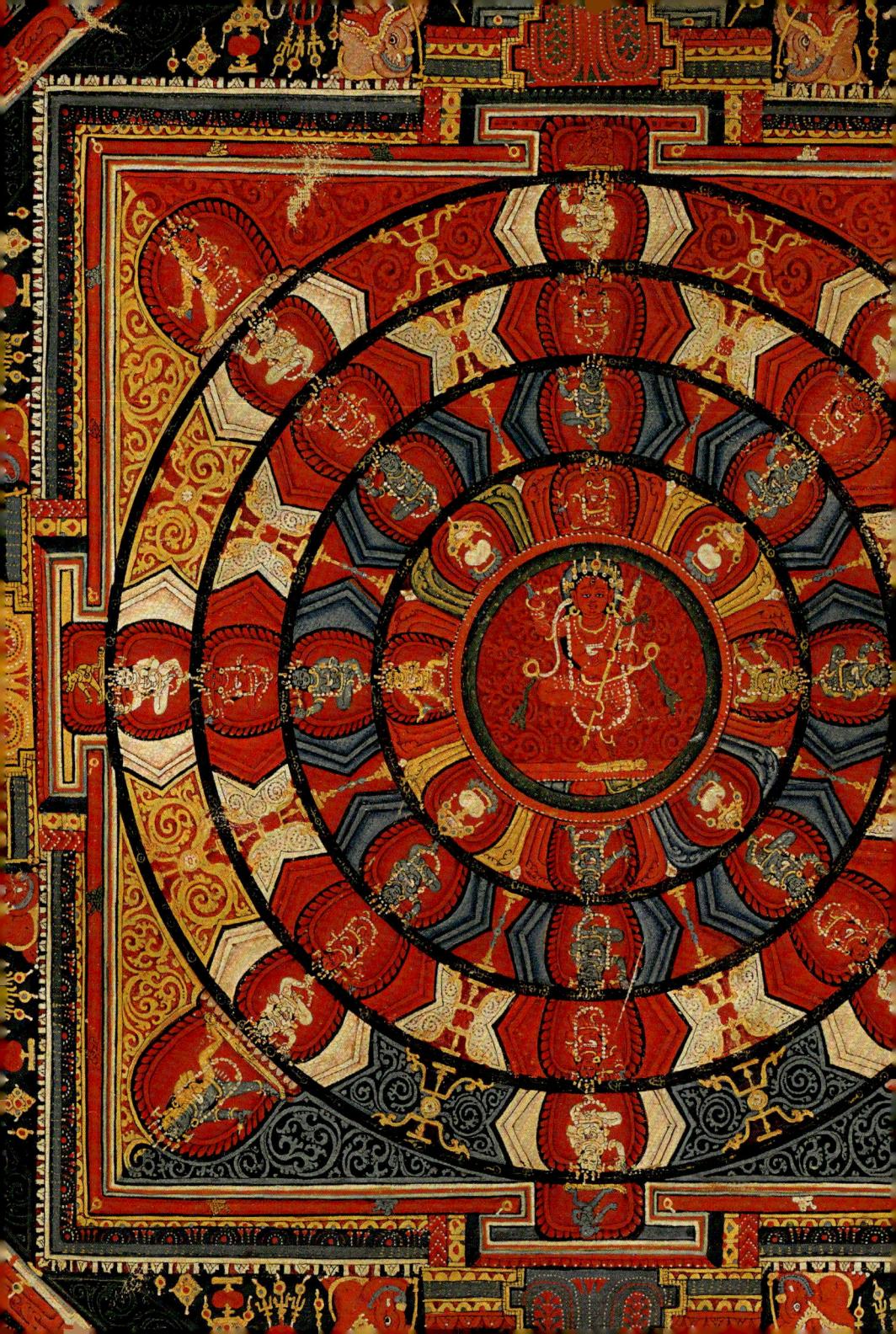

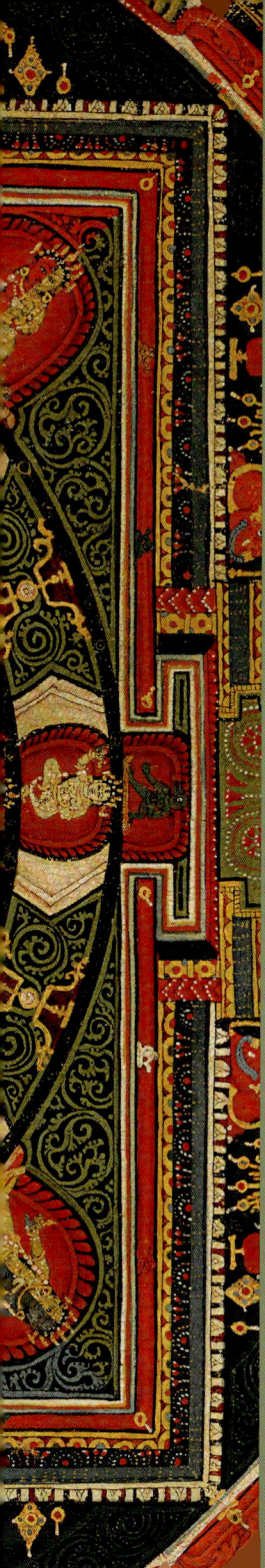

Mandalas and Ritual Objects

Ornate implements such as bowls and bells remind us of the myriad ways Buddhism is lived and performed every day. They are also a powerful reminder that all Buddhist objects, including sculptural and painted images, can be considered ritual objects insofar as they have religious use. Whether a practitioner's intentions are devotional or meditative, all objects in Buddhist contexts have a function and serve as an expression of Buddhist ideas.

Mandalas are noteworthy for their beauty and complexity. Considered loci of divine power and protection, these concentric patterns have several uses. Mandalas appear in many Buddhist contexts, but they are most closely associated with tantric practices.

Although they are often two-dimensional, mandalas are understood to depict palaces in which a primary buddha, bodhisattva, or deity resides. They serve as an aid to meditation for devotees who create these spaces, either in their minds or through constructed forms, and visualize traveling toward the mandalas' sacred cores.

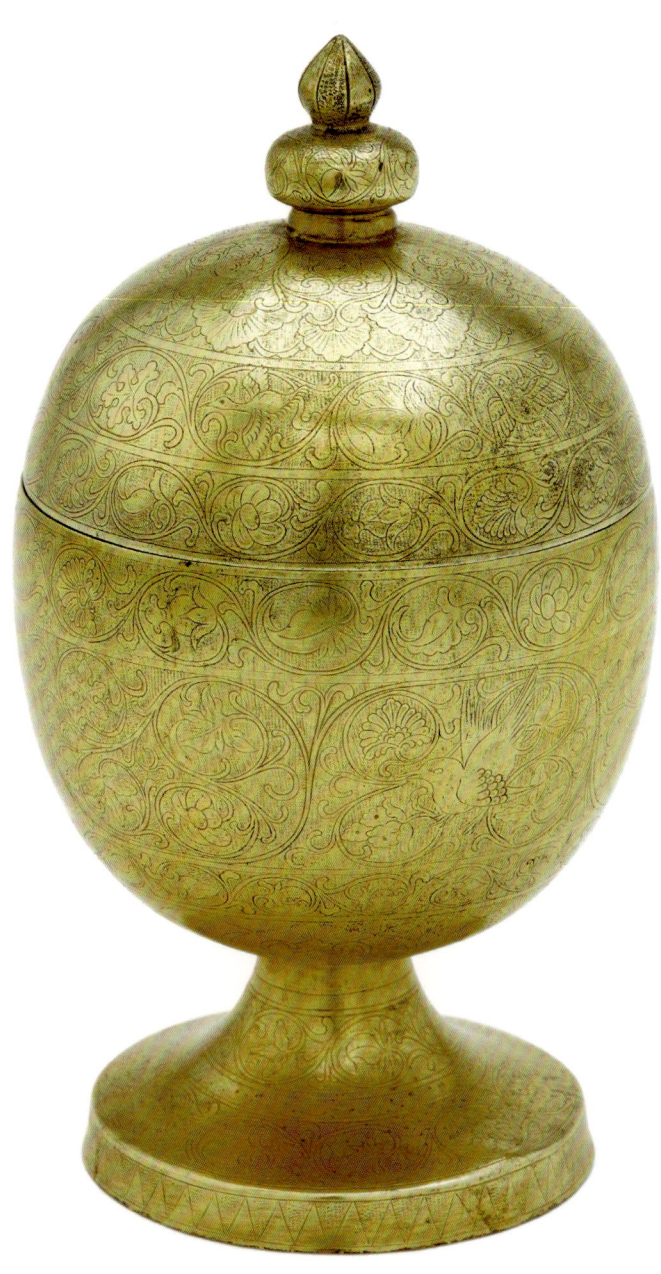

Lidded container with birds and floral scrolls
China, probably Shaanxi Province, Chang'an (Xi'an), Tang dynasty, 8th century
Cast, hammered, and turned silver with chased and ring-punched decoration and mercury gilding
12.3 × 7.1 cm
Purchase, Freer Gallery of Art, F1931.17a–b

This object has often been described as a Buddhist reliquary, a container for holding relics. But no similar piece has been discovered in a context that confirms its intended function, secular or sacred. And while the container's patterns also are found on objects made for temple rituals, they are not specifically Buddhist. For these reasons, we cannot confirm that this is in fact a "ritual object."

Despite its small size and seemingly simple form, this gilt silver box is a hybrid that reflects converging styles and techniques. The surface is almost completely covered with shallow incised decoration, created using a technique called "chasing." Bands of flowers on scrolling vines encircle the vessel. In the central band on both the top and bottom, birds fly above the scrollwork. An experienced master must have created these rhythmic, flowing lines, taking advantage of the silver, which is relatively soft.

These techniques and materials were not traditionally favored by Chinese craftsmen. They preferred casting, by pouring molten metal in molds, to cold metalworking, and they favored bronze—a mixture of copper, tin, and lead—over gold and silver. With the growing exchange of goods across the pan-Asian trade routes now called the Silk Road, however, Chinese taste changed, and foreign styles and customs were adopted. This container reflects the practices of metropolitan workshops that thrived in the early Tang dynasty capital at Chang'an (modern Xi'an).

KW

Deity from the Nganjuk mandala
Indonesia, Java, Nganjuk, late 10th century
Bronze
7.9 × 5.1 × 3.7 cm
Loan of Ann and Gilbert Kinney, Arthur M. Sackler Gallery,
LTS2015.3.8

In 1913, two farmers in a small village in Indonesia's Nganjuk Province discovered a hoard of bronzes while cultivating a new patch of land. The majority of these bronzes came into the possession of the National Museum in Jakarta, where archaeologists soon noticed their distinct style and unique characteristics. This particular bronze has many of the features that set the Nganjuk group apart. The figure is ornamented with a diadem and crown, a heavy necklace, a band around the chest, and three bands around each arm. As with the other Nganjuk bronzes, the halo behind his tilted head converges in a pointed tip.

From the beginning, scholars recognized that the Nganjuk bronzes must have had a special meaning as a group. Through comparative analysis of Japanese tantric Buddhist drawings and Indian iconographic treatises, they were able to identify many of the figures. Scholars discovered that, together, the bronzes form the mandala of the adamantine sphere (*Vajradhatumandala*). Centered on Vairochana, the primordial buddha, this mandala is one of the most important in tantric Buddhism. It probably was set up in a temple before its many parts, for unknown reasons, were buried.

Three-dimensional representations of mandalas, such as the one to which this sculpture belonged, are extremely rare. This bronze likely represents one of the many attendant deities in the *Vajradhatumandala*. The bell (*ghanta*) in his right hand is an important implement in tantric Buddhist rituals.

JE

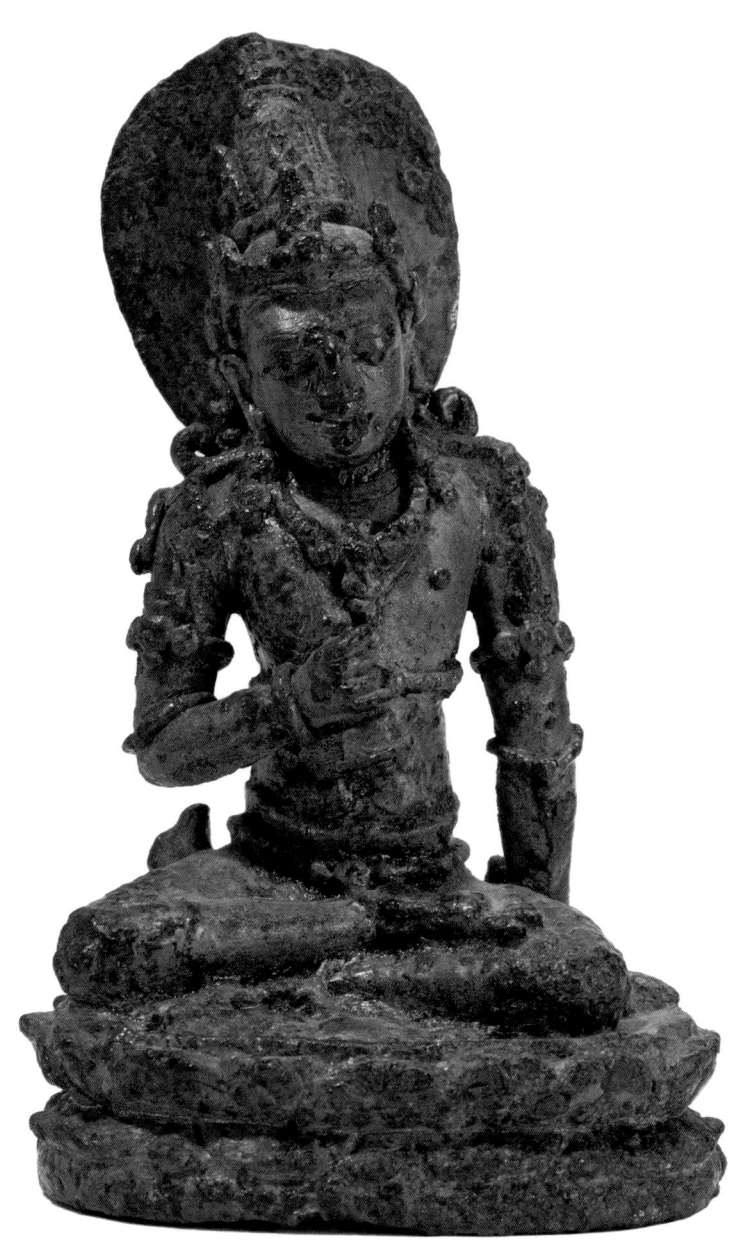

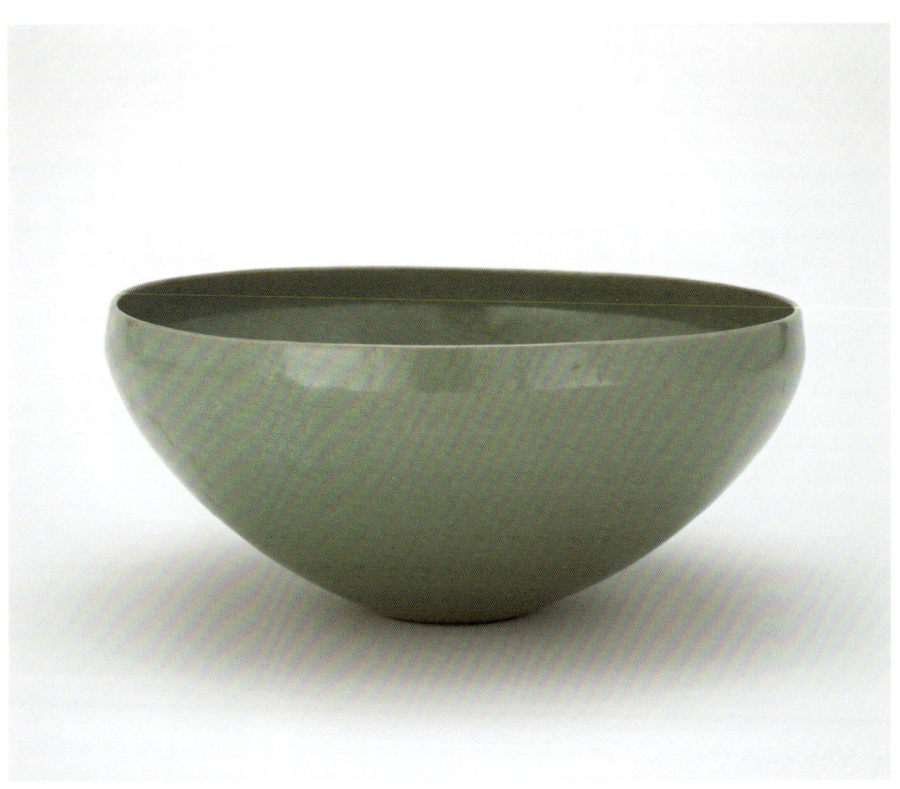

Alms bowl
Korea, Jeollanam-do Province, Gangjin kilns
Goryeo period, 12th century
Stoneware with celadon glaze
9.8 × 22.7 cm
Gift of Charles Lang Freer, Freer Gallery of Art, F1909.14

The rules and regulations for Buddhist monastic communities traveled with the spiritual knowledge of Buddhism as it spread throughout Asia. According to the vinaya (discipline), as those documents are known collectively, the alms bowl (in Sanskrit, *patra*) is one of the essential possessions permitted to Buddhist monks and nuns. Monastics carry such bowls as they make their rounds each morning to collect food. Contrary to popular misconception, the alms bowl is not a "begging bowl," for the monastic does not beg; rather, he or she presents the opportunity for lay members of the religious community to earn merit by placing food in the bowl.

This Korean bowl approximates the hemispherical form of an alms bowl, with a narrow, rounded base and slightly inverted rim. A close precedent is found in polished black pottery alms bowls made in China during the Tang dynasty (618–907). The materials of this Korean bowl, however—pale-gray stoneware with a smooth, lustrous celadon glaze—are more luxurious and less practical than the Tang-dynasty examples. Celadon-glazed bowls of this sort were made in four sizes, of which this is the largest. Even so, it is smaller than most functional Southeast Asian alms bowls. This bowl and its smaller versions instead may have served a role in making offerings on an altar or in another ritual context.

LAC

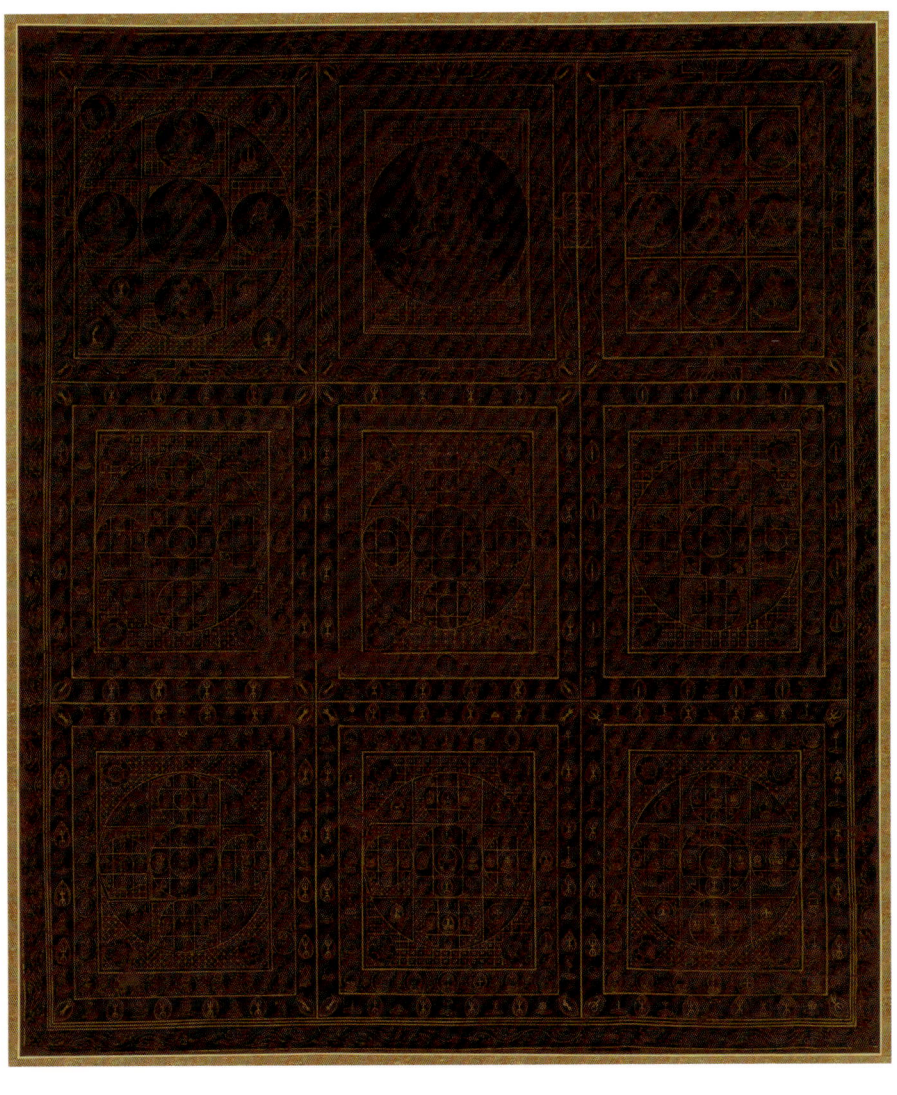

Ryokai mandara (mandalas of the two worlds)
Japan, Kamakura period (1185–1333)
Gold on purple silk
166.3 × 81.8 cm; 166.8 × 82 cm
Purchase, Freer Gallery of Art, F1966.4–.5

Mandalas come in several forms. Some, such as the geometrically precise and orderly vision of an invisible spiritual universe, help believers grasp the connection between the everyday and the sacred nature of all things. Other types of mandalas impose sacred images over topography, suggesting that there is an invisible but important reality that supports the everyday.

The *ryokai mandara*, or mandalas of the two worlds, derive from Chinese paintings introduced to Japan in the eighth century. These paired diagrams represent complementary aspects of the universe. The womb world (*taizokai*) mandala, with its central lotus, represents the individual, particular, and relative. The diamond world (*kongokai*) mandala, with its nine-square configuration, represents the unconditioned, universal, and absolute. By contemplating both together, the practitioner seeks to unite with and take in the power and perfection of the Buddhist cosmos.

After the Japanese capital moved from Nara to Kyoto in the early ninth century, esoteric Buddhism emerged as Japan's preeminent Buddhist system. For important esoteric ceremonies, such as the ordination of monks, the mandalas of the two worlds are hung at the ends of the ordination hall, with the altar between them. Each initiate tosses a flower or sprig of anise onto other mandalas laid flat on the altar to determine which deity will be his focus in meditation and worship.

JU

Altar pendant (keman)
Japan, Kamakura period (1185–1333)
Copper, gold, and silver
44.8 × 31.5 × 2.2 cm
Purchase—Charles Lang Freer Endowment, Freer Gallery of Art, F1974.13

Keman are pendants made of gilt metal, painted leather, or wood. Often decorated with floral motifs, they are thought to derive from garlands of fresh flowers that were offered to deities in India. In Japan, pairs or sets of matching *keman* were created to hang overhead, across the altars of Buddhist temples. A *keman* with a design identical to this one's is in Japan's Nara National Museum.

This *keman* is made of copper that was gilded and silvered to highlight four characters in the graceful Indian Siddha script. Each character represents a Sanskrit syllable. In esoteric Buddhism (in Japanese, *mikkyo*), characters written in Sanskrit, the ancient original language of the Buddha's teachings, were believed to hold spiritual power. While sacred Buddhist texts are written in classical Chinese throughout East Asia, translations sometimes retain the original Sanskrit. This is especially true for syllables of magical incantations (dharani) and for mystical symbols and phrases (mantra) recited to reach spiritual union with a deity.

Placed above lotuses, the characters on this *keman* are encircled by silver disks that resemble the halos of Buddhist deities. On the front of the pendant, "bhai" appears twice, symbolizing a deity whose name begins with that syllable. On the back are the characters "ba" and "kya." We can presume that the written symbols on the face of the *keman* represent Bhaisajyaguru (Yakushi Nyorai), the medicine buddha (see p. 52).

AY

MANDALAS AND RITUAL OBJECTS 127

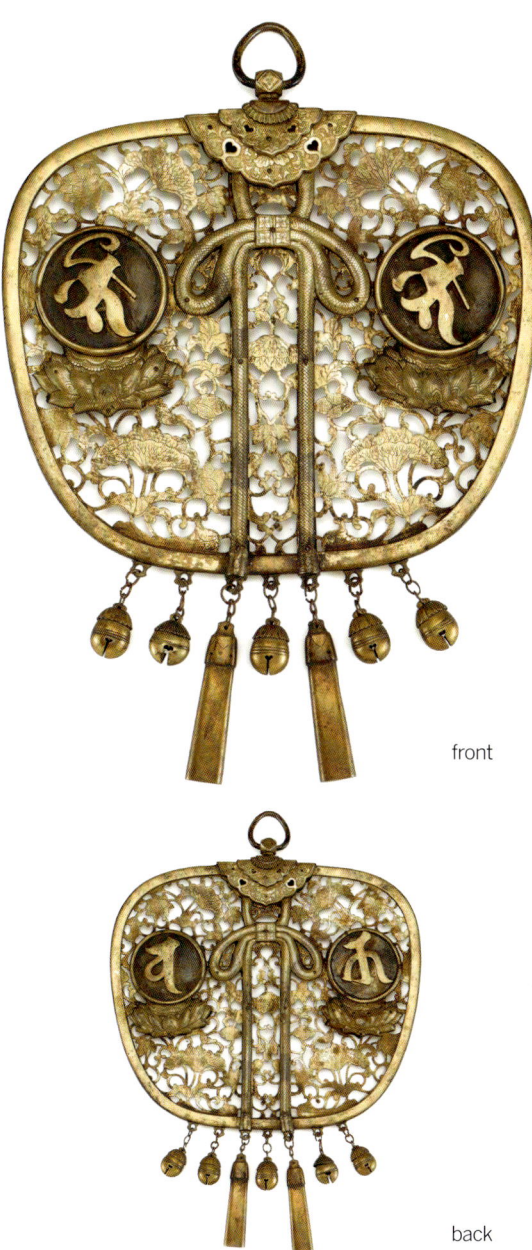

front

back

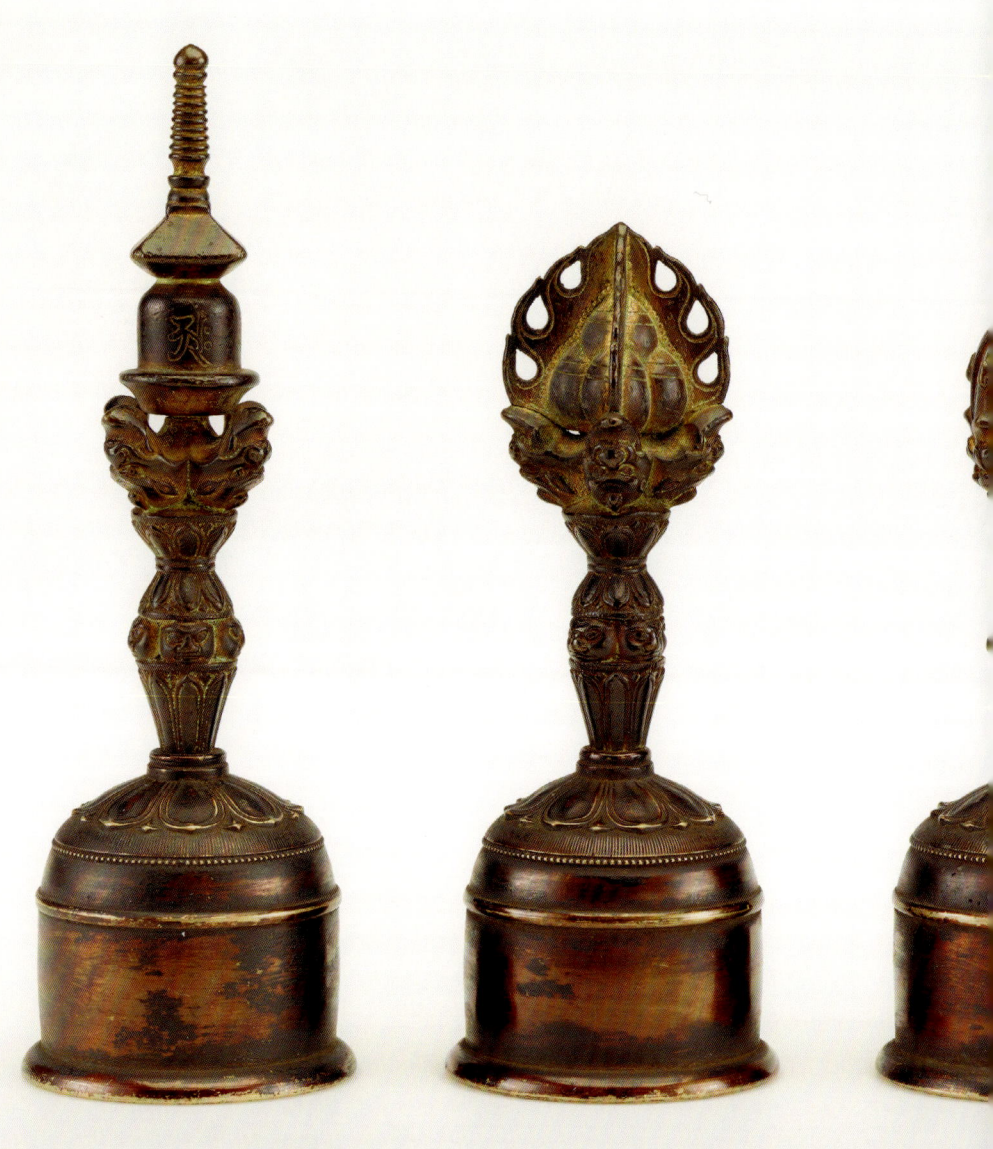

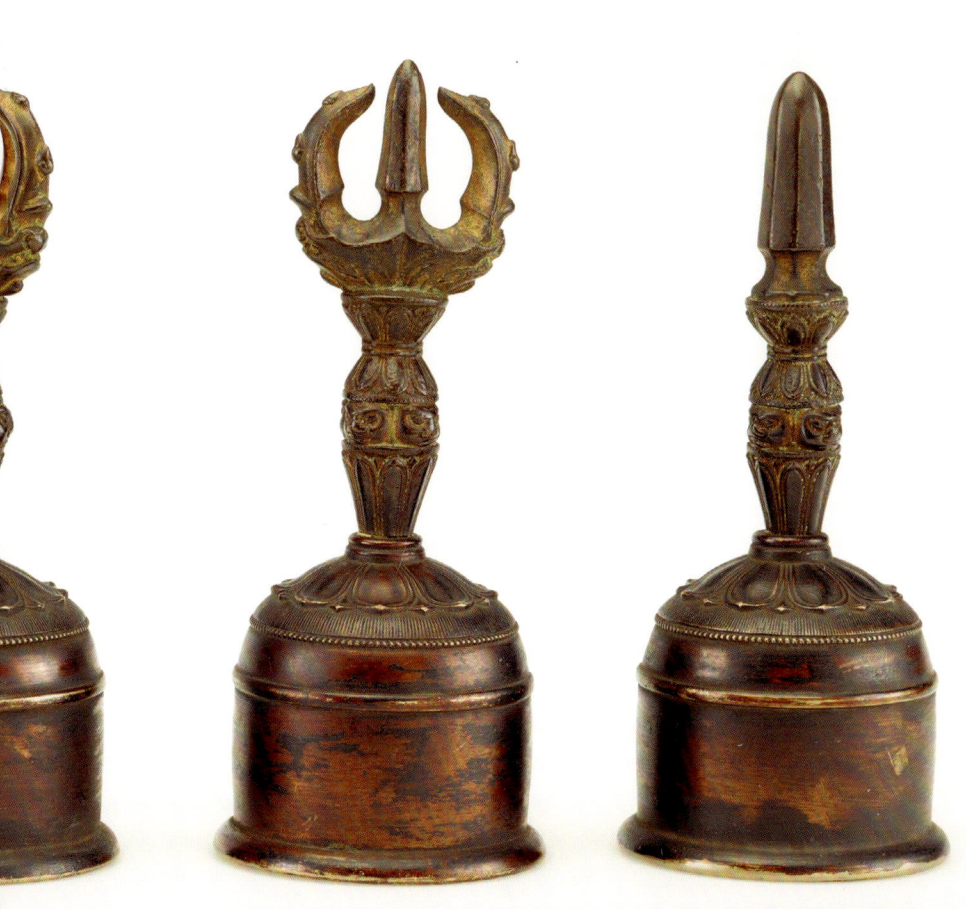

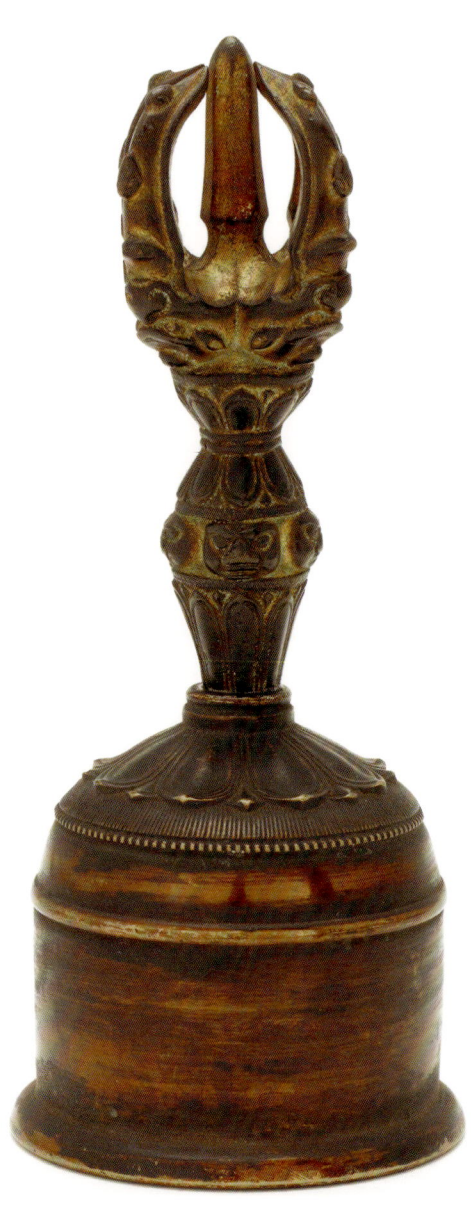

Ritual bells
Japan, Kamakura period (1185–1333)
Bronze
18.7 × 6.3 cm
Gift of Charles Lang Freer, Freer Gallery of Art, F1903.292–96

This set of five bronze bells was used in the rituals of esoteric Buddhism, known in Japanese as *mikkyo* ("concealed" or "secret" teaching). Only the initiated priesthood knows and performs this school's complex doctrines and rituals, which are essential to esoteric practice.

In some rituals, these bells were placed on a square altar. The bell with a pagoda surmounting its handle represents Mahavairochana (in Japanese, Dainichi Nyorai), the central buddha of the cosmos; accordingly, it was placed at the altar's center. The other four bells, representing the buddhas associated with the cardinal directions, were placed in the altar's corners. Esoteric priests would have rung bells to summon deities, to recognize their arrival, and to accompany their departure. The sound of a bell also awakens the enlightened mind.

Elements of esoteric practices were assimilated into other Japanese Buddhist schools, such as Tendai. But the principal proponents of esoteric Buddhism in Japan belonged to the Shingon school, headquartered at Mount Koya (Koyasan). They traced their lineage back to Chinese and Indian masters.

AY

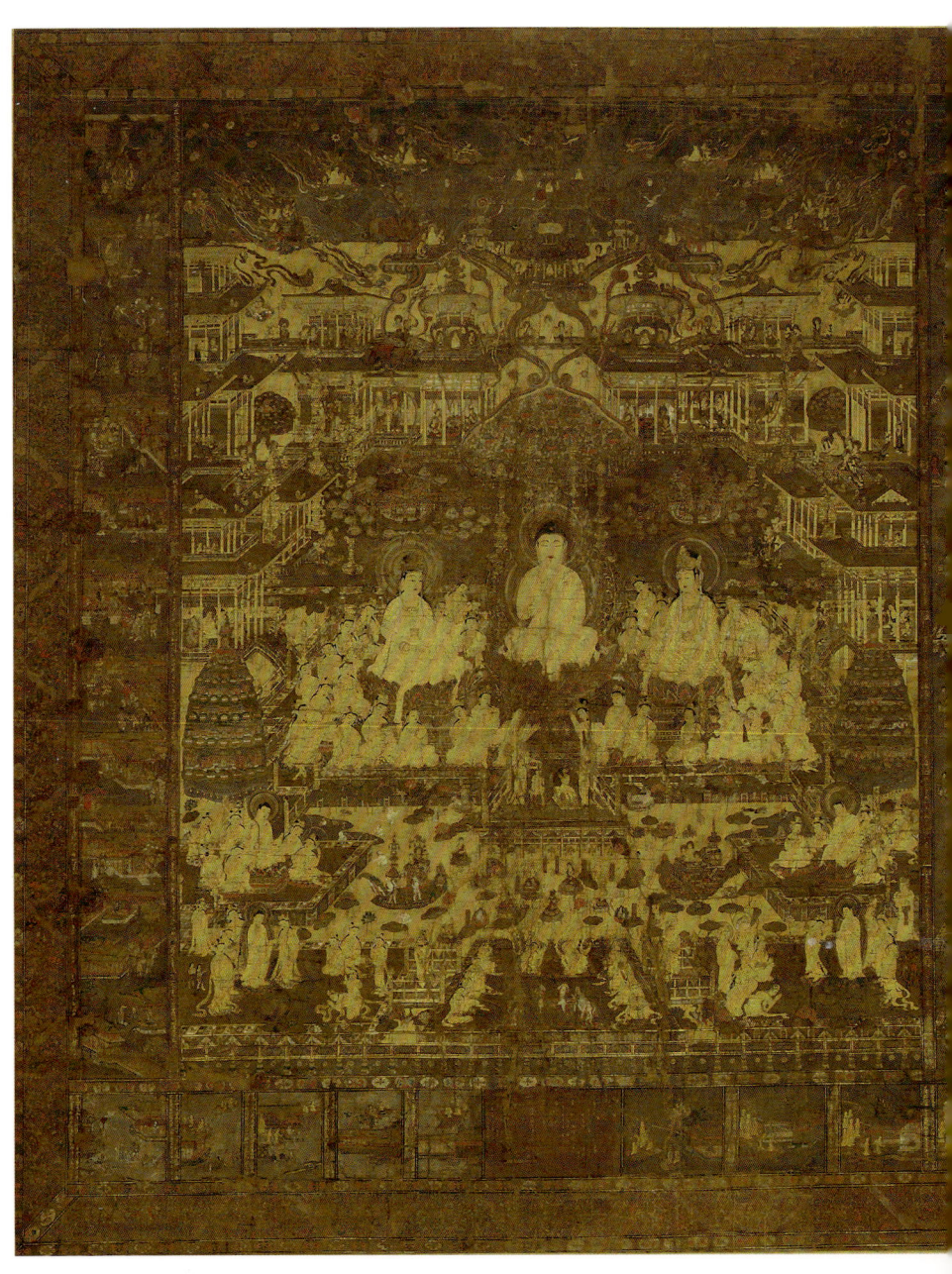

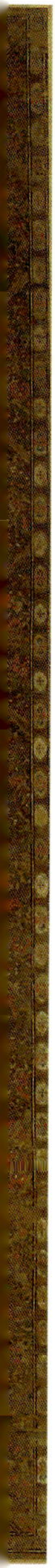

Taima mandala
Japan, Kamakura period, 13th century
Panel-mounted hanging scroll; ink, color, and gold on silk
179.8 × 163.9 cm
Gift of Charles Lang Freer, Freer Gallery of Art, F1906.5

Taimadera, a temple in the ancient Japanese capital of Nara, houses a magnificent silk tapestry imported from China in the eighth century. The tapestry's imagery encapsulates Pure Land Buddhism's core beliefs, which center on Amitabha's (in Japanese, Amida) promise that believers will escape suffering when reborn in his Western Paradise, or Pure Land. The painting shown here, one of many inspired by the tapestry, faithfully depicts Amitabha's heavenly realm.

Analyzing this painting reveals multiple sources of text and imagery that can be traced to China and India. Depicted on the perimeter are images of Indian royalty searching for enlightenment. Buddha Amitabha appears presiding over the Pure Land; he also is seen greeting the reborn as they emerge from lotus flowers and begin to savor the pleasures of paradise.

In the legend of the original tapestry, Buddha Amitabha, disguised as a nun, visited a princess. The nun ordered the noblewoman to gather a hundred horse-loads of lotus stems, which were spun into thread and dyed five colors. Then the bodhisattva Avalokiteshvara (Kannon), who also appeared as a nun, wove the threads. The beautiful tapestry, more than fourteen feet square, was miraculously completed overnight.

JU

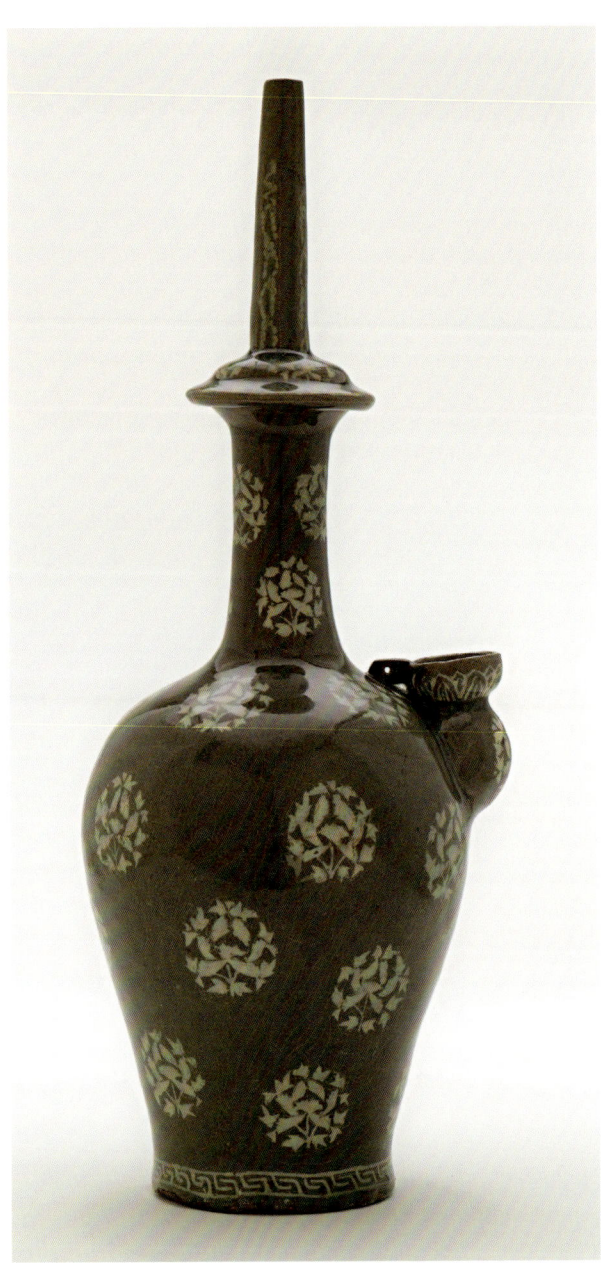

Ritual water sprinkler
Korea, Jeolla-do Province, Gangjin or Buan kilns
Goryeo period, first half of 13th century
Stoneware with white slip inlay under celadon glaze
35.8 × 14.4 × 13 cm
Gift of Charles Lang Freer, Freer Gallery of Art, F1909.45

Like the alms bowl (p. 123), the bottle for collecting water is one of the personal belongings permitted to monks and nuns in the vinaya, the body of regulations for monastic establishments. Known as the *kundika* in Sanskrit, the vessel has a distinctive shape. A short spout on the shoulder is used to fill the oval body, and the long neck is topped with a slender tube through which water is poured out. Originating in South Asia as a practical container for storing drinking water, the *kundika* became a ritual implement employed in Buddhist ceremonies to sprinkle water for purification and offering. Made of metal or ceramic, the vessel appeared in many cultures where Buddhism took hold.

During the Goryeo dynasty in Korea, the *kundika* form (in Korean, *jeongbyeong*) was made in celadon-glazed stoneware as well as in bronze. Kilns in Gangjin and Buan, which served the court and nobility, developed a distinctive form of decoration for celadon ceramics: motifs incised or stamped into the clay were inlaid with white and black clay solutions before the celadon glaze was applied. This bottle bears peony medallions that appear to be inspired by textile motifs, such as those on the silk gauze garments represented in a Korean painting of Buddha Amitabha (p. 66).

LAC

Water pot
Japan, Kamakura or Muromachi period, 13th–14th century
Bronze
27.5 × 13.5 cm
Purchase—Charles Lang Freer Endowment, Freer Gallery of Art, F1965.26a–c

Water vessels (in Japanese, *suibyo*) were among the few possessions Buddhist monks were permitted to own. Such containers had a variety of uses in monasteries, such as for carrying and pouring clean water for washing. Some bronze examples, often shaped like gourds, were used to pour hot water for tea, which was served to monastery guests.

Ewers also were used to contain and pour water in Buddhist rituals. This example has a clear, sharp profile and restrained decoration, including a lion surmounting the hinged lid. Similar pots with lions on their lids are among the objects placed on altars at Shingon temples, suggesting an association with esoteric ceremonies.

AY

MANDALAS AND RITUAL OBJECTS   137

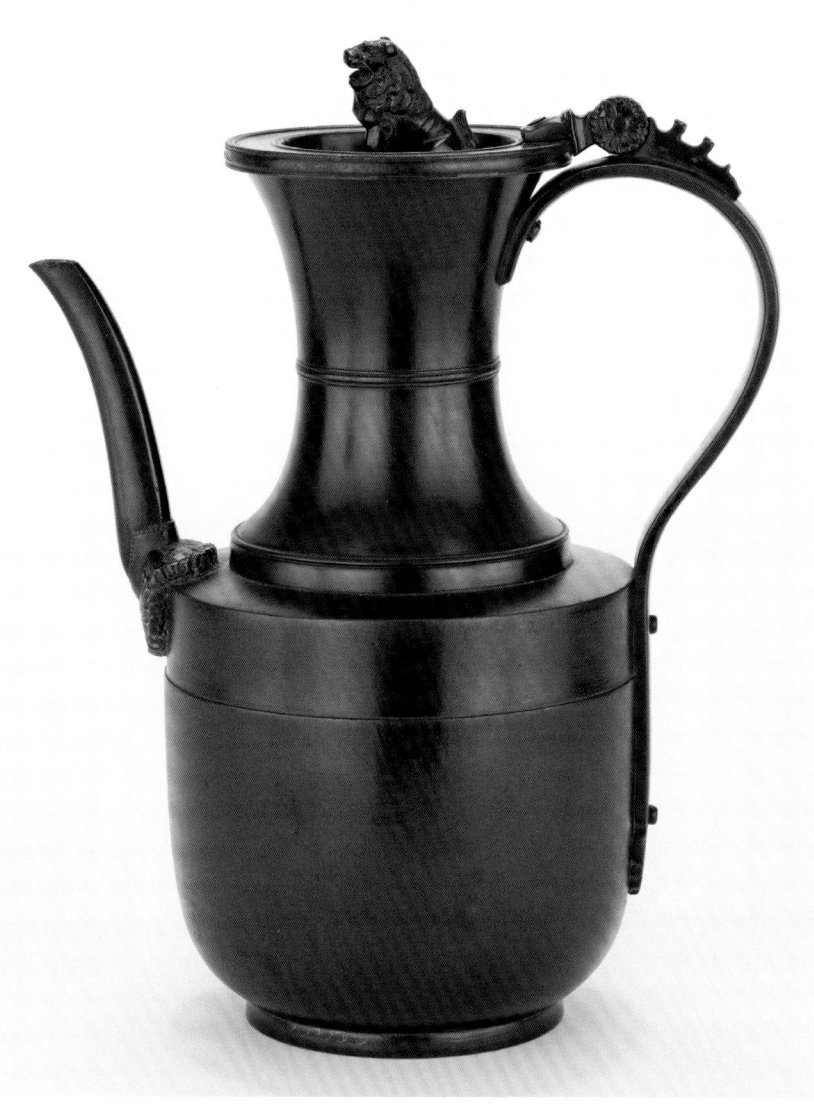

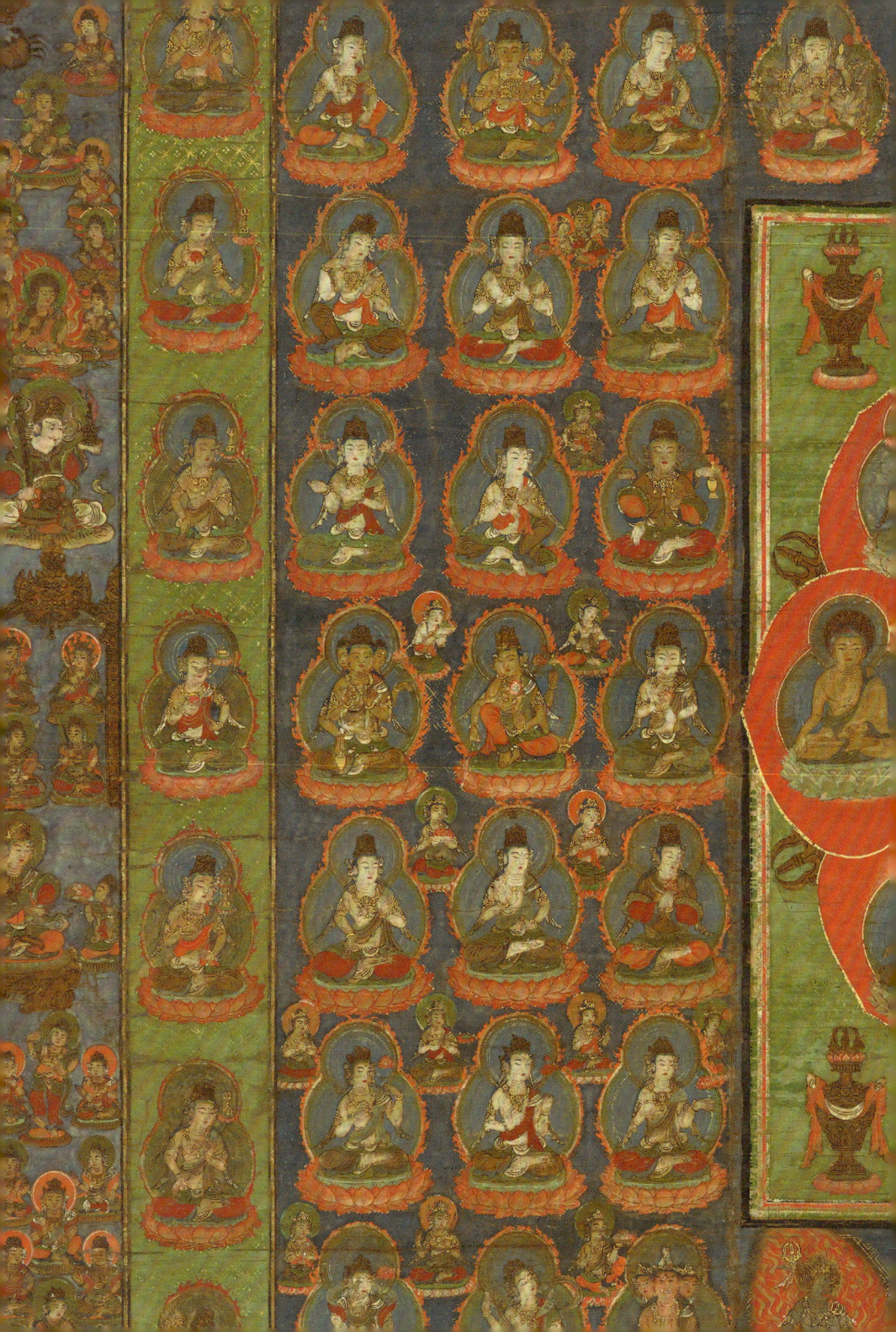

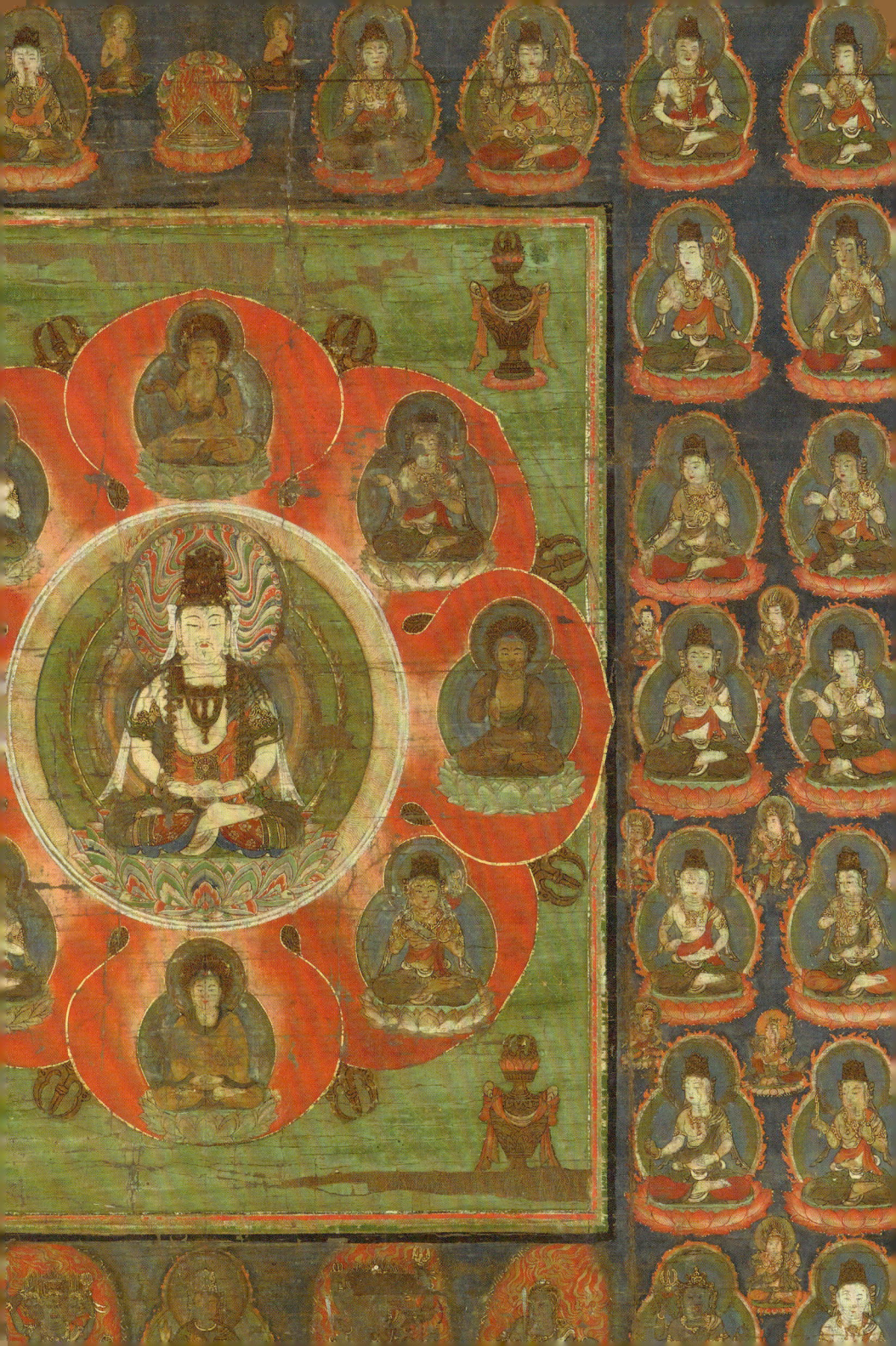

Garbhadhatu (taizokai) mandala
Japan, Kamakura period, mid-13th century
Hanging scroll; color on silk
219.5 × 142.8 cm
Purchase, Freer Gallery of Art, F1998.1

Representing the womb world mandala (*taizokai*), this powerful painting must have been half of a set of mandalas of the two worlds (*ryokai*). Given its scale and skill of execution, this fine work likely was produced for an esoteric Buddhist temple of great importance.

Deriving from iconography that Japanese monks brought home from China in the ninth century, this image is usually paired with the diamond world (*kongokai*) mandala. Together, the mandalas of the two worlds are the focus of prolonged meditation. The practitioner's ultimate goal is to awaken to the unified nature of reality within Vairochana, the mandalas' central figure, and within himself or herself.

JU

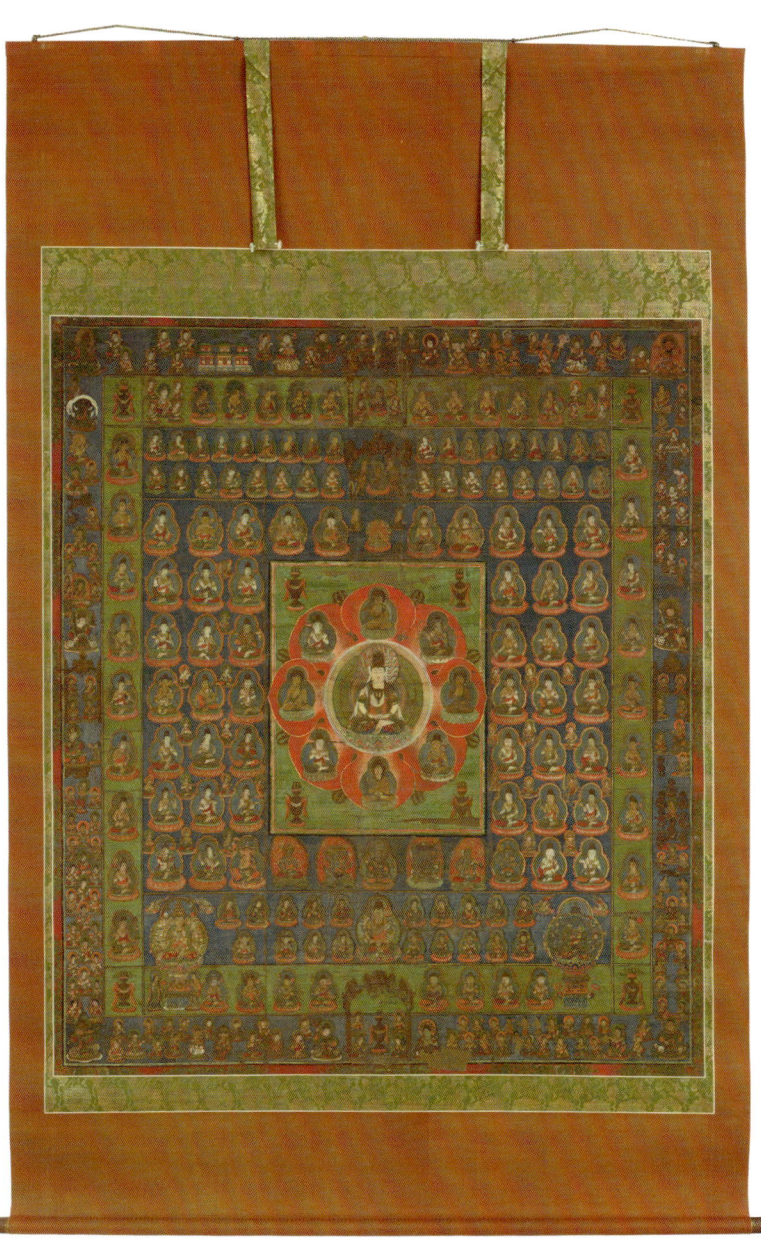

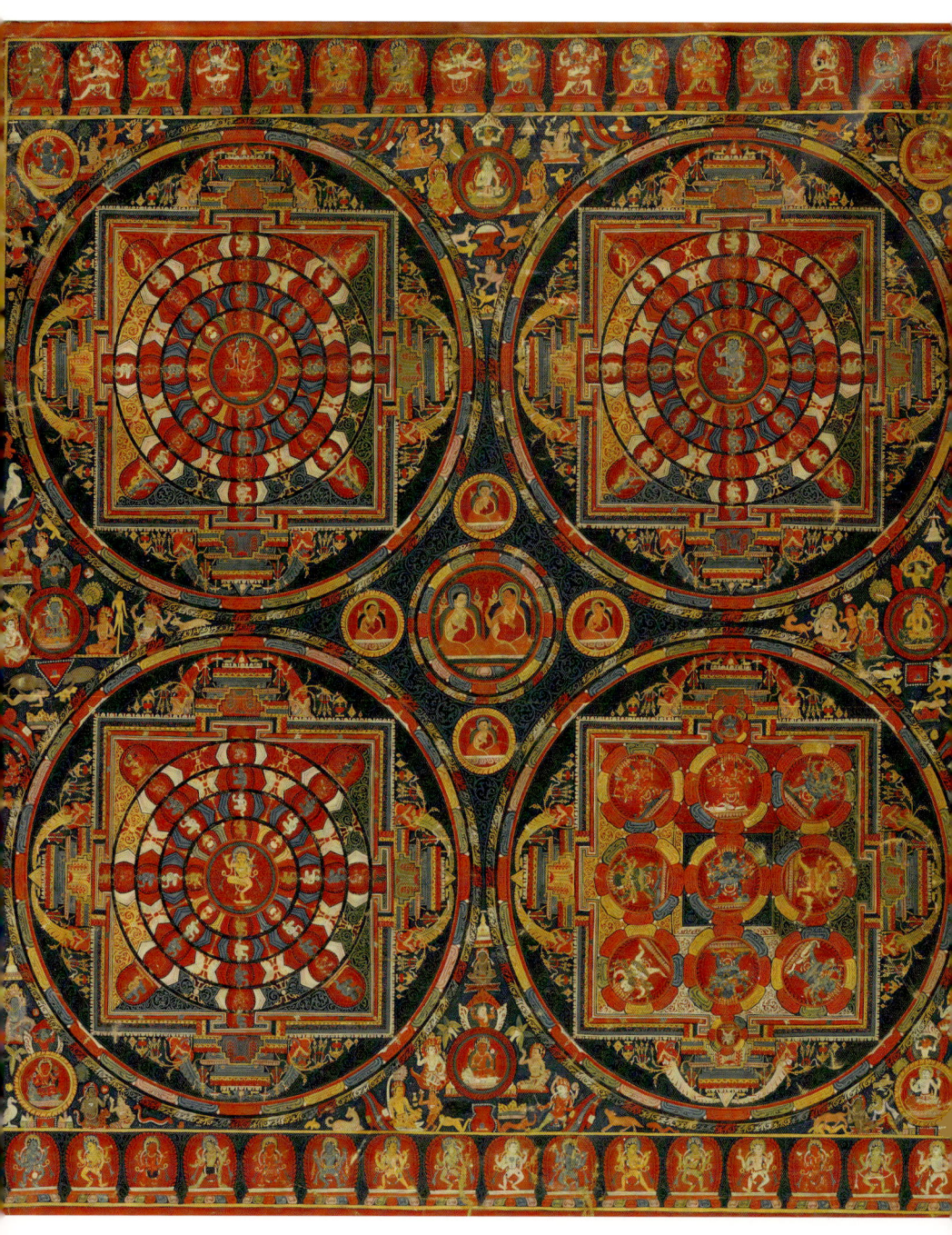

Four Mandalas from the Vajravali
Tibet, Ngor Monastery, ca. 1430
Opaque watercolor on cloth
87.7 × 78 cm
Purchase—Charles Lang Freer Endowment, Freer Gallery of Art, F1997.22

Around 1430, a group of Newar painters from the Kathmandu Valley of Nepal arrived at Ngor Monastery in central Tibet. Their appearance fatefully coincided with the decision of the monastery's abbot, Ngorchen Kunga Zangpo, to commission a series of mandala paintings in memory of his teacher. The artists and their workshop produced Ngorchen's famously exquisite set of mandalas and related series, including this painting. This distinctive and innovative body of work inspired generations of painters and patrons.

Mandalas have many forms and functions within Tibetan Buddhism. Drawn or painted, a mandala is a blueprint-like representation of a three-dimensional palace. The deity residing at the palace's center, the structure's apex, is the most important one. In initiation rituals, mandalas are essential tools that introduce a student to the deities and visualizations of a given practice. Once initiated, a meditator builds the mandala in his or her mind. To effectively aid these practices, an artist must consult and follow a source text containing detailed descriptions of the mandala's appearance and deities. Still, the artist's unique touch is often apparent in the execution and embellishments of the design.

The source text for Ngorchen's mandalas is a cycle of teachings known as the Vajravali. Because of their ability to produce enlightenment or supernatural powers, the Vajravali teachings, like many Tibetan Buddhist practices, are secret. A practitioner may only receive them from his or her guru during an initiation ritual, transmissions that form Tibetan Buddhist lineages. One such exchange is represented by the two monks in the center of this composition. The teacher memorialized by this set of paintings is the very guru from whom Ngorchen received his own Vajravali initiation.

RB

Base for an offering mandala
China, Ming dynasty, probably Yongle reign (1402–24)
Cloisonné (brass, enamel, wire, traces of gilding)
7.7 × 31 × 31 cm
Purchase—Charles Lang Freer Endowment, Freer Gallery of Art, F1998.295

During the early fifteenth century, the Chinese court often invited Tibetan prelates, or spiritual leaders, to conduct Buddhist rituals in Beijing. These visitors and rites were especially frequent during the Yongle reign, when the emperor commissioned many Buddhist ceremonies in his parents' memory. This splendid object probably was a gift from the Yongle emperor or his successor to a visiting Tibetan lama or religious dignitary. It is made of cloisonné, a favorite court luxury, chosen to show high respect for the Tibetan visitors.

The object is the base for a three-dimensional offering mandala, a cosmic diagram representing the entire universe, for use in Tibetan Buddhist ritual. By making such a mandala and offering it to a deity, buddha, or guru, a devotee could accumulate merit and wisdom. Decorated with lotus flowers and the eight auspicious symbols, the mandala base represents absolute space, the foundation of the Buddhist universe. Small holes on the sides indicate where metals rings were originally attached, allowing worshippers to wrap a white cloth around the base as a symbol of Buddhist purity.

The base supported a telescoping tower of metal rings, which helped worshippers visualize sacred Mount Meru and the continents of our world. Depending on their wealth, worshippers placed grains of pulverized gems, barley, rice, or colored sands inside each ring. A "flaming Buddhist jewel" was inserted at the top.

To make cloisonné, an artist creates a design on a metal base by bending wires to form small cells (cloisons). These cells are filled with colored enamel, which is fused by firing the object to a high temperature; this process is repeated several times. Final steps include polishing the surface and gilding the wires.

JS

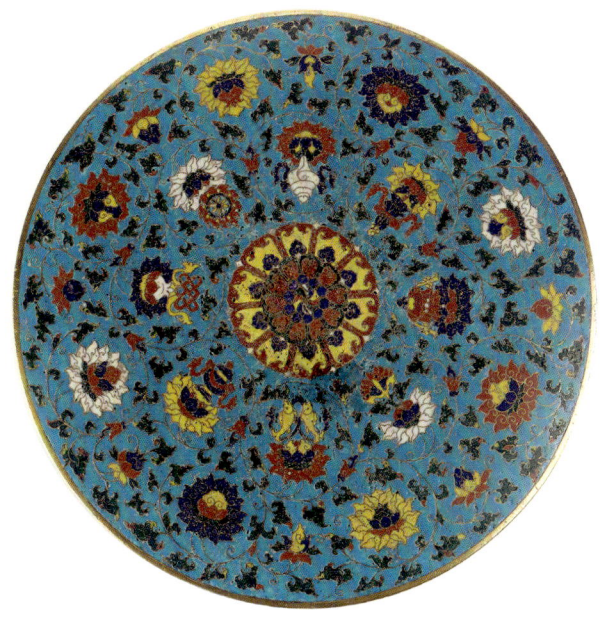
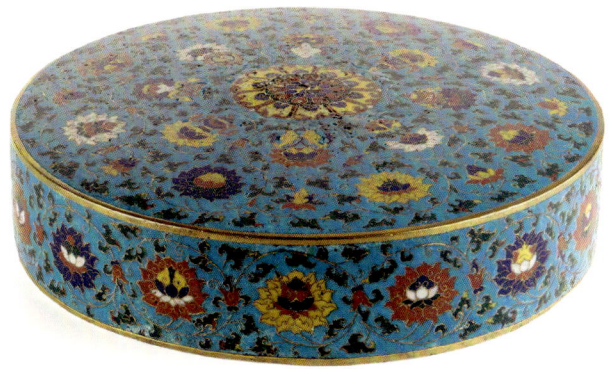

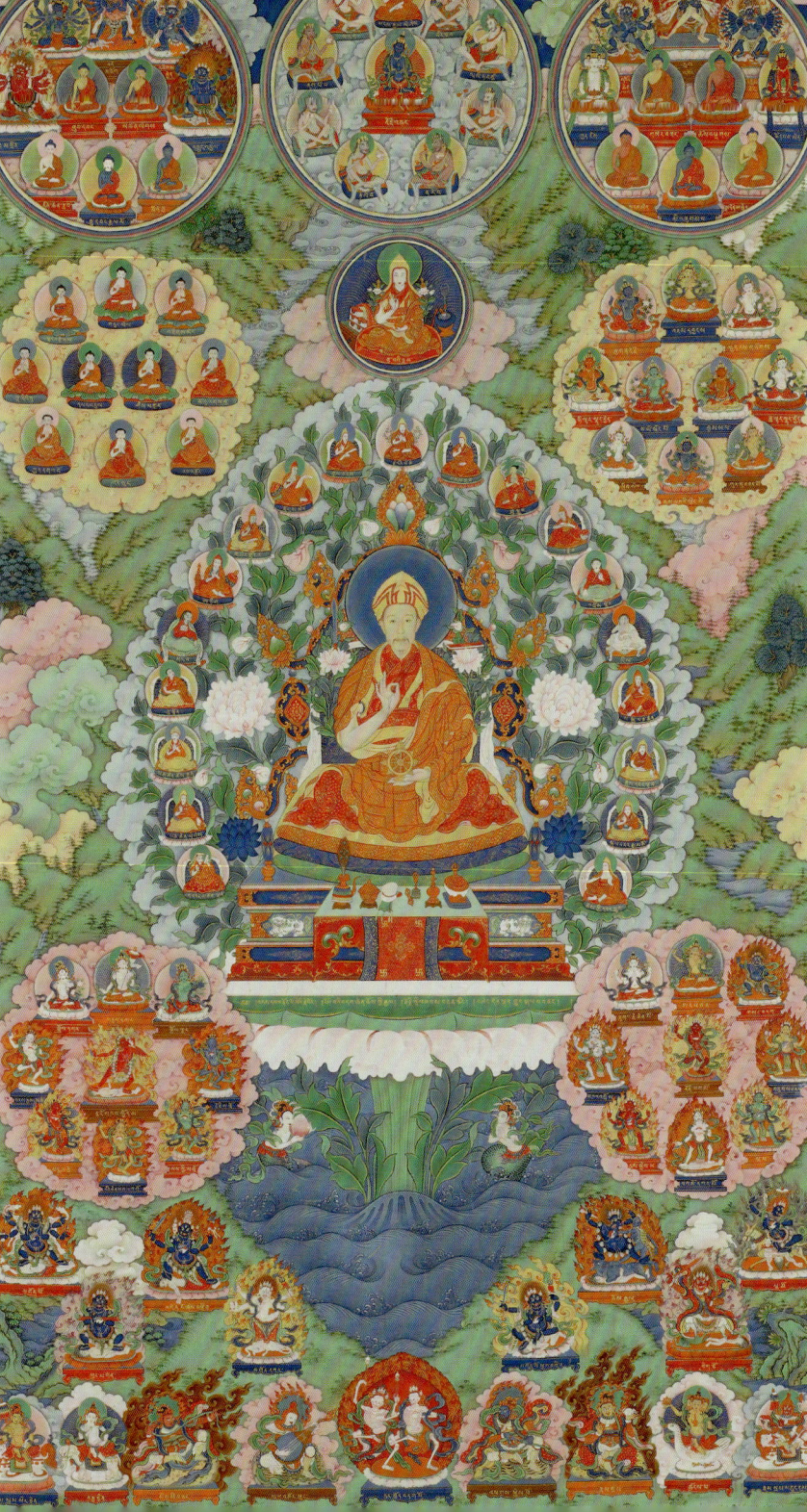

Qianlong Emperor as Manjushri
Imperial workshop; face by Giuseppe Castiglione (1688–1766)
China, Qing dynasty, mid-18th century
Unmounted thangka; ink, color, and gold on silk
113.6 × 64.3 cm
Purchase—Charles Lang Freer Endowment and funds provided by an anonymous donor, Freer Gallery of Art, F2000.4

Wearing a headdress of the Yellow Hat (Gelukpa) order of Tibetan Buddhism, an exquisitely robed figure sits with folded legs on an elaborate throne. With thumb and index finger joined in a circle, his right hand forms the *vitarka* mudra, symbolizing the explication and transmission of Buddha's teachings. His left hand holds the wheel of the law, identifying him as a *chakravartin*, or universal sovereign. A lotus flower appears at each shoulder, one supporting a flaming sword and the other the text of a sutra. These are emblems of Manjushri, the bodhisattva who personifies Buddha's transcendent wisdom.

Distributed in a symmetrical arrangement from top to bottom, 108 Buddhist figures surround the bodhisattva. Tibetan names written in gold identify the figures, providing a spiritual lineage that proclaims the emperor Qianlong (reigned 1735–96) to be a reincarnation of Manjushri. The text marshals a broad range of enlightened beings to support the emperor: human teachers and reincarnated lamas, buddhas and bodhisattvas, guardian and tutelary deities, gods and goddesses, and even the Lords of the Charnal Grounds, twin dancing skeletons.

Meticulous detail and jewel-like colors attest to the painting's origin in a Tibetan-Chinese workshop at the imperial court in modern Beijing. Giuseppe Castiglione, a master painter and longtime Jesuit missionary at the Qing court, almost certainly executed the sensitive face, which provides a naturalistic portrait of Qianlong.

SDA

Stupa
China, probably Beijing, Qing dynasty, Qianlong reign (1735–96)
Cloisonné (metal, enamel, gilt wire)
66.6 × 24.8 × 28.1 cm
Purchase—Charles Lang Freer Endowment, Freer Gallery of Art, F1991.6

Hollow stupas that held religious relics or written prayers were important accoutrements in Tibetan Buddhist practice, which flourished at the Chinese court during the Qing dynasty (1644–1911). The expensive and labor-intensive art form of cloisonné was a favorite material for Buddhist objects because its opulence signaled a donor's high regard for the faith. This stupa was probably commissioned by the Qianlong emperor (reigned 1735–96), who was devoted to Buddhist teachings and practice. He also knew the strategic benefits of protecting and promoting the Tibetan faith for social and political benefits in his expansive, multiethnic empire.

The style of this stupa reflects the close intermingling of Tibetan and Chinese imagery during Qianlong's reign. It is decorated with an intricate design of Buddhist lotuses and the eight auspicious symbols. A gilded staircase leads to an opening occupied by a lotus-shaped throne, symbolizing the presence of the Buddha. The ornament over the opening is a curious hybrid of a *garuda*, a mythical bird that is a Tibetan symbol for conquering obstacles, and a Chinese bat motif. The Chinese word for bat (*fu*) is a homophone for the word for "good fortune," making the bat an auspicious animal. Feathery incised lines in the wings force the viewer to see this creature as both *garuda* and bat.

The spire consists of thirteen telescoped rings that resemble ceremonial parasols, a standard design symbolizing the stages of enlightenment. Most Tibetan stupas have a crescent moon and flaming pearl at the top, but here the ornament is probably a Buddhist "temple vase of abundance." Yet, it also resembles the non-Buddhist, Chinese symbol of a gourd that represents the unity of heaven and earth.

JS

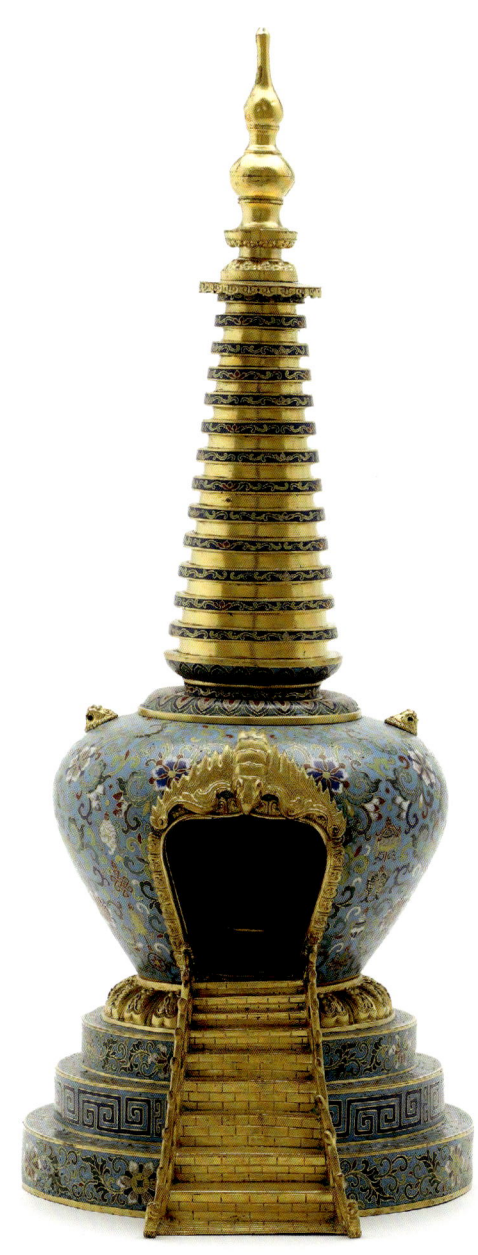

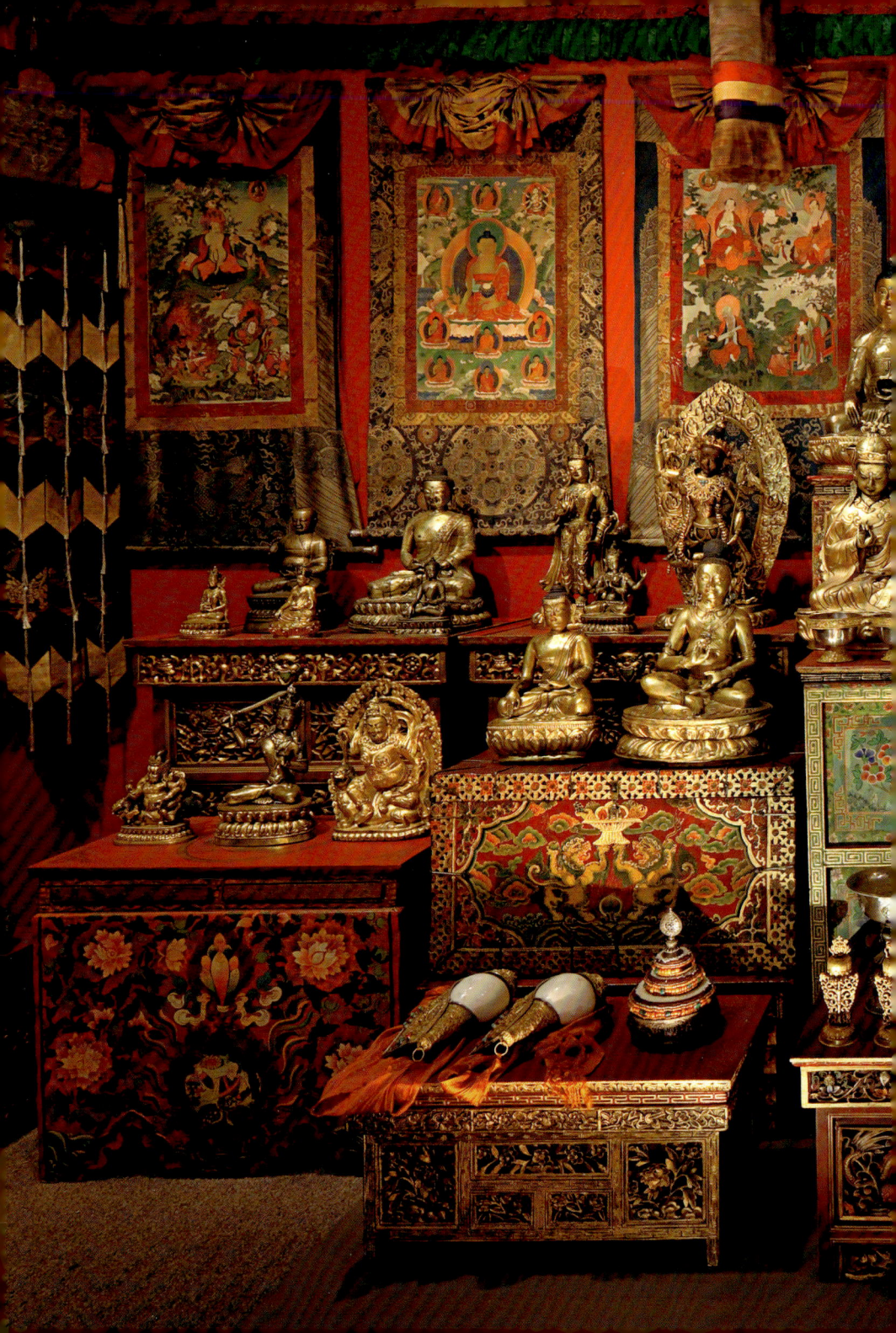

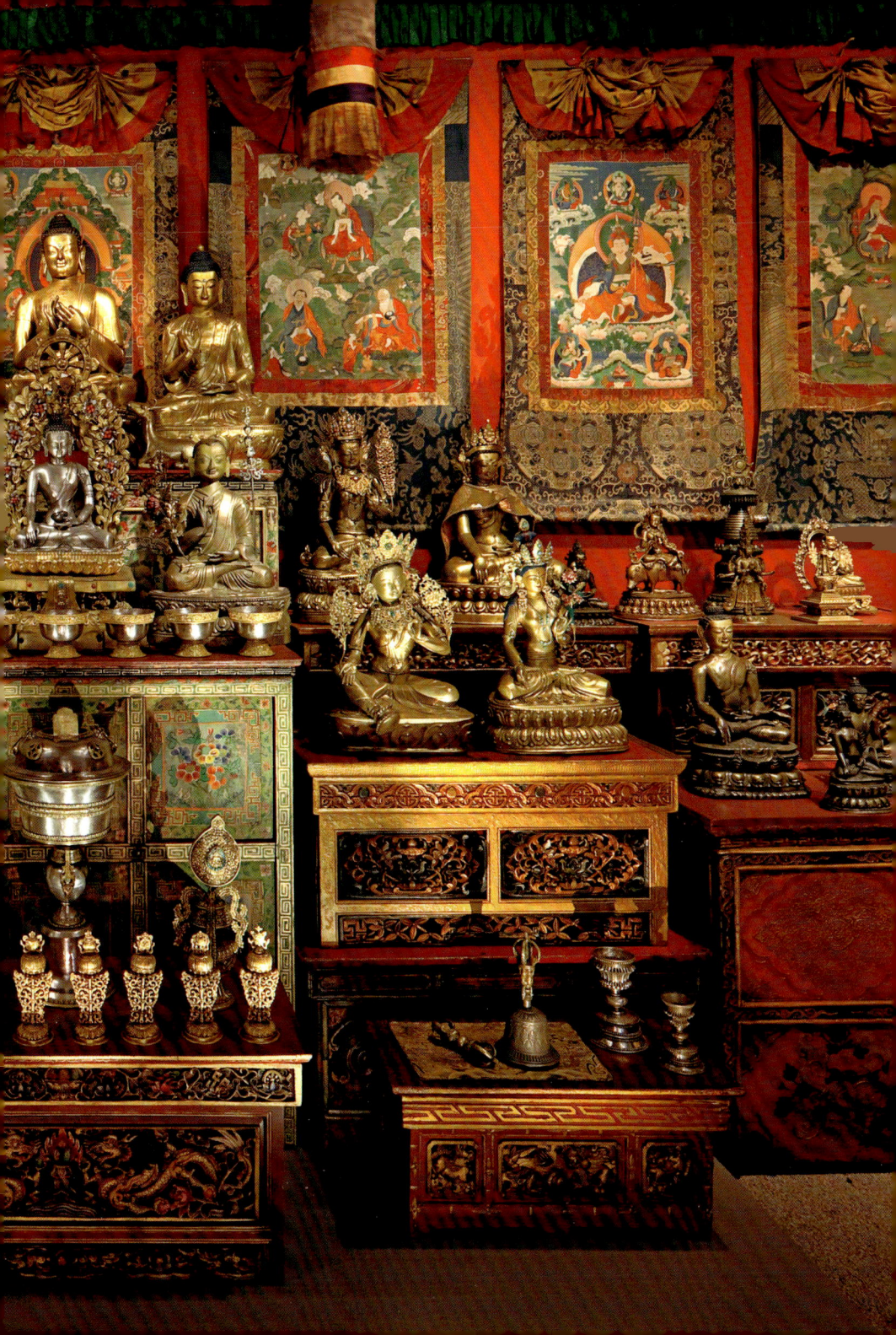

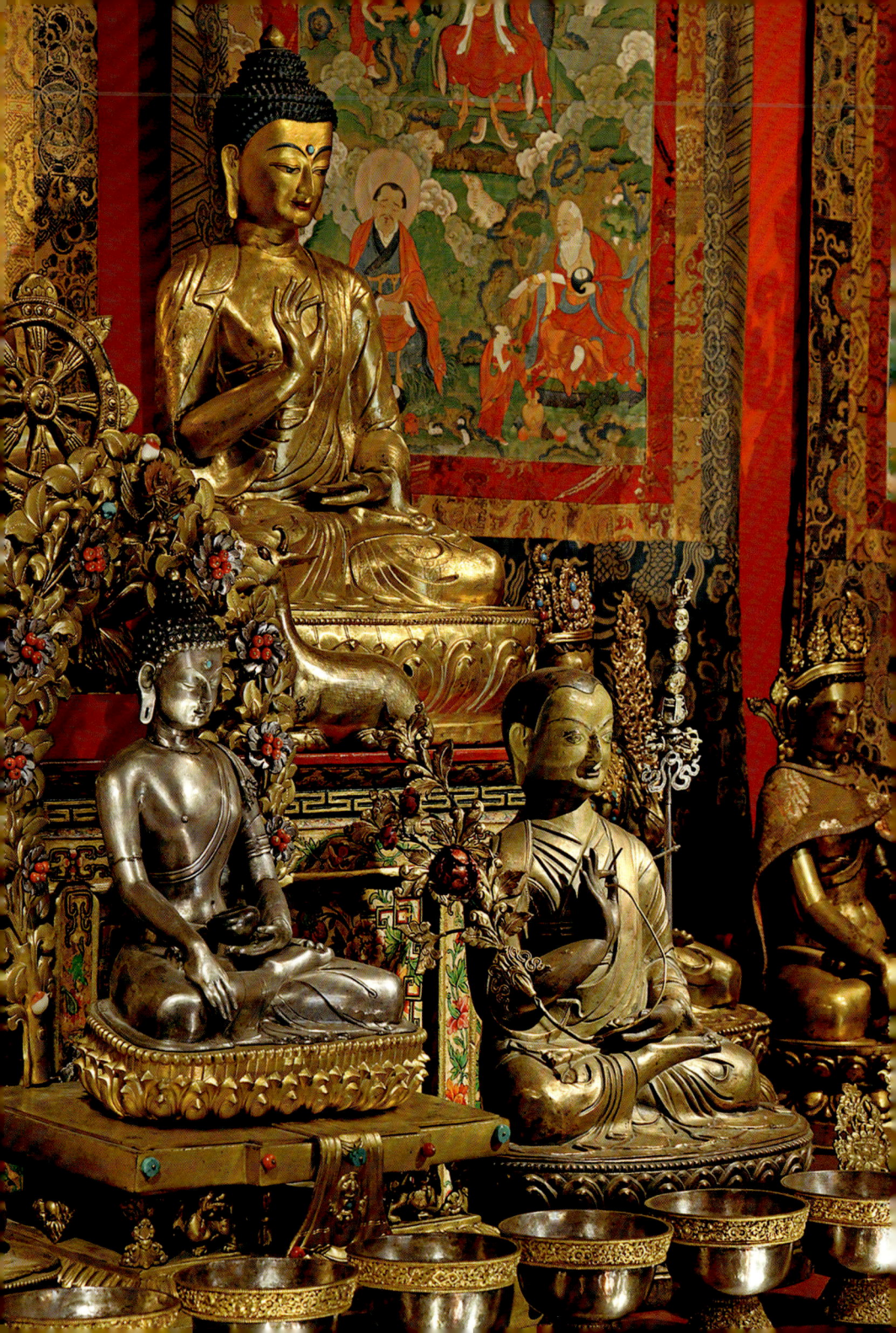

The Shrine Room of Alice S. Kandell
First installed 2010
Mixed media
The Alice S. Kandell Collection, see page 222

Whether small domestic altars or grand temple halls, the diverse worlds of Tibetan Buddhist worship are crowded with vibrant figures that may be human or divine, wrathful or peaceful, protective or awakened. These sacred spaces are carefully orchestrated to present a hierarchy of enlightened (and unenlightened) beings and to facilitate the choreography of ritual movement. When they are removed from temples and shrines and relocated to the secular sphere of a museum, Tibetan Buddhist objects are transformed—from icons to artifacts, from living images to inanimate artworks. A profound change occurs as these objects are viewed outside of the vivid context of a sanctified space and apart from their multidimensional relationships with other sacred images.

As an antidote to conventional museum displays, in 2010, the Arthur M. Sackler Gallery acquired a shrine that the New York collector Alice S. Kandell had assembled over many years. Installed at the museum with the guidance of a Tibetan lama, the shrine is an immersive environment, inviting visitors to encounter Tibetan Buddhist art in a manner that evokes the sacred precincts of the Himalayas. The experience is multisensory, as flickering lights evoke butter-lamp offerings and the sonorous chanting of Tibetan monks fills the room. More than two hundred objects are exhibited on painted furniture rather than in glass cases, hung among traditional textiles rather than on white walls, and presented without the mediation of labels. This display conjures the crowded, overlapping placement of objects typical of Tibetan shrines, in contrast to the open spaces of traditional museum galleries. Reflecting Tibetan Buddhist concepts and customs, the arrangement of sculptures and paintings seeks to restore the objects' contextual relationships.

RB

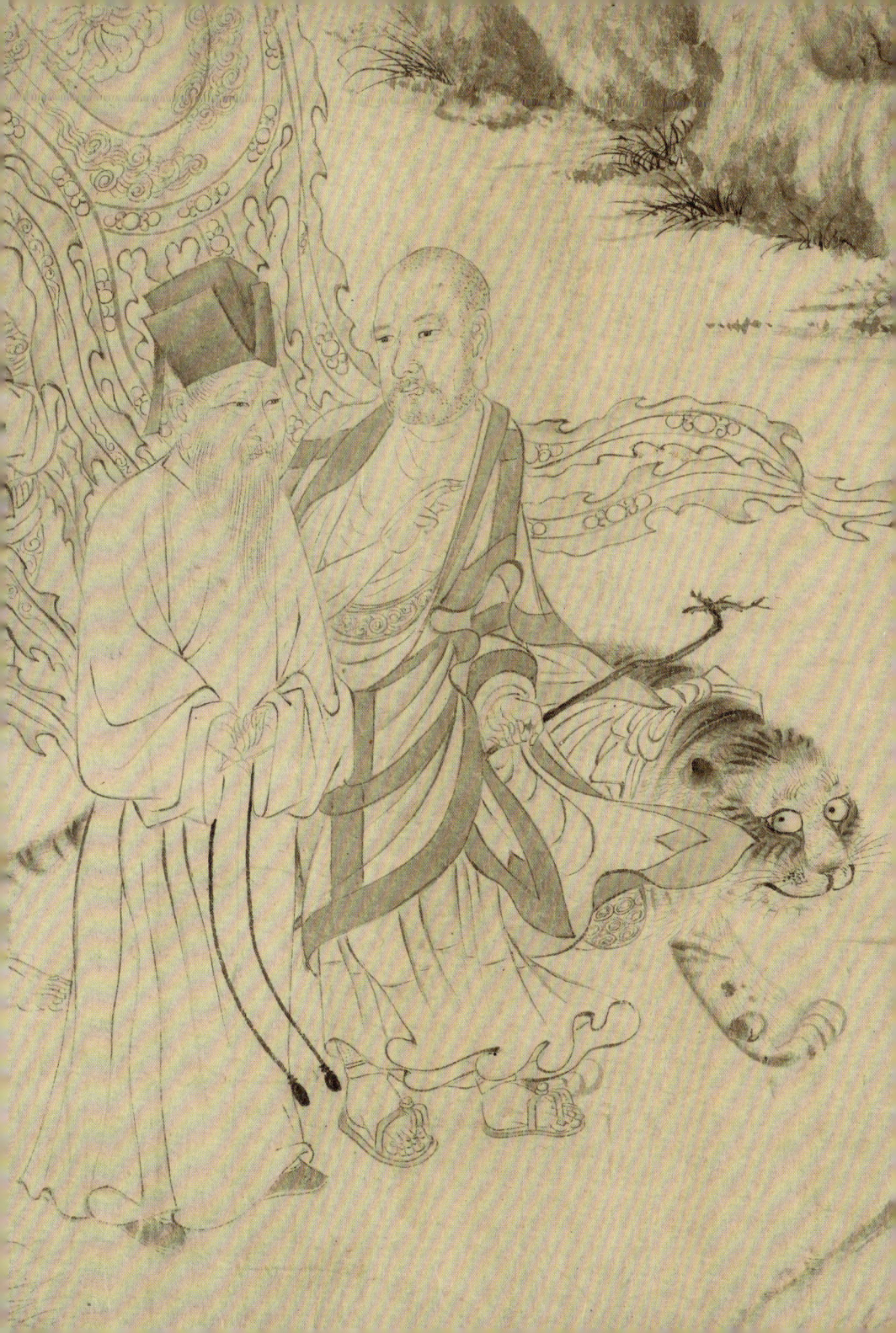

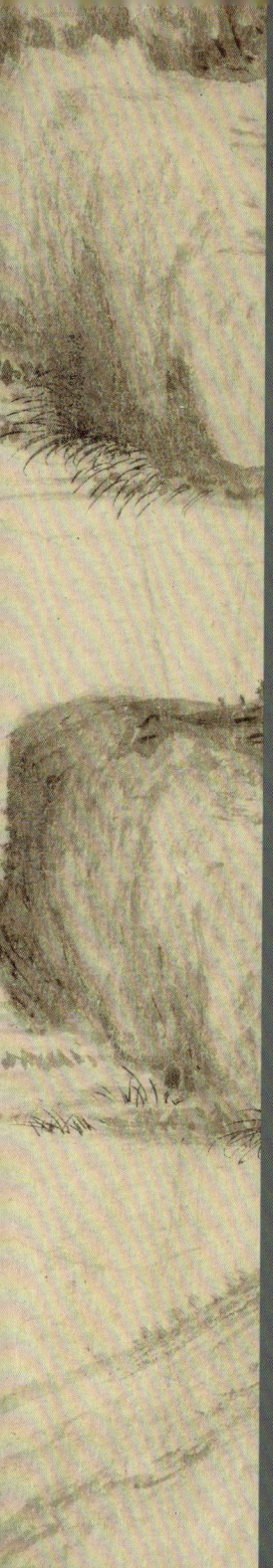

Teachers and Teachings

"Sutra," a word related to "suture," literally means "string" or "thread." In Buddhism, sutras are texts of central importance, as their words preserve the core strands of the Buddha's teachings (dharma). Although primarily intended for recitation and memorization, sutras also may serve as foci of veneration. Their creation is invariably seen as a praiseworthy act.

Teachers who translate texts and instruct students are equally essential. These masters also create a thread, linking modern devotees with all who have shared the dharma before. Various Buddhist traditions honor different teachers and founders, and do so to different degrees.

Alongside ordinary teachers are a host of figures who transcend human limits and serve as protectors and defenders of the dharma. Prajnaparamita, for example, embodies the perfect wisdom imparted by the texts that share her name. And the arhats, a group of enlightened and nearly immortal monks, protect the dharma until the Future Buddha, Maitreya, appears.

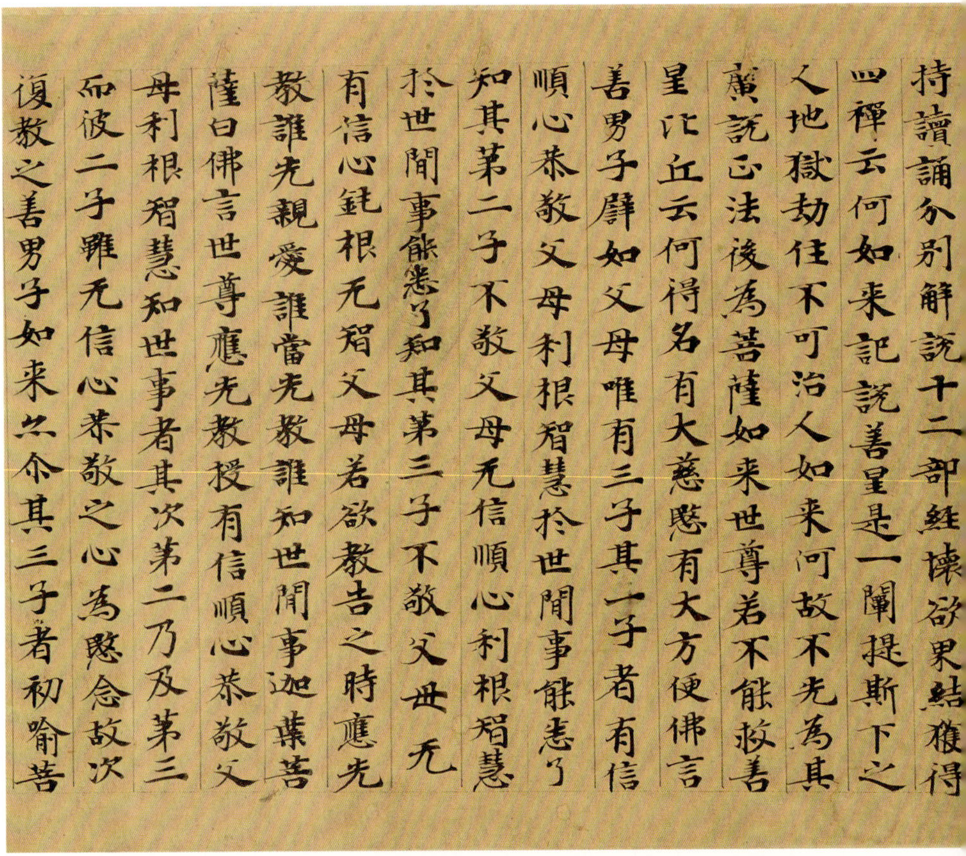

持讀誦分別解說十二部經壞欲界結獲得
四禪云何如來記說善星是一闡提斯下之
人地獄劫住不可治人如來何故不先為其
廣說正法後為菩薩如來世尊若不能救善
星比丘云何得名有大慈愍有大方便佛言
善男子譬如父母唯有三子其一子者有信
順心恭敬父母利根智慧於世間事能憨了
知其第二子不敬父母无信順心利根智慧
於世間事能愍了知其第三子下敬父母无
有信心鈍根无智父母若欲教告之時應先
教誰先親愛誰當先教誰知世間事迦葉菩
薩白佛言世尊應先教授有信順心恭敬父
母利根智慧知世事者其次第二乃及第三
而彼二子雖无信心恭敬之心為愍念故次
復教之善男子如來亦介其三子者初喻菩

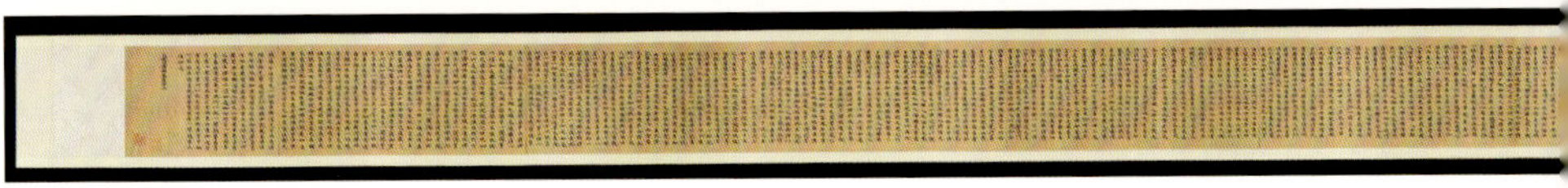

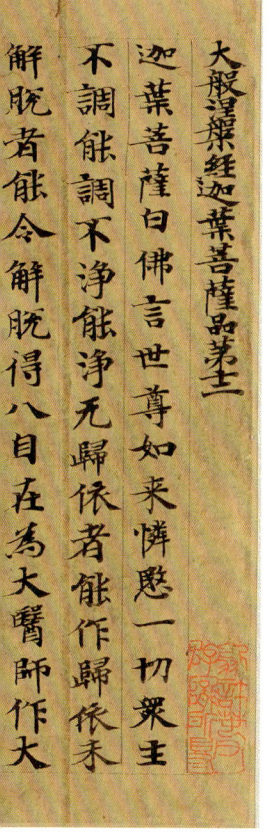

Mahaparinirvana Sutra (Sutra of the Great Demise)
Anonymous scribe
China, Gansu Province, Dunhuang, Sui dynasty, ca. 580s
Handscroll; ink on paper
20.9 × 380.3 cm
Purchase—Charles Lang Freer Endowment, Freer Gallery of Art, F1982.2

The text on this scroll excerpts the thirty-third chapter of the *Mahaparinirvana Sutra* (Sutra of the Great Demise), as translated into Chinese during the 420s by the eminent Indian monk Dharmakshema. Superseding all previous teachings, the sutra purports to preserve the last and most advanced lessons that the Buddha gave his disciples before his physical demise. One of the essential scriptures of the Tathagatagarbha school (in Chinese, Rulaizang), the *Mahaparinirvana Sutra* preaches that the eternal and immutable buddha-nature lies concealed in all sentient beings. Even the worst of these beings possesses an innate capacity to achieve enlightenment and transcend the endless cycle of birth, death, and rebirth (samsara).

Chapter 33 records several conversations between the Buddha and Kashyapa, one of his closest disciples, who asks a series of questions. Many concern the monk Sunakshatra, the Buddha's oldest son from his time as a prince. Kashyapa asks why the Buddha declared his son to be utterly unfit for salvation, seeming to contradict the teaching that salvation is available to all.

The scroll was discovered in 1900, along with many others, in a sealed cave outside the oasis town of Dunhuang, Gansu Province, where it was produced more than thirteen hundred years before. Professional scribes, either monks or laymen, transcribed sutras primarily for donation to Buddhist shrines and temples. Believers commissioned transcriptions of a selected chapter or group of chapters to acquire spiritual merit for themselves and for family members, both living and dead.

SDA

Section of "Ananda's Perfect Memory"
Japan, Nara period, 8th century
Hanging scroll; ink on paper
27.3 × 44.5 cm
Gift of Sylvan Barnet and William Burto in honor of Mitsuru Tajima, Freer Gallery of Art, F2014.6.2a–g

In this passage from the *Sutra of the Wise and Foolish* (Kengukyo), Shakyamuni explains that his disciple Ananda's past virtuousness has earned him a perfect memory. This trait would prove immensely important: Buddhist tradition holds that all sutras record the Buddha's words as precisely recounted by Ananda.

This section is from a copy of *Kengukyo* traditionally attributed to Emperor Shomu (reigned 724–49), who unified Japan and established Buddhism as its official religion. Accordingly, the copy is known as Ojomu (Great Shomu). The scrolls of the Ojomu manuscript originally were dedicated to Todaiji, the renowned Buddhist temple that Emperor Shomu ordered to be built in Nara.

The majesty of the Ojomu scrolls' calligraphy is unmatched among sutra manuscripts of the period, and its attribution to Emperor Shomu confers exceptional prestige. It is written in large characters on *dabishi*, paper believed to contain relics of Shakyamuni. Here, the paper is made of hemp mixed with white clay and particles of incense wood. The text is written in vertical columns of twelve or thirteen characters rather than the usual seventeen. Imposing and stable, the characters strongly reflect contemporary Chinese calligraphic styles. Some modern scholars thus have suggested that Ojomu originated in Tang-dynasty China rather than in Japan.

Later, the Ojomu became a model for Japanese calligraphers. Sections cut from its handscrolls were later preserved in albums of calligraphy samples (*tekagami*). In such albums, the Ojomu fragment would be the first sample, followed by a section of a sutra copied by Empress Komyo (701–760), who is also revered for her devotion to Buddhism.

AY

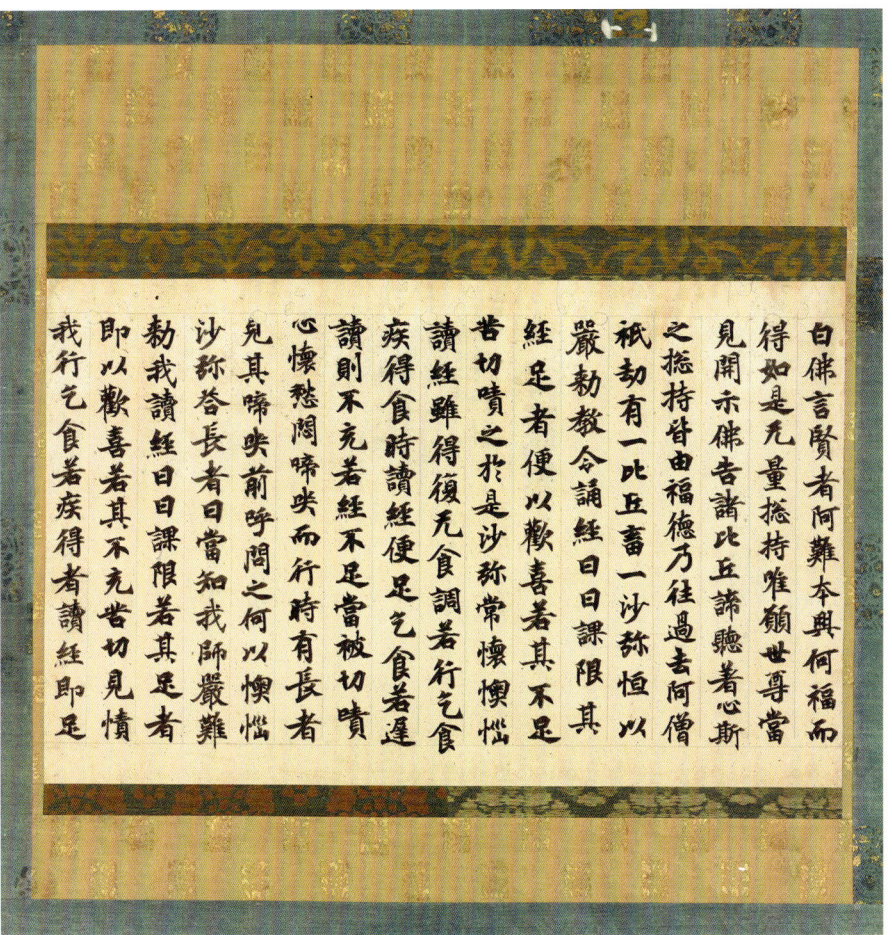

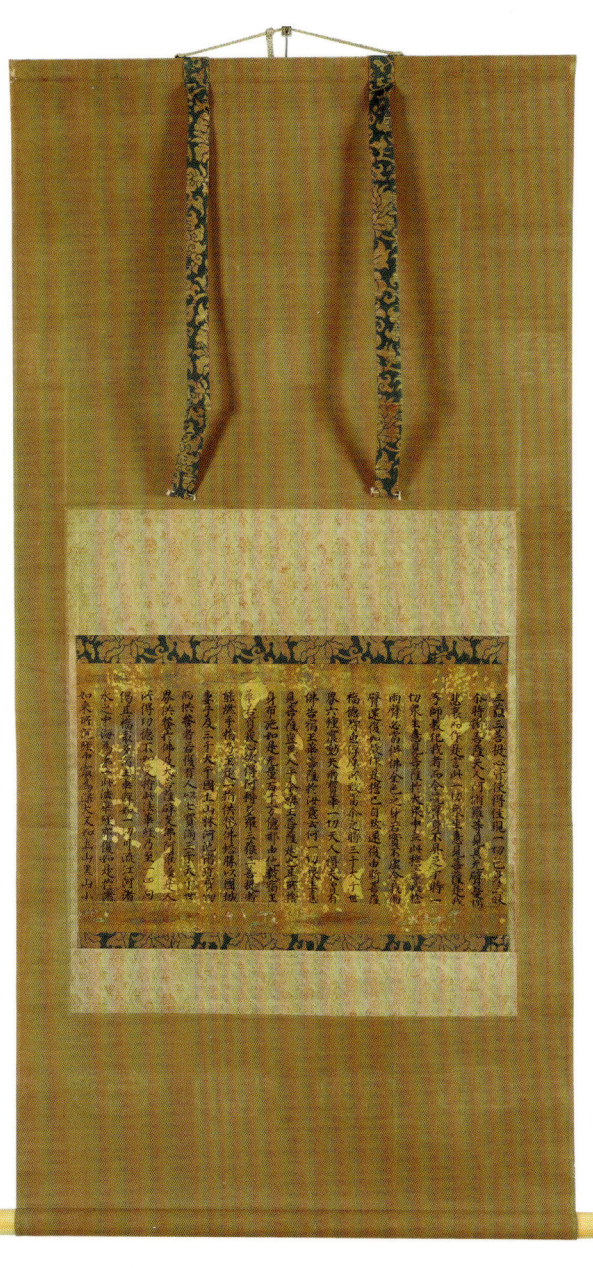

Section of the Lotus Sutra, chapter 23
Japan, late Heian period, mid-12th century
Hanging scroll; ink, color, gold, and silver on paper
24.7 × 40.7 cm
Gift of Sylvan Barnet and William Burto in honor of Tajima Mitsuru, Freer Gallery of Art, F2014.6.5

Brilliantly decorated sutra copies (in Japanese, *soshokukyo*) were created as offerings to Buddhist deities. The outstanding skills of Japanese specialists in paper decoration, who received generous aristocratic patronage, are evident in this rare fragment, an outstanding example of *soshokukyo*. Gold and silver are meticulously layered on the paper's surface. Delicate paintings of a lotus pond below the text and silver clouds above carry a sensitive naturalism that contrasts the disciplined regularity of the writing. This ornamentation represents the light that emanates from Amitabha (Amida) in the Pure Land, where, in the Lotus Sutra (Hokkekyo), he promises that the faithful will be reborn.

The text is from the twenty-third chapter of the *Lotus Sutra*. By the twelfth century, Japanese Buddhists found themselves in the last age of Buddhist law (*mappo*). They believed that copying, reading, and donating the *Lotus Sutra* would bring release from the cycle of suffering in this dark age, which would only end with the Future Buddha's birth.

Chapter 23 describes two episodes from the former lives of Bhaishajyaraja (Yakuo), the medicine king bodhisattva, in which self-sacrifice resulted in his perfect universal enlightenment. In one episode, Bhaishajyaraja wrapped himself in jeweled robes, poured fragrant oil over his head, and set himself afire as an offering to the Buddha. After burning for 1,200 years, he earned rebirth through his great sacrifice. When the Buddha passed into nirvana, Bhaishajyaraja again sacrificed himself, this time burning both of his arms. Because of his merit and wisdom, the bodhisattva's arms reappeared.

AY

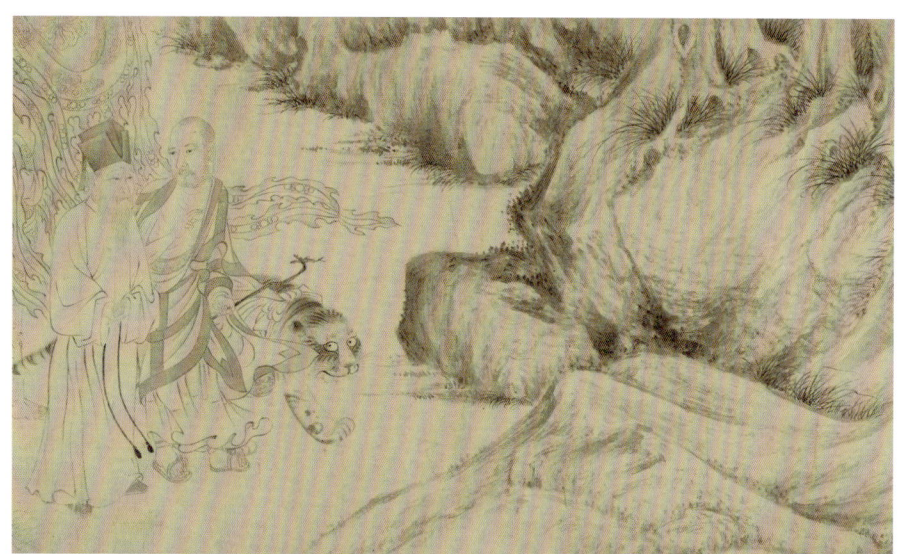
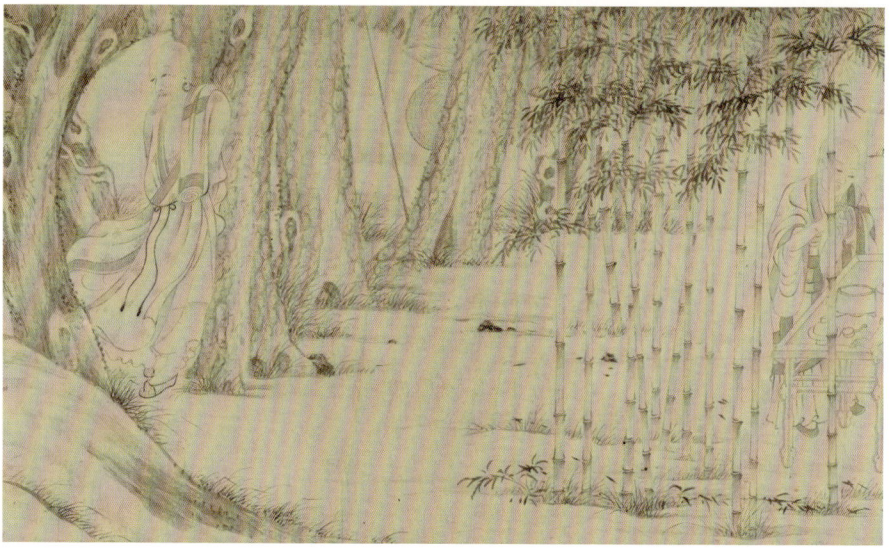

Sixteen Arhats (Luohan)

Fanlong (act. mid-12th century)
China, Southern Song dynasty, mid-12th century
Handscroll; ink on paper
30.5 × 1062.5 cm
Purchase—Charles Lang Freer Endowment, Freer Gallery of Art, F1960.1

Over its full thirty-five-foot length, this scroll depicts sixteen arhats (in Chinese, *luohan*) with their disciples and attendants in a series of independent compositions. Often seated on high-backed chairs, nine of the arhats are portrayed as Chan patriarchs receiving the submission or obeisance of different individuals or groups. The remainder appear in natural settings, such as in the section shown here. An arhat converses with a tall-hatted Confucian scholar as they emerge through a mountain ravine, escorted by a tame tiger and two demon-like earth spirits bearing banners, along with a third demon carrying a monkey on his shoulders. Although Chinese scholars were adherents of Confucianism, which frowned on strong religious belief, in fact many were practitioners of Buddhism in their private lives.

Considered protectors of the Buddhist law, or dharma, arhats are devout individuals who have attained profound spiritual realization and thus acquired transcendent powers over nature, matter, time, and space. Still, they remain in the world until all sentient beings have achieved spiritual liberation. Appearing in the guise of Buddhist monks, arhats conventionally are shown in groups of four, sixteen, eighteen, and even five hundred. Originally depicted as Indian ascetics in Chinese art, by the time of this painting, arhats were often thoroughly Chinese in appearance.

The artist Fanlong, a Chan Buddhist monk, followed the style of the earlier scholar-painter Li Gonglin, whose technique of thin, precise line drawing is well represented in this scroll. This painting is the only surviving work credibly attributed to Fanlong, whose barely visible signature can be found among the rocks to the right of the emerging figures.

SDA

Arhats (Luohan) Laundering
Lin Tinggui (act. late 12th century)
China, Southern Song dynasty, 1178
Hanging scroll mounted on panel; ink and color on silk
112.3 × 53.5 cm
Gift of Charles Lang Freer, Freer Gallery of Art, F1902.224

In the guise of ordinary Buddhist monks, five arhats (in Chinese, *luohan*) of various ages, followed by an attendant with grotesque features, emerge from a cleft in the rock. Under a darkening sky, they stoop to launder their garments in a swirling wilderness stream, then wring them out and hang them to dry on nearby branches. Immortal guardians of the Buddha's teachings, arhats epitomize the ideals of monastic life. They often are shown engaging in everyday tasks and activities, in either nature or a monastery setting.

Arhats sometimes appear as a group of five hundred monks, usually spread over multiple scrolls or sculptures. This pair of paintings (this page and p. 166) comes from a series of one hundred scrolls, each depicting five arhats together with other incidental figures. Two otherwise unknown painters created the set between 1178 and 1188 for a temple near modern Ningbo in Zhejiang Province, China. Each painting is by a different artist, but both had local sponsors, and both are dated in now-invisible inscriptions to the first year of the project.

SDA

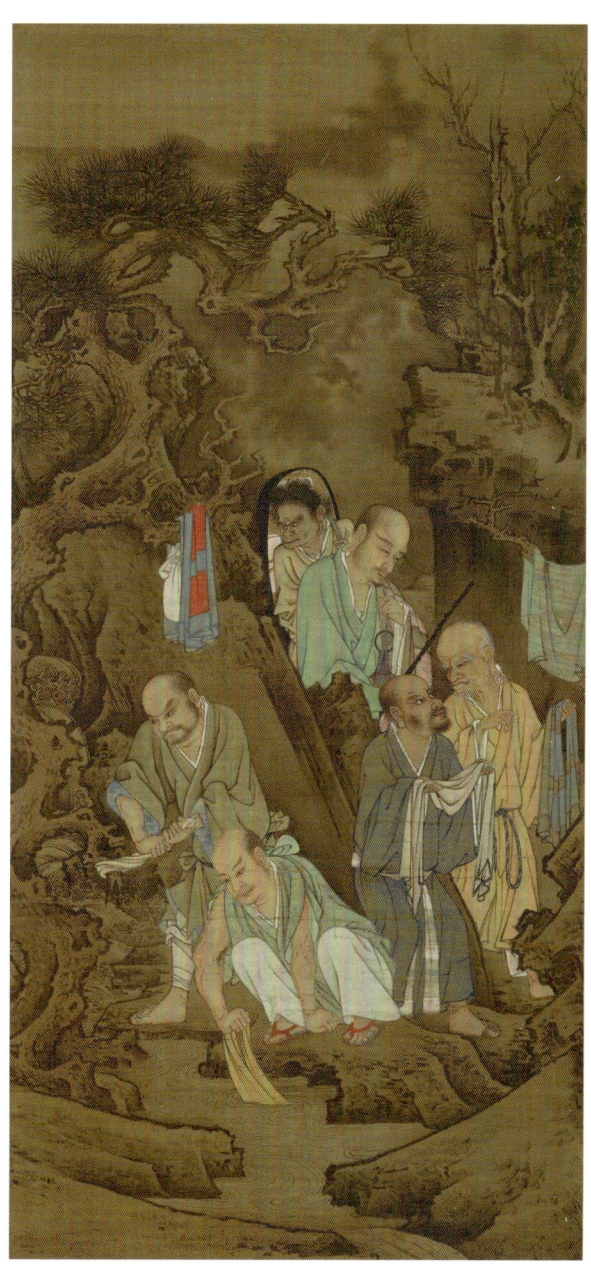

Rock Bridge at Mount Tiantai
Zhou Jichang (act. late 12th century)
China, Southern Song dynasty, 1178
Hanging scroll mounted on panel; ink and color on silk
109.9 × 52.7 cm
Gift of Charles Lang Freer, Freer Gallery of Art, F1907.139

China's Mount Tiantai, meaning "heavenly terrace," is reputedly the haunt of gods and immortals. Located a short distance inland from the coastal city of Ningbo, the mountain also is known for its famous sights, particularly a natural rock arch spanning a waterfall. Buddhists believe this landform was a pathway to heaven, where the five hundred arhats (in Chinese, *luohan*) worship and dwell among magnificent celestial temples. Here, three arhats stand on a swath of clouds in the foreground as two others stroll the clouds above, patrolling the temple gates.

Both groups observe the devout monk Tanyou (died 396), who is attempting to gain access across the rock bridge. According to Tanyou's story, initially the large stone at the far end thwarted him. But because of his persistence and sincerity, the arhats opened a door in the stone, allowing the monk to enter their heavenly abode and participate in their monastic routine. After this brief taste of bliss, he was sent back to his earthly monastery to live another ten years. This painting captures the moment just before the arhats first welcomed pious Tanyou into paradise.

SDA

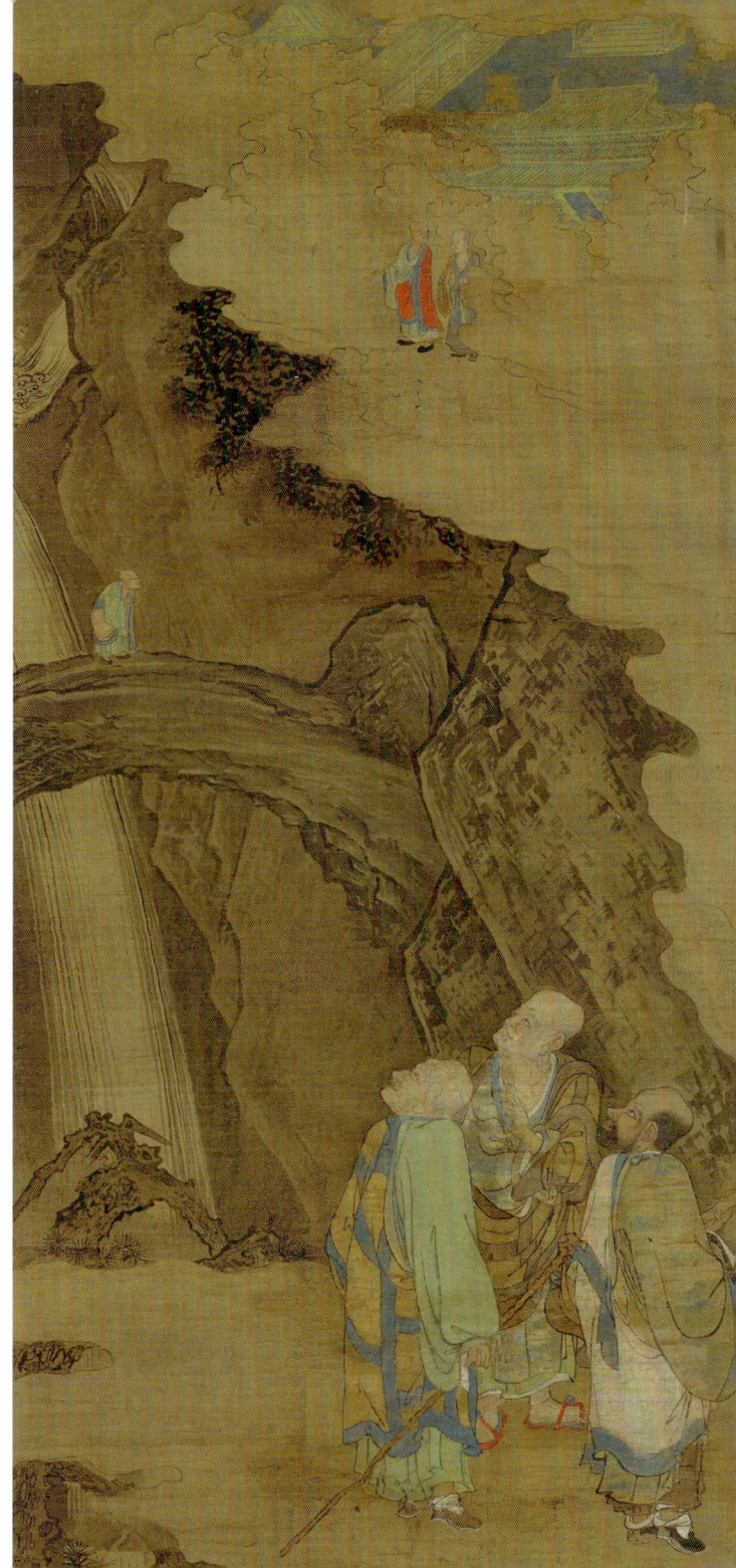

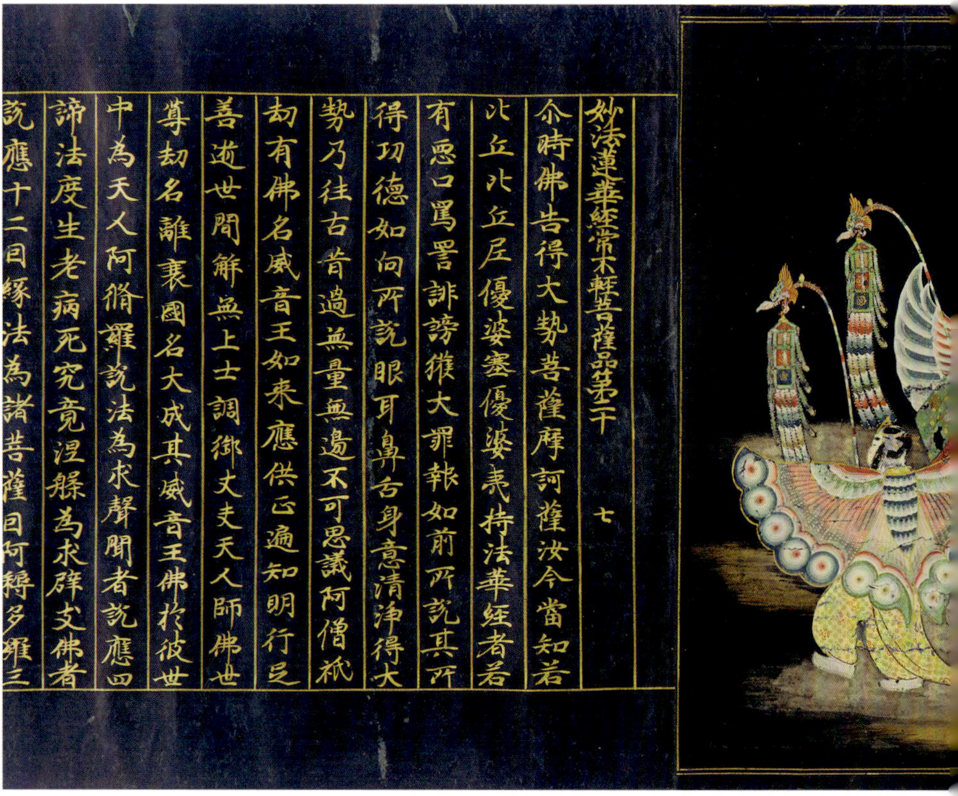

妙法蓮華經常不輕菩薩品第二十

七

爾時佛告得大勢菩薩摩訶薩汝今當知若
比丘比丘尼優婆塞優婆夷持法華經者若
有惡口罵詈誹謗獲大罪報如前所說其所
得功德如向所說眼耳鼻舌身意清淨得大
勢乃往古昔過無量無邊不可思議阿僧祇
劫有佛名威音王如來應供正遍知明行足
善逝世間解無上士調御丈夫天人師佛世
尊劫名離衰國名大成其威音王佛於彼世
中為天人阿修羅說法為求聲聞者說應四
諦法度生老病死究竟涅槃為求辟支佛者
說應十二因緣法為諸菩薩因阿耨多羅三

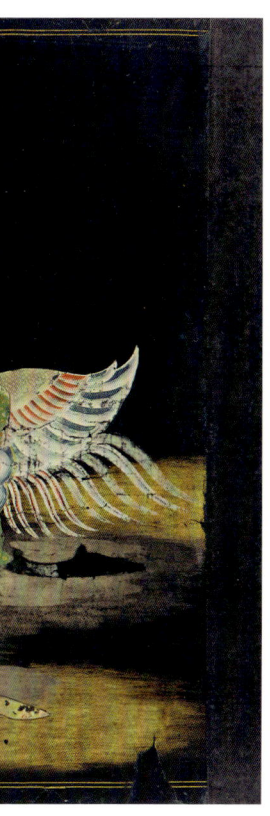

Lotus Sutra
Japan, Heian period, 1180
Handscroll; ink, color, gold, and silver on indigo-dyed paper; rock-crystal roller knobs
26 × 877.3 cm
Purchase—Charles Lang Freer Endowment, Freer Gallery of Art, F1980.199

Dancers in elaborate costumes grace this scroll from a *Lotus Sutra* set. One costume resembles a butterfly; the other is of a *kalavinka* (in Japanese, *karyobinga*), a creature with a bird body and human head that dwells in the Buddhist paradise and sings with unearthly beauty. Both performers carry banners as offerings. Their costumes and movement evoke ancient ritual dances that are still performed at some Japanese Buddhist temples and Shinto shrines.

Along with their subject matter, the illustrations in this set of *Lotus Sutra* scrolls are unusual in style and material. They are painted in full color with gold and silver pigment and cut gold leaf. Such delicate work, involving layered pigments and meticulous detail, is rare in sutra illustrations on indigo paper, which usually are rendered in only silver and gold (p. 170). These paintings represent Japanese artists' exquisite achievements at the height of imperial court patronage in the late Heian period.

The calligrapher copied the sutra text in gold on indigo-dyed paper, continuing a tradition that had begun in Japan by the eighth century. The text, which begins with a title to the left of the illustration, is written in Chinese characters, seventeen per column, as was customary for sutra copies.

AY

Sutra of Meditation on the Bodhisattva Samantabhadra (Fugen)
Japan, Heian period, late 12th century
Handscroll; silver and gold on indigo-dyed paper
25.4 × 76.9 cm
Purchase—Charles Lang Freer Endowment, Freer Gallery of Art,
F1968.60

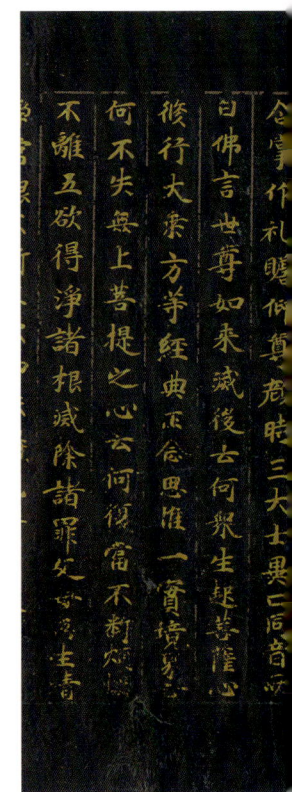

"I will mount my kingly white elephant and manifest myself in his presence," declares the bodhisattva Samantabhadra (in Japanese, Fugen) in the *Lotus Sutra*. The sutra's closing text, which is recorded in this scroll, and its final chapter both relate Samantabhadra's teachings and compassionate vows. Among them is his pledge to appear to a faithful Buddhist who recites the sutra sincerely and continuously for three days. The bodhisattva also promises to help the reader reach a complete understanding of the sutra and to provide dharani, potent incantations of aid and protection.

The frontispiece of this scroll illustrates Samantabhadra's descent from the east, riding enthroned upon his six-tusked white elephant. A monk sits reading and reciting a sutra, sheltered in a cave in a mountainous landscape. Painted in gold and silver with fine lines and tonal washes, the soft forms of the forested mountains evoke the Japanese landscape. The bodhisattva emanates rays of light toward the devout monk, underscoring the miracle of the deity's presence in the earthly world.

This scroll was once part of a *Lotus Sutra* set now in Toshodaiji, a Buddhist temple in Nara, Japan. It is an exceptionally fine example, produced at the height of an intensive period of sutra copying and decoration. Twelfth-century Buddhists believed that the final long age of Buddhist law (dharma) had commenced and that it would bring suffering and disorder until the birth of the next buddha, Maitreya (Miroku). Thousands of scrolls were copied as the urgent quest for salvation spread.

AY

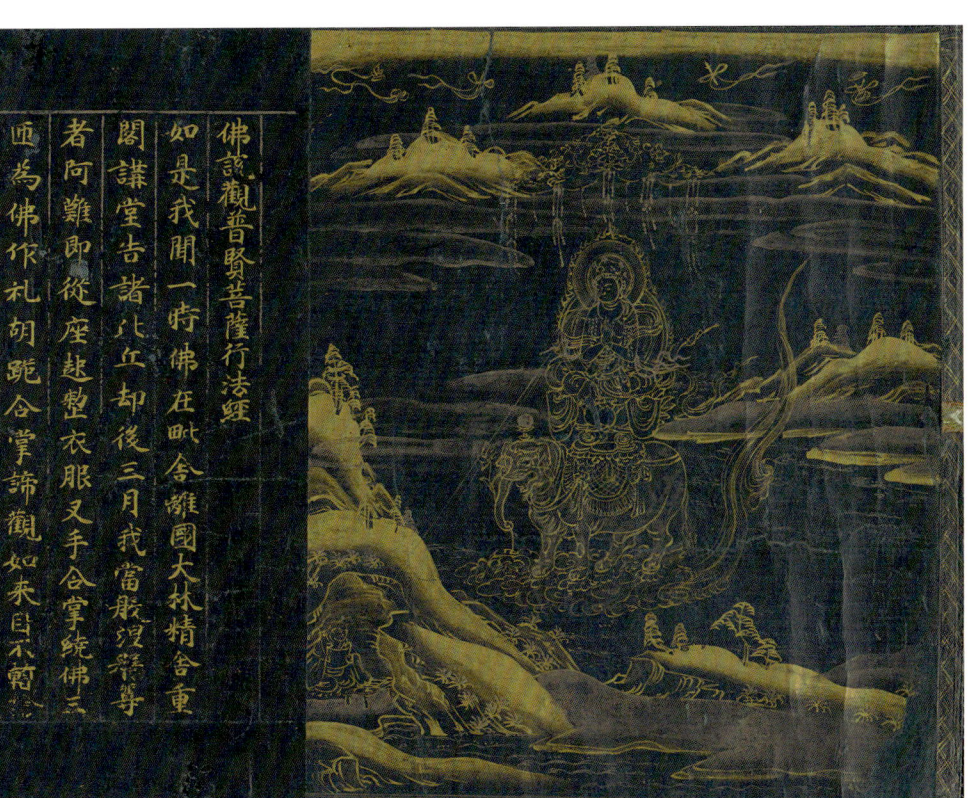

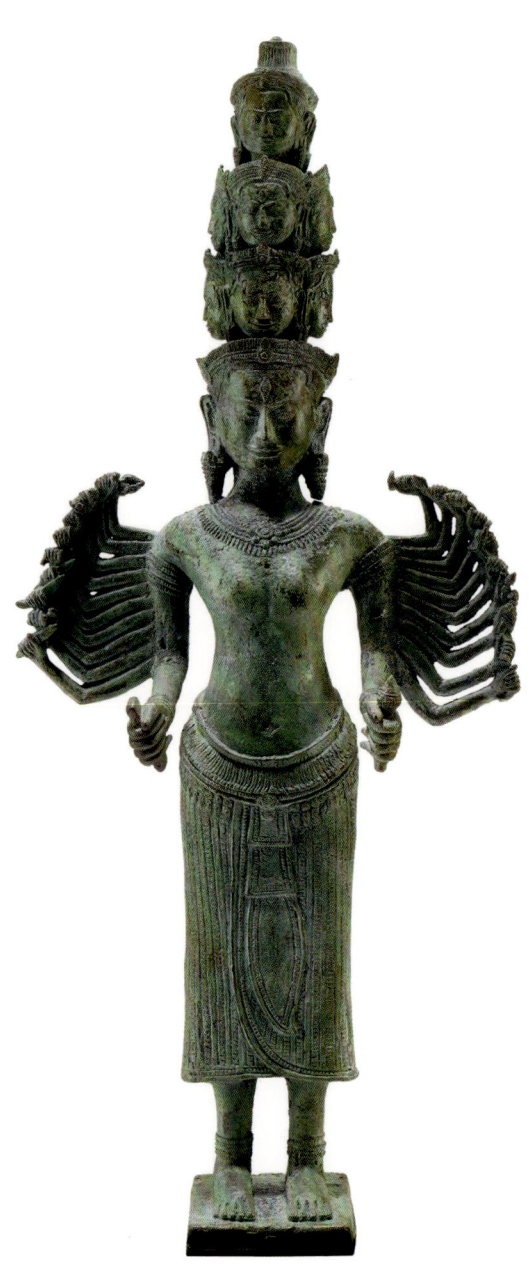

Prajnaparamita
Cambodia, ca. 1200
Copper alloy
52.1 × 23.5 × 10.2 cm
Gift of Ann and Gilbert Kinney, Arthur M. Sackler Gallery, S2015.26

Literally translated, *prajnaparamita* means "perfection of wisdom." This is the sixth and ultimate perfection—after giving, morality, patience, effort, and concentration—that a bodhisattva must achieve on his or her way to buddhahood. The perfection of wisdom requires a level of understanding well beyond conventional wisdom: it calls for a profound knowledge of the true nature of reality. Accordingly, a collection of texts aptly named the *Prajnaparamita Sutras* explains what one must understand. These Mahayana teachings are invaluable to cultivating the wisdom that a practitioner needs to achieve awakening.

As buddhahood arises from attaining this wisdom, Prajnaparamita is considered the mother of all buddhas. Personified as a goddess, she holds a lotus bud in her lower left hand as a symbol of purity. In her lower right hand is a palm-leaf manuscript, undoubtedly containing the very teachings she embodies. Her other twenty hands hold many more attributes, including ritual implements such as a thunderbolt scepter (*vajra*) and a dagger. These are important in Vajrayana rituals.

Twelfth- and thirteenth-century Cambodian artists frequently depicted Prajnaparamita in stone bas-relief and in small bronze triads, together with Avalokiteshvara and the Buddha. In these cases, she has a single head and two or four arms. In the pantheon of the Vajrayana tradition, deities have many arms and heads to symbolize their complex natures and diverse abilities. The multiple arms and heads we see here indicate that Prajnaparamita has a place in Vajrayana Buddhism as well.

JE

Prince Shotoku and Attendants

Japan, Kamakura period, 13th century
Hanging scroll; ink, color, and gold on silk, 212 × 94 cm
Purchase—funds provided by the Parnassus Foundation, courtesy of Jane and Raphael Bernstein; Mr. and Mrs. Frank H. Pearl; Jeffrey P. Cunard; and the Charles Lang Freer Endowment, Freer Gallery of Art, F2001.1

Prince Shotoku (574–622), son of Emperor Yomei, never became emperor of Japan, but he held the powerful title of regent. Along with unifying the nation under a constitution, his accomplishments included promoting Buddhist teachings and building major temples: Shitennoji in Osaka and Horyuji in Nara. He became a symbol of the formative period of the Japanese imperial state and of Buddhism.

The events and accomplishments of his life were codified in biographies. Modeled after the life of the Historical Buddha, the texts include episodes that extol Shotoku as an exemplar of filial piety. Devotion to one's parents was a primary virtue of the Confucian ideals at the Japanese state's foundation.

Painted some six centuries after his death, during a revival of a cult that venerated Shotoku, this portrait illustrates an episode in which, at age sixteen, the prince prays for his father's recovery from illness. Shotoku wears a priest's vestments and carries an incense burner. His attendants carry a sutra scroll and a canopy.

The sources for this portrait reflect Shotoku's dual religious and secular roles. Its composition and style preserve elements of his earliest portrait, painted in the seventh century. Shotoku's vestments, on the other hand, underscore his role as an early advocate for Buddhism. The figures also are reminiscent of Buddhist sculptures in which a deity stands between two smaller attendants. The painting evokes a strong emotional and spiritual resonance as the younger figures turn toward the prince. He seems to contemplate the gravity of his duty to his father and of his future role in the complex political and religious contests of his time.

AY

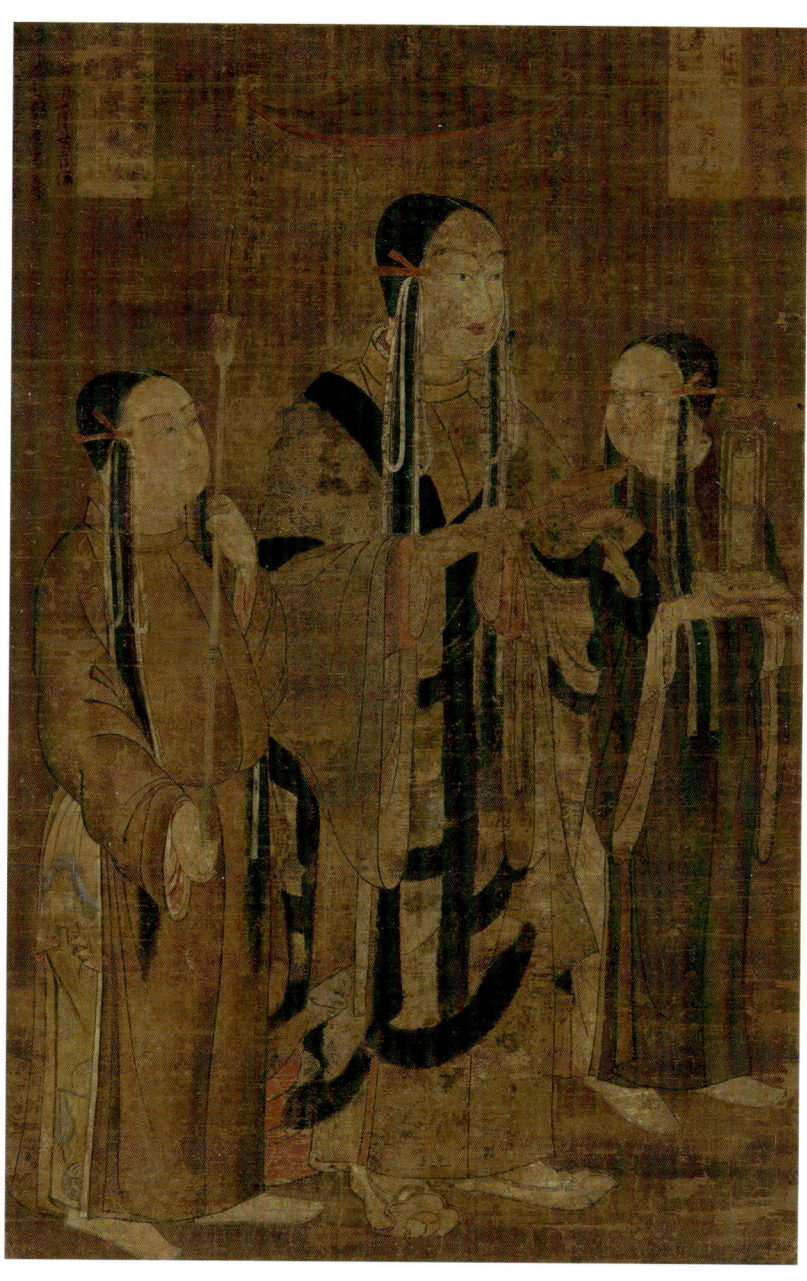

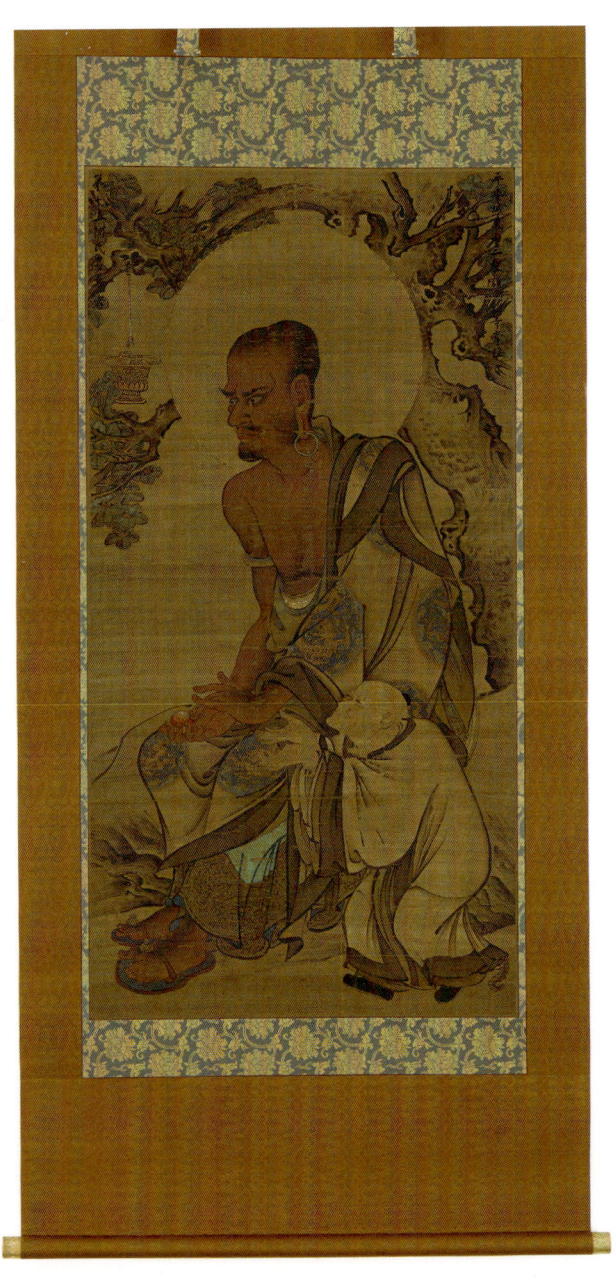

Arhat (Ashita Soja-Ajita)
Ryozen, ca. 1328–ca. 1360
Japan, Nanbokucho period, mid-14th century
Ink and color on silk
208.3 × 79.1 cm
Gift of Charles Lang Freer, Freer Gallery of Art, F1904.309

Images of arhats (in Japanese, *rakan*)—homely, sometimes grotesque monk-like figures—date to as early as the eighth century in Japan. As recounted in the *Lotus Sutra*, the Buddha once addressed a vast audience that ranged from royalty to paupers, monks, nuns, animals, and creatures of the spirit world. Five hundred of the assembled listeners achieved instant enlightenment upon hearing the Buddha's words.

This group became the arhats. As their spiritual attainments afford them mystical powers, including extreme longevity, the arhats are charged by the Buddha himself to protect the dharma until the arrival of Maitreya, the Future Buddha. They traverse the universe as miracle-working manifestations of the Buddha's compassion, teaching believers how to live in accordance with Buddhist principles.

Like Kshitigarbha (in Japanese, Jizo), arhats are always depicted as Buddhist monks. But unlike the handsome bodhisattva, they were rendered as bizarrely unattractive. This portrayal underscores the superficiality and fleeting nature of perceived beauty.

This painting comes from a set of seventeen. Charles Lang Freer acquired it, along with other selections from the set, from the estate of the prominent Japanese painter Shibata Zeshin (1807–1891). Zeshin in turn had purchased them from Tofukuji, a Zen temple in Kyoto, where the paintings likely were created.

JU

Portrait of Tendai Daishi
Japan, Nanbokucho period (1333–92)
Hanging scroll mounted on panel
87.7 × 55.8 cm
Purchase—Charles Lang Freer Endowment, Freer Gallery of Art,
F1976.16a–c

The Chinese Buddhist priest and theologian Zhiyi (538–597) established China's Tiantai school of Buddhism. His focus and scholarly commentaries on the *Lotus Sutra* formed the basis of Tiantai teachings.

Some of the earliest portraits of Zhiyi were painted at China's Mount Tiantai. The Japanese Buddhist monk Saicho (767–822) traveled to the mountain. Upon his return to Japan, he founded the Tendai school. Saicho established Tendai's head temple, Enryakuji, at Mount Hiei, located near Kyoto, home of the emperor and his court. Enryakuji and the Tendai school gained power and wealth as its priests were called upon to perform rituals to protect the emperor and the country.

Saicho also brought sketched portraits of the Chinese Tiantai patriarchs back to Japan, where they served as models for paintings that commemorated the historical lineage of Tendai Buddhism. This Japanese portrait depicts Zhiyi—known in Japanese as Tendai Daishi, meaning "great master of Tendai"—in a meditation pose. The priest is seated on a low, Chinese-style wooden chair. A meditation weight, which aids in maintaining a perfectly erect posture and is a distinguishing feature of Tendai Daishi portraits, sits atop the cowl that covers his head and shoulders. The wood grain of the chair is realistically delineated, and the facial features, brushed in fine ink lines, resemble a Japanese technique developed in the thirteenth century for portraits of important subjects.

The symmetrical, static pose and unmodulated outlines of this portrait suggest that it may have been based on a sculpture. A eulogy might once have been inscribed above the figure.

AY

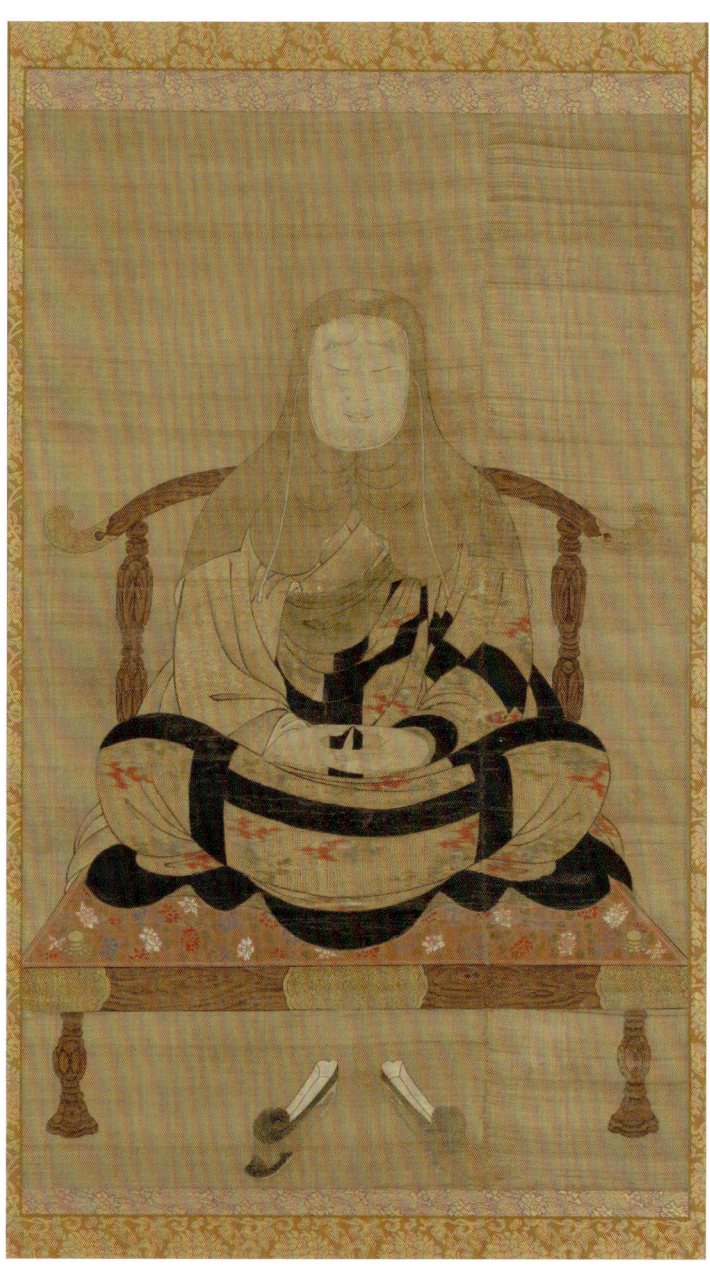

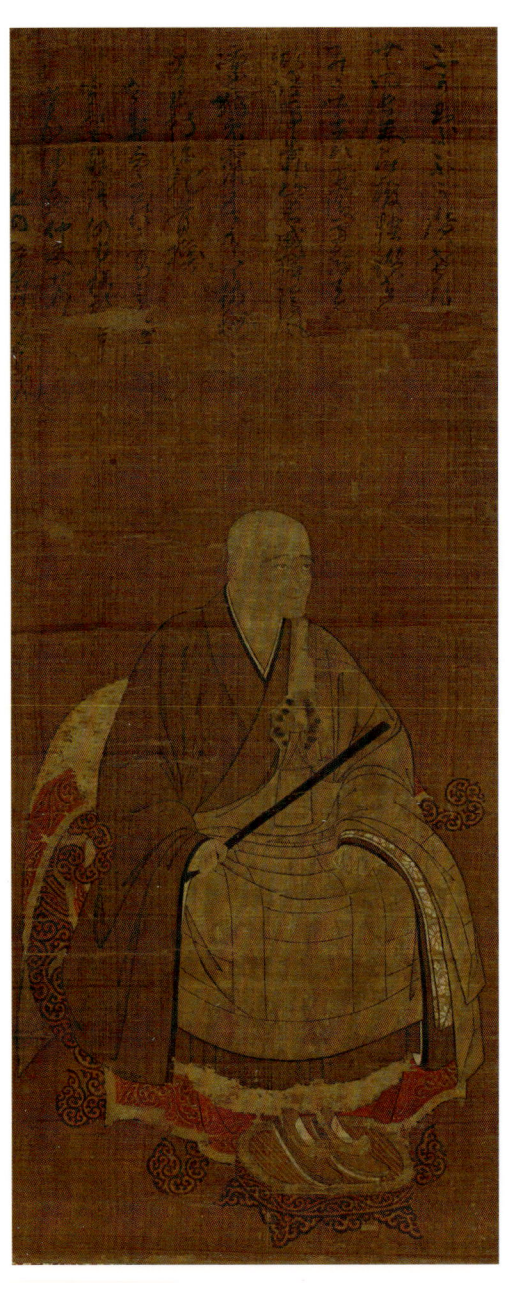

Portrait of Getsuan Shuko
Japan, Nanbokucho period, 1382
Hanging scroll; ink and color on silk
180.6 × 52.4 cm
Purchase—Charles Lang Freer Endowment and funds provided by Peggy and Richard Danziger, Freer Gallery of Art, F1983.4

In this formal portrait, the Zen priest Getsuan Shuko sits with his legs crossed beneath his robes, holding a rod in his right hand and clenching his left hand. These gestures underscore Getsuan's strong character and spiritual authority.

The priest sits on a Chinese carved lacquer chair, with his shoes placed on a matching footstool. Portraits known as *chinso*, in which the subject sits formally in a chair, are distinctive to Zen Buddhism, following Chinese models and customs. In Japanese portraits of priests in other Buddhist schools—as well as of nobles, shoguns, and even emperors—the subject is seated on a mat (tatami). Only the highest-ranking individuals were given a slight elevation or low platform (see p. 178).

Scholars once thought that *chinso* were created as certificates of enlightenment, conferring a place in the lineage of dharma transmission from master to disciple. Recent studies, however, have suggested that *chinso* were painted for memorial rites and for a Zen master's followers, serving as reminders of their teacher. When a disciple departed to serve in another temple, he often received a *chinso* of his master as a gift to carry with him.

In most *chinso*, facial features are highly detailed and naturalistic, while the subject's heavy vestments appear more formulaic. It is possible that the faces were based on life sketches and the robes and setting were based on generic models. Artists followed a similar process for other types of Japanese portraits.

AY

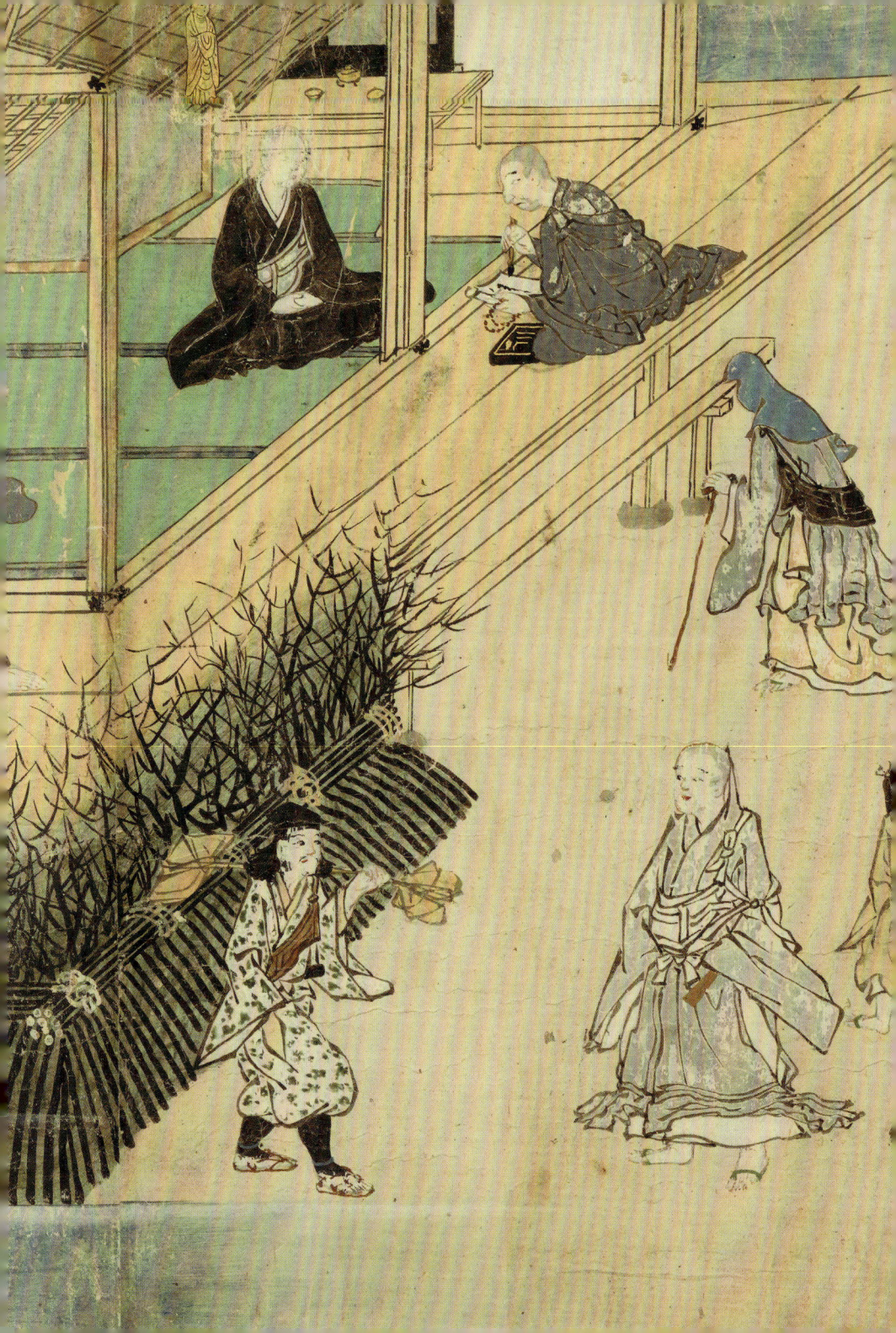

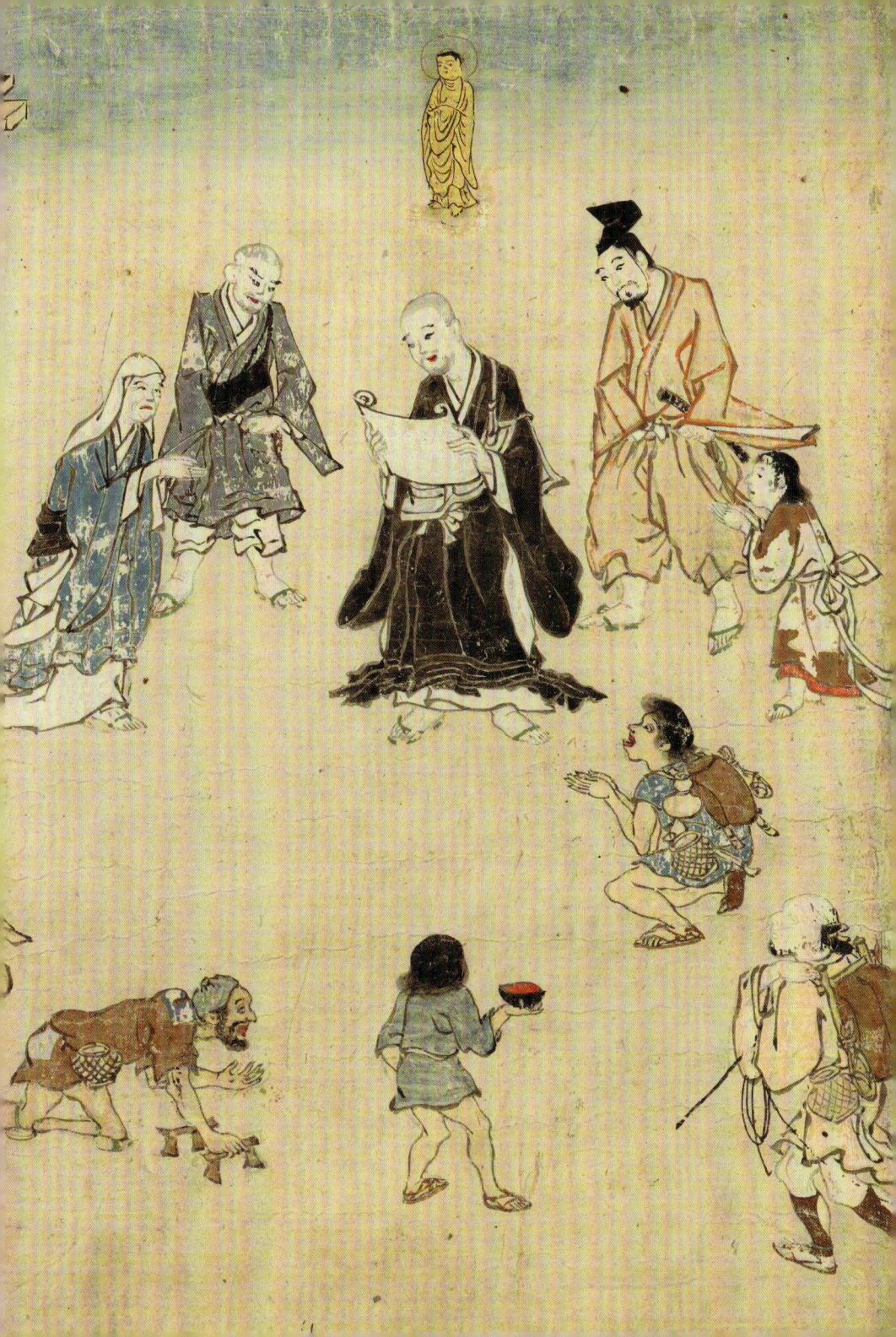

Yuzu nembutsu engi (account of the origins of the Yuzu Nembutsu Buddhist sect)
Japan, Kamakura period, 1329
Handscroll; ink and color on paper
29.2 × 1155 cm
Purchase, Freer Gallery of Art, F1958.11

The Japanese monk Ryonin (1073–1132) formed a theory around the concept of *yuzu*, or the interrelatedness of all things, from which he developed a novel program of practice. This system was premised on the notion that an individual's meritorious actions or prayers benefited everyone. Ryonin thus proposed that all beings are engulfed in a world of interconnected merit, and he traveled the countryside proselytizing his beliefs.

This handscroll is one of several illustrated biographies of Ryonin and his so-called Yuzu Nembutsu sect. As is typical of such accounts, this example comprises two handscrolls: the first detailing Ryonin's life and the second recounting miraculous events visited upon Yuzu believers after his death. The scroll recounts that through the power of Amitabha (in Japanese, Amida), both people and deities would join the faith. Even those who had fallen into hell could be saved by belief in the Buddha.

Nembutsu is a repetitive invocation of Buddha Amitabha's name. Yuzu Nembutsu practitioners endorse the ritual repetition of the invocation "All honor and praise to the Amida Buddha." Another distinction of Ryonin's sect was his insistence on registering all adherents in membership books. Some of the most charming and evocative episodes in this handscroll depict the monk enrolling devotees from every social class and even demonic figures from the netherworld.

JU

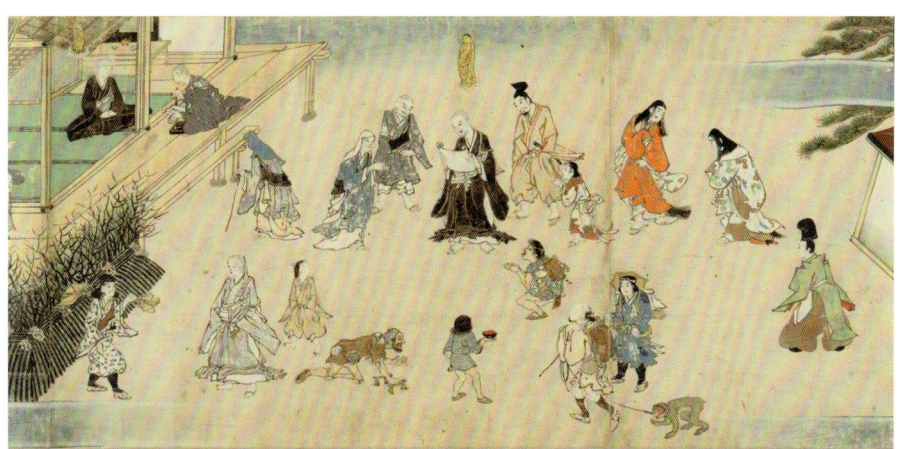

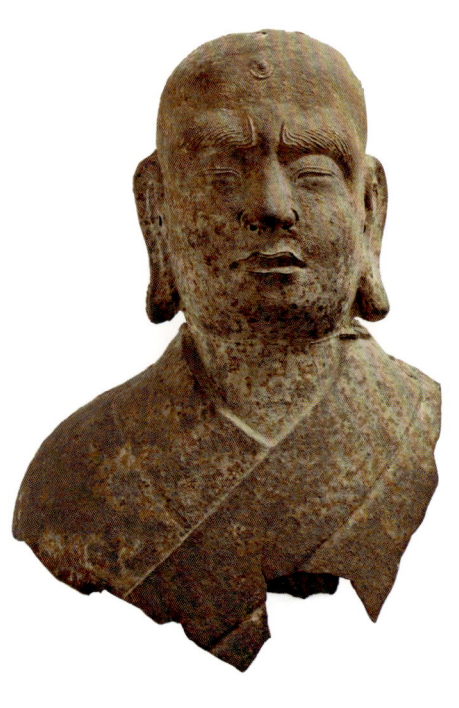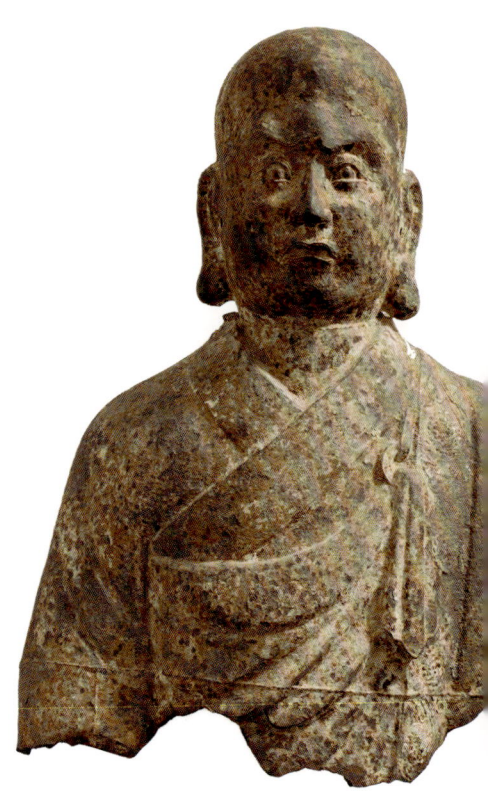

Busts of two arhats (luohan)
China, Ming dynasty, probably second half 15th century–16th century
Iron, traces of gesso and earth encrustation
42.7 × 32.4 × 21.8 cm; 54.8 × 44.7 × 23.4 cm
Gift of Charles Lang Freer, Freer Gallery of Art, F1913.77 and .79

Arhats (*luohan*) represent the original followers of the Historical Buddha. Portrayed wearing monk's robes, arhats in Chinese art were usually depicted in groups of sixteen or eighteen. Exaggerated features represented both their Indian origins and their enlightened state of mind.

Museum founder Charles Lang Freer acquired these two torsos together, but it is impossible to know whether they originally belonged to the same group. Regardless, the pairing allows us to see how effectively Chinese sculptors could communicate emotions. One figure is withdrawn in contemplation, while the other, with his adamantine stare, expresses his fierce guardianship of the Buddhist faith. Such sculptures were placed in temples near a statue of the Buddha to serve as protectors of the faith.

While cast iron sculptures have been made in China since at least the eighth century, the medium became highly popular for Buddhist statuary during the Ming dynasty (1368–1644). Invariably, these iron statues were vividly colored and highly finished, but their surface decoration is prone to damage. Each was cast in multiple parts, as indicated here by the thick lines seen at the necks now that their covering of clay, lacquer, and pigment has worn away.

JS

Encounter of Yunmen Wenyan and Fayan Wenyi
Kenko Shokei (act. ca. 1480–1506/18)
Japan, Kamakura or Kyoto, Muromachi period, late 15th century
Hanging scroll; ink, color, and gold on paper
49.1 × 39.4 cm
Gift of Charles Lang Freer, Freer Gallery of Art, F1905.266a–b

Zen (in Chinese, Chan) Buddhism seeks to free the mind from illusion and other impediments to enlightenment. The practice centers on direct, mind-to-mind interactions with masters. In the presence of a master's enlightened mind, and with his guidance, the disciple experiences his own transcendence.

Encounters between masters and disciples became an important subject of Zen painting. For this "encounter painting," the Japanese priest and artist Kenko Shokei followed a model by the Chinese artist Ma Yuan (circa 1160/65–1225) in the collection of Tenryuji, a major Zen monastery in Kyoto. Both works depict the priest Fayan Wenyi (885–958) meeting the master Yunmen Wenyan (862/4–949) in a natural setting dominated by an overhanging pine tree. These two men each headed a prominent branch of Chan Buddhism.

Ma Yuan's original painting likely entered Japan between the thirteenth and fifteenth centuries, during a period of commercial and religious exchange. Large Japanese Zen monasteries became centers not only of Buddhist practice but also of Chinese literary and historical studies and distinguished collections of Chinese art. Zen monks and their warrior patrons favored the Chinese style, of which Shokei was an accomplished painter. He spent two years in Kyoto, during which he had privileged access to the shogun's collection of Chinese paintings. His interpretation of Ma Yuan's encounter painting attests to Shokei's broad knowledge of Zen subjects and to the importance that Zen Buddhists accorded the Chinese masters of the past.

AY

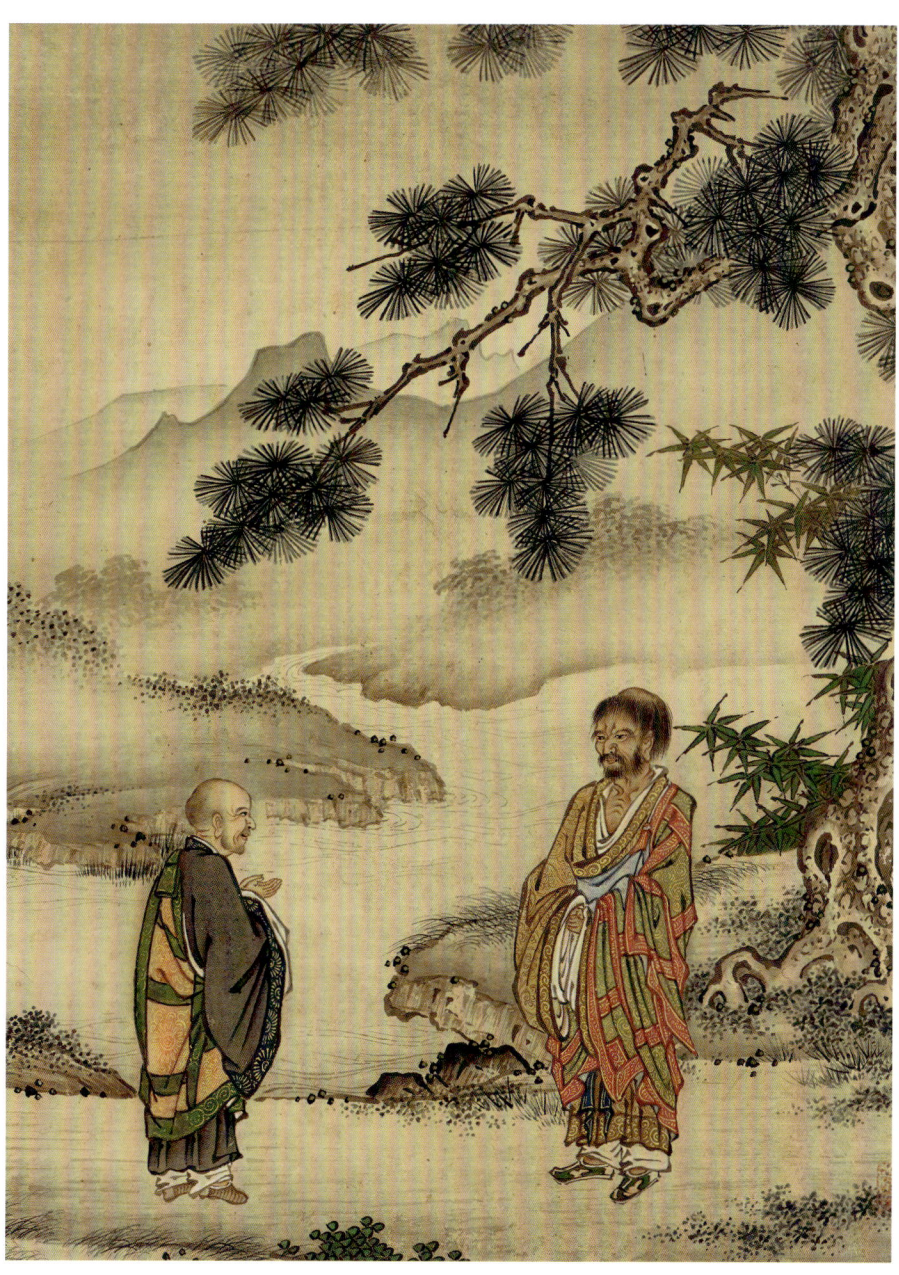

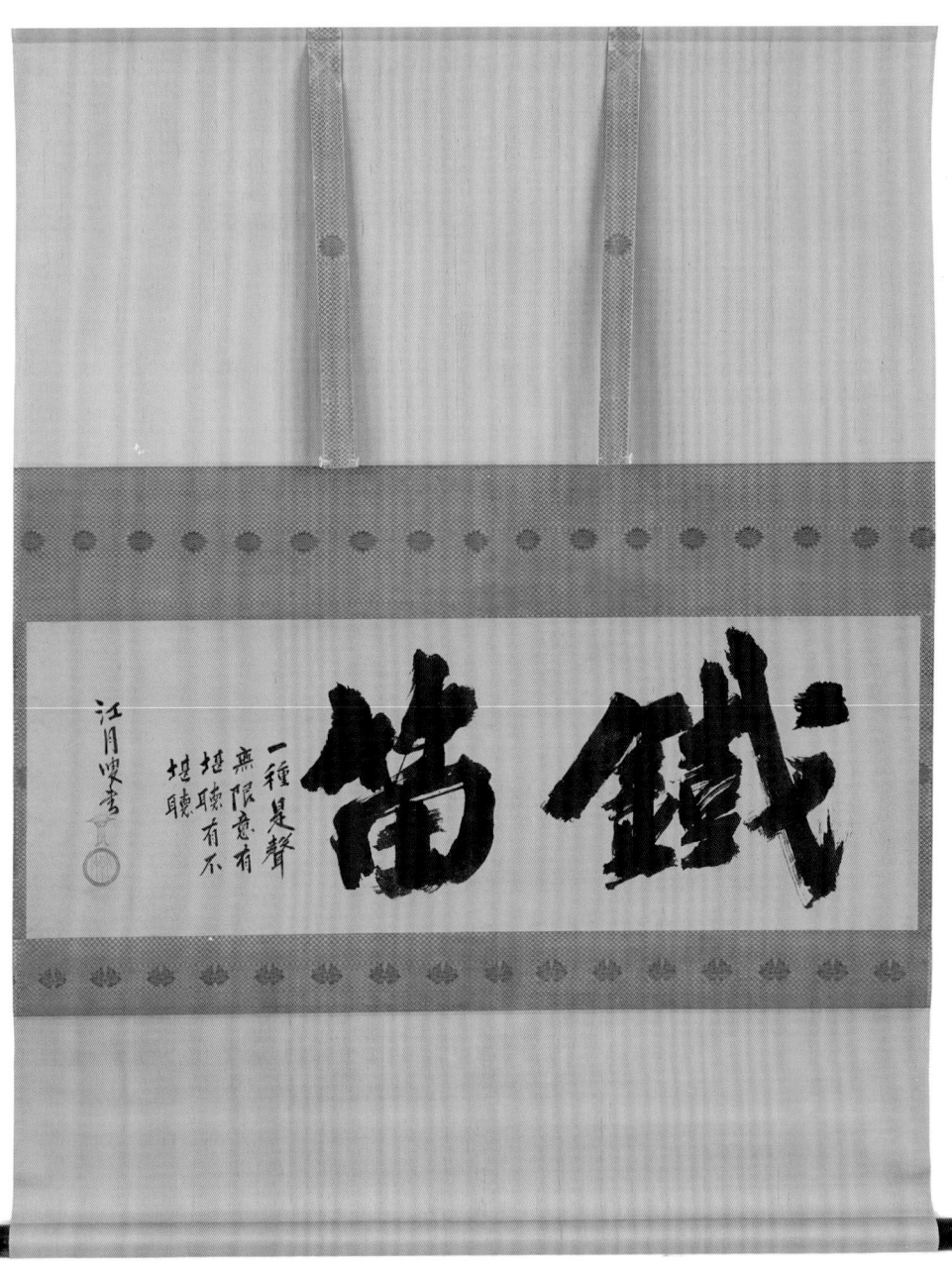

Iron Flute
Kogetsu Sogan (1574–1643)
Japan, Edo period, early 17th century
Hanging scroll; ink on paper
30.6 × 90.6 cm
Purchase—Charles Lang Freer Endowment, Freer Gallery of Art,
F1981.12

Bokuseki, or "ink traces," is the Japanese term for calligraphy written by a Zen Buddhist monk. Such writings are direct expressions of strong character and enlightenment: when a *bokuseki* scroll is displayed, it evokes the writer's spirit. These scrolls were handed down within temples, given as gifts from master to disciple, or exchanged as tangible embodiments of dharma transmission and community.

Early Japanese Zen Buddhist monasteries were centers of learning that fostered Chinese studies and cultural practices. They were instrumental in introducing new forms of Chinese calligraphy for display and contemplation. Calligraphy by earlier masters served as models for later calligraphers, and the appreciation of *bokuseki* eventually spread beyond monasteries to culturally sophisticated laypeople, such as tea masters.

This scroll was written for display in an alcove of a tearoom. Two bold characters reading "Tetteki" (iron flute) dominate the inscription. This phrase may allude to a Chinese story of a magical iron flute that was given to Sun Shouyung, a blind fortuneteller who lived in the thirteenth century. Following to the left in smaller characters is an enigmatic Chinese couplet: "A sound that has infinite resonance is audible yet inaudible."

The calligrapher, Kogetsu Sogan, was the son of tea master Tsuda Sogyu. He entered Daitokuji, a prominent Zen monastery in Kyoto, as a child. In 1610, he became the temple's 156th abbot. A distinguished calligrapher in the tradition of Daitokuji abbots, he played a prominent role in the political and cultural life of the early Edo period (1579–1647).

AY

Padmasambhava
Central Tibet, ca. 1700–1750
Gilt copper alloy, pearl, and turquoise; traces of pigments
51.5 × 35 × 25.2 cm
The Alice S. Kandell Collection, Arthur M. Sackler Gallery,
S2014.18a–b

Padmasambhava is one of the most widely worshipped and universally beloved figures in the Tibetan Buddhist tradition. A great Indian master of tantric Buddhism, Padmasambhava possessed remarkable spiritual attainments and magical powers. Most significantly, he used these rare and potent skills to subjugate local deities across Tibet and the Himalayas, converting them from enemies to protectors of Buddhism.

In this lively sculpture, Padmasambhava's power is vividly conveyed in his forceful countenance. His lifted eyebrows meet at a furrow above his wide-open eyes, forming a penetrating gaze. His hand gestures—one meditative and one threatening—complement his facial expression, creating the overall impression of a fearsome figure whose power derives from spiritual mastery. As signified by his third eye, marked here by an inlaid pearl, Padmasambhava is believed to have achieved full buddhahood.

Along with clearing obstacles to the spread of Buddhism, Padmasambhava is venerated for contributing to the development of tantric Buddhism in Tibet. There, he is known as Guru Rinpoche, or "precious teacher." During the eighth century, Padmasambhava exercised his enlightened wisdom by transmitting to Tibetan disciples new teachings centered on tantric practices. Here, the delicately cast, skull-topped staff (*khatvanga*) he holds in the crook of his left elbow features the macabre symbolism ubiquitous in tantric ritual and art. Tantric Buddhist practices employ such mortuary imagery in meditative visualizations and artistic representations to encourage practitioners to confront their fear of death.

RB

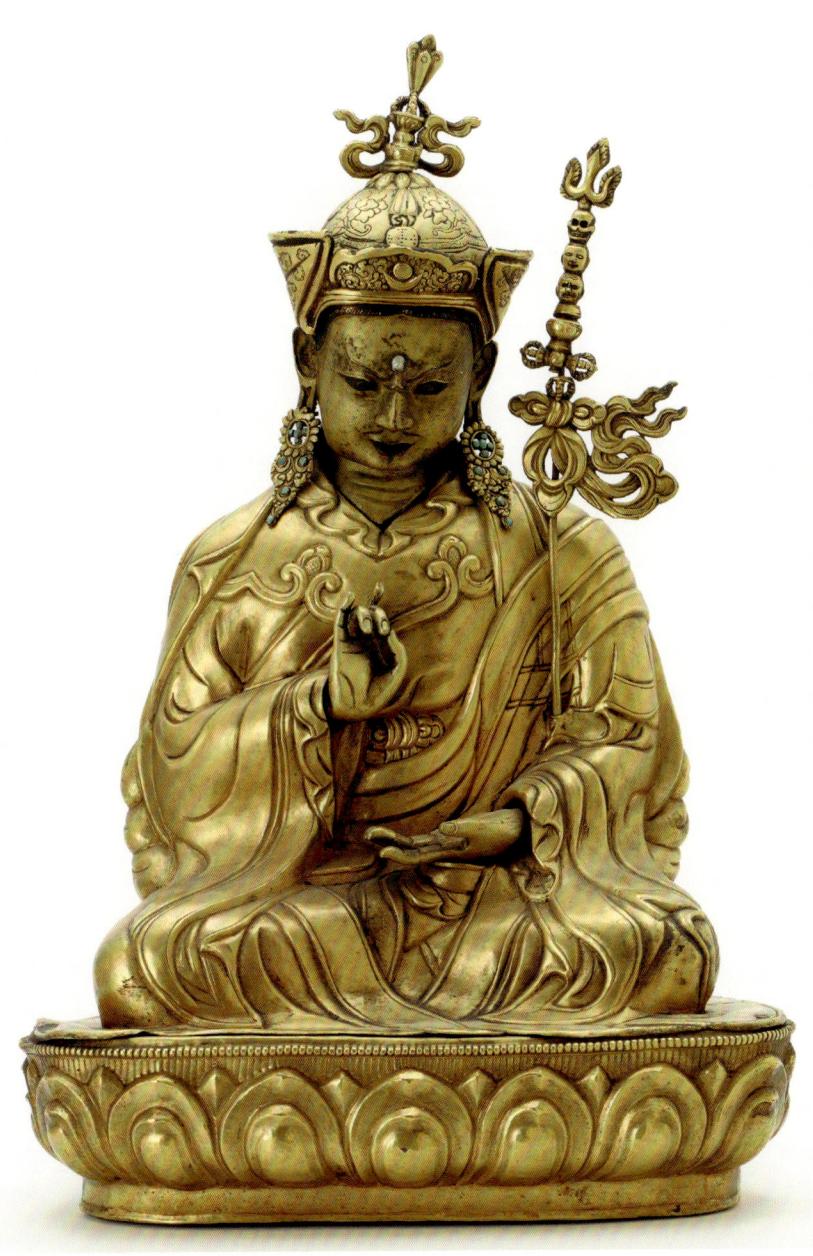

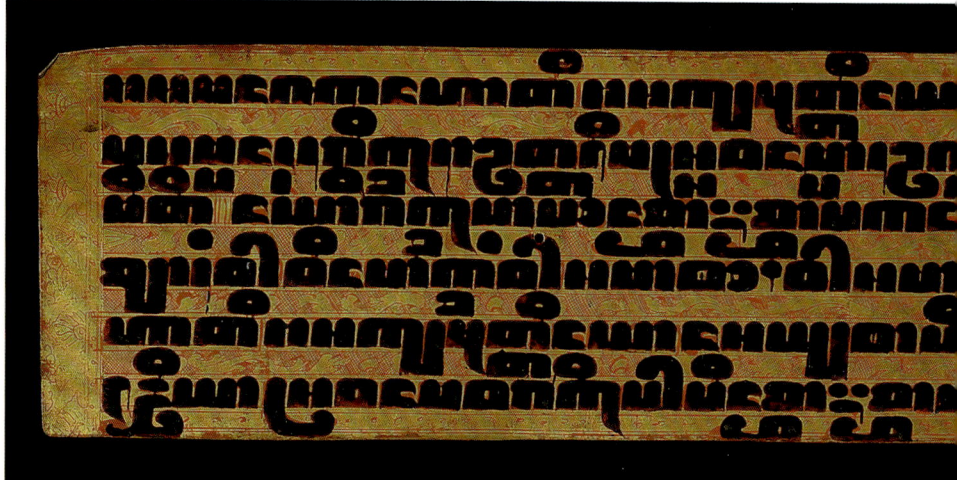

**Kammavacha manuscript
(excerpts from the monastic code of discipline)**
Anonymous scribe
Myanmar, ca. 1800
18 copper leaves with decorated wood covers; gold, wood, and enamel on copper
10.6 × 54.4 cm
Purchase—Smithsonian Unrestricted Trust Funds, Smithsonian Collections Acquisition Program, and Dr. Arthur M. Sackler, Arthur M. Sackler Gallery, S1986.487.1–.20

The monastic order plays an important role in Myanmar's Theravada Buddhism. It is customary for boys aged seven and older to become ordained as novices. Following ordination, they are required to stay in a monastery for a period of time (usually around three months) and become immersed in the Buddha's teachings. At the age of twenty, they may choose to be fully ordained as a monks.

As part of the ceremony that marks a boy's ordination, his parents often donate a *kammavacha* manuscript, which contains

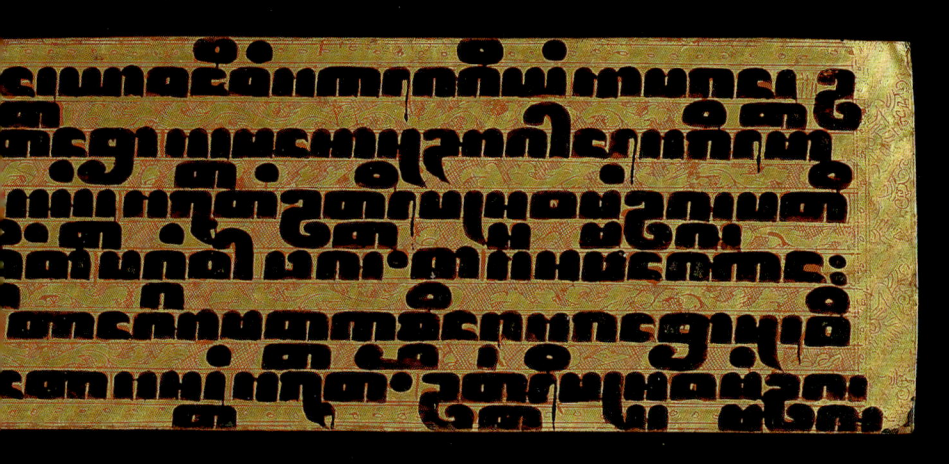

excerpts from the monastic code of discipline. These manuscripts are written in dark, square letters resembling tamarind seeds; accordingly, the style is called the tamarind seed script. The pages are richly decorated sheets of palm leaf, ivory, or even metal. Commissioning and donating such a manuscript earns the lay donors considerable merit, which gives them access to a higher rebirth in a future life.

This manuscript consists of eighteen lacquered copper plates and two decorated wooden covers. Between the lines and in the margins of the plates, the text is embellished with floral and geometric decorative patterns, drawn in red on a gold background. The finely decorated copper leaves were bound together between the covers with a ribbon.

JE

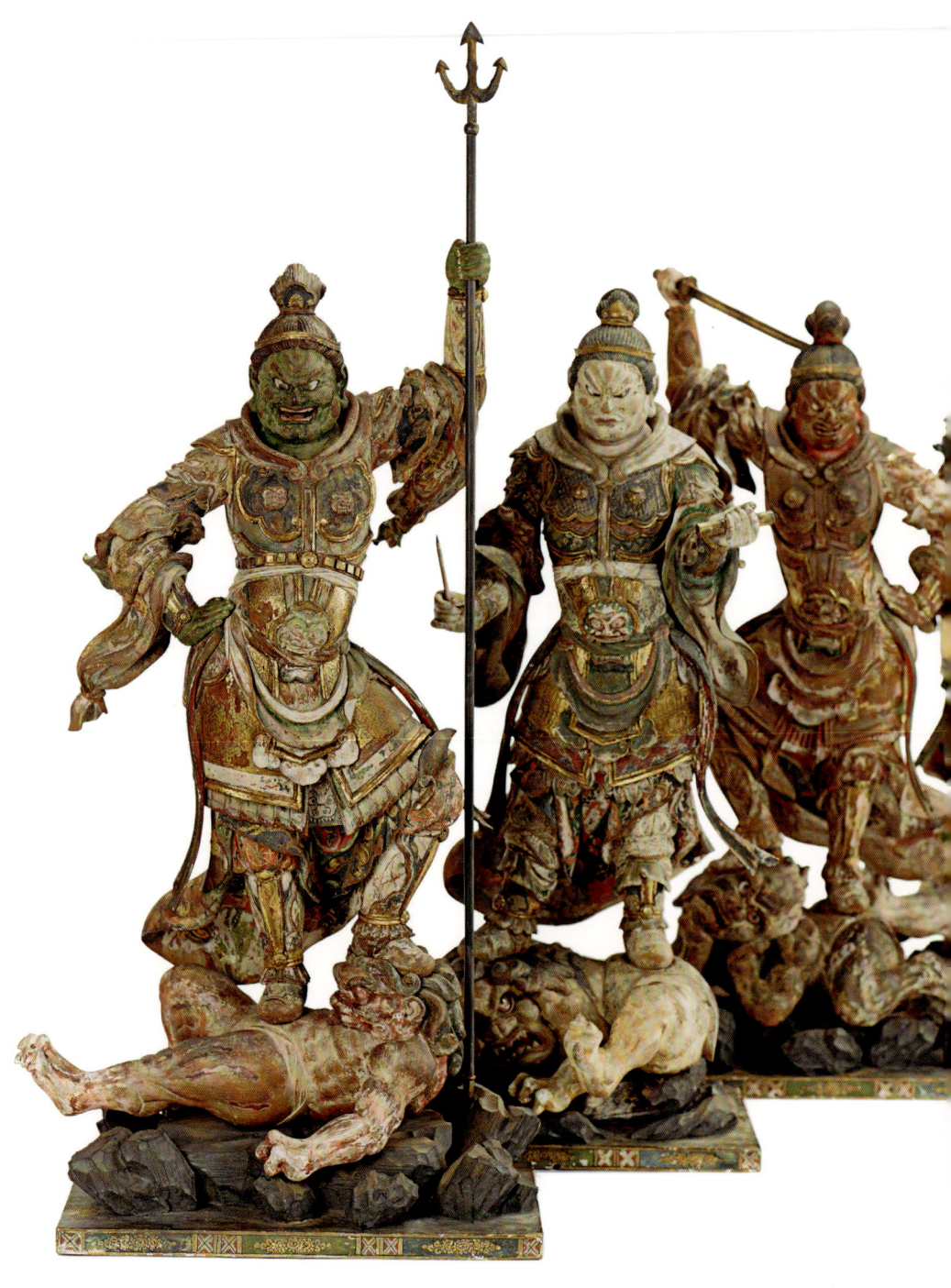

Attendants and Protectors

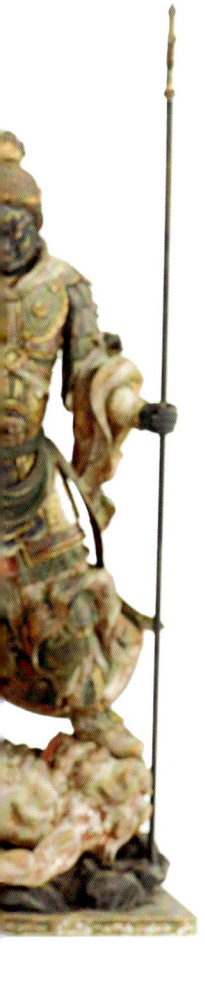

Buddhism, like many religions, spread through conversion— but not all of the converts were human. The Buddhists also brought in regional divinities, many of which were associated with other religious traditions. These gods are not exempt from karma and eventual rebirth, so even they can benefit from the dharma. Such figures often became protectors and guardians, depicted flanking monastery entrances or images of buddhas. Devotees often appeal to these deities for help with the worldly concerns of everyday life.

While many of these guardians remained culturally specific, others traveled beyond their places of origin. Among the figures co-opted by Indian Buddhists is a group of directional deities known as world-protectors (*lokapala*). They appear as fierce military figures, brandishing weapons and crushing demons. While these guardians were not popular in South Asian art, they were redefined in East Asia, where they took on greater significance and visibility.

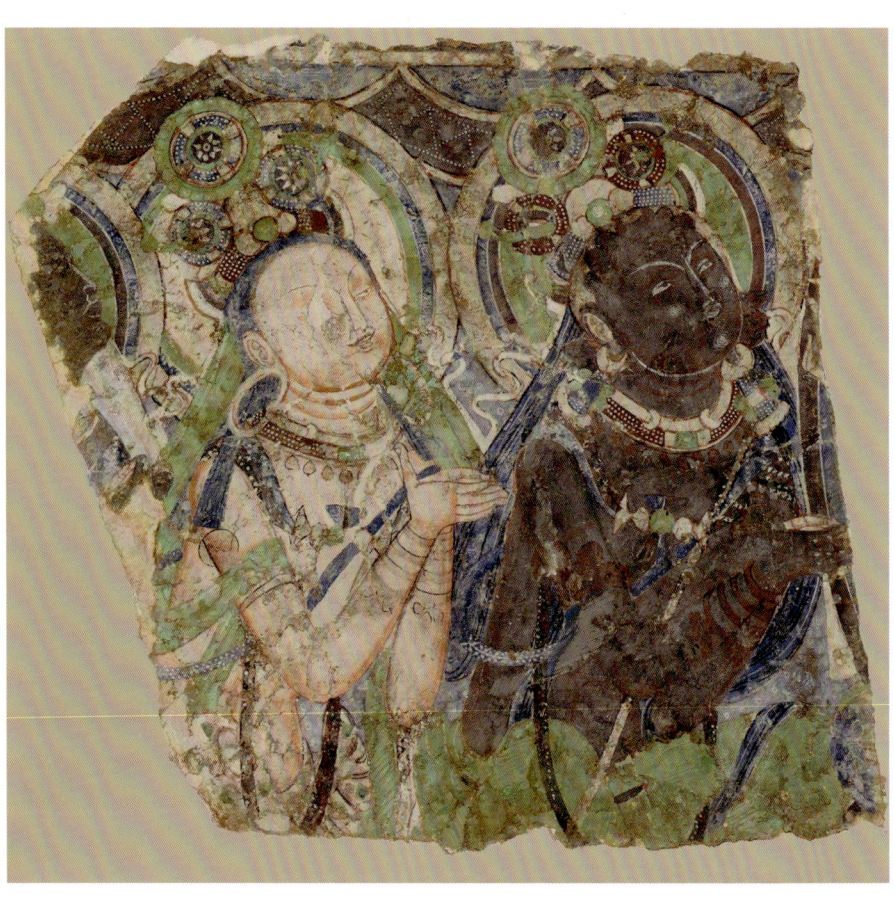

Two celestial beings
China, Xinjiang Province, Kucha, Kizil, probably Cave 224
6th century
Gypsum plaster with pigment, 71.1 × 76 cm
Smithsonian American Art Museum, Gift of John Gellatly; now on loan to the Arthur M. Sackler Gallery, 1929.8.325.13, LTS1985.1.325.13

Showing two devotional figures, likely celestial beings (devas) descended from their heavens, this detail is from a large mural once inside a cave chapel. It was given to the Smithsonian in 1929 along with fifteen other fragments. Each example belongs to a composition featuring buddhas preaching to gods, celestial beings, monks, and ascetics. This range was intended to convey the doctrine's broad appeal to beings both mortal and divine. In this painting, the celestials are portrayed in rapt attention.

Most of the sixteen fragments have German inscriptions associating them with specific manmade caverns at Kizil (or Qizil), a cave complex associated with the ancient kingdom of Kucha and now in China's Xinjiang Province. Two German expeditions studied the site between 1905 and 1914. In addition to documenting the Buddhist center, which thrived from the fourth through the eighth century along the northern Silk Road, the German teams carefully removed hundreds of wall sections. Most are still housed in Berlin's Museum fur Indische Kunst, but some were sold in the 1920s to help pay for the conservation and installation of the rest. The fragments now kept in the Freer|Sackler must have left Germany at that time.

With more than two hundred Buddhist caves, Kizil represents the earliest major cave-temple complex in China and the largest group in Xinjiang. The patrons of the site were likely local Central Asians. Based on the caves' paintings, however, the patrons were in contact with all surrounding empires. The paintings' subjects celebrate themes belonging to the Sarvastivada school of Buddhism, which focuses on Shakyamuni and does not believe in the multiplicity of bodhisattvas. Although the figures in this fragment resemble bodhisattvas, we can conclude that they are devas instead.

KW

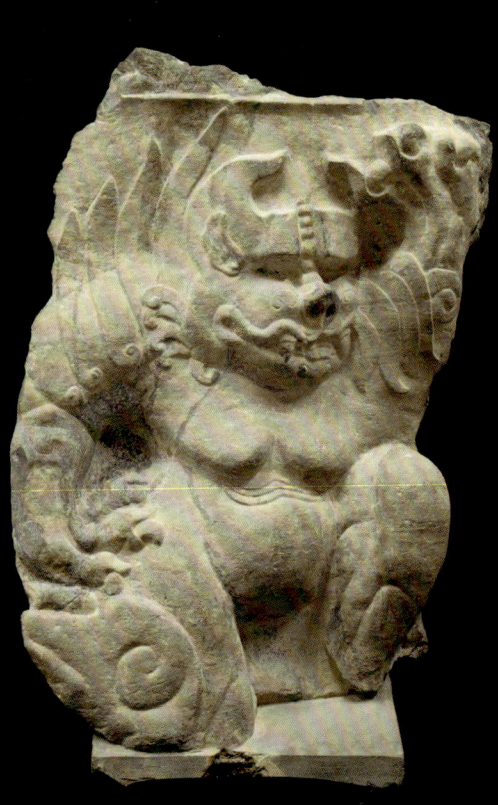 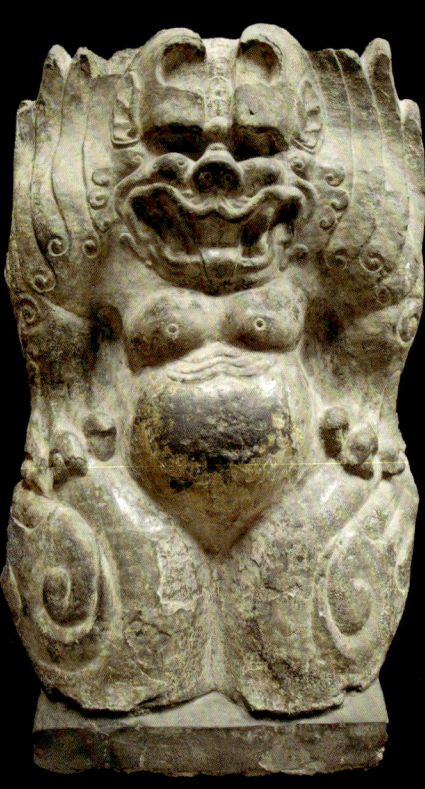

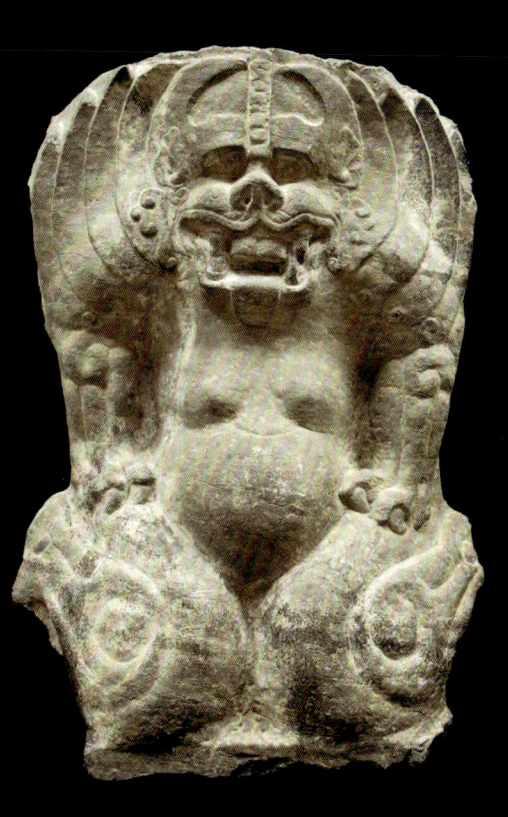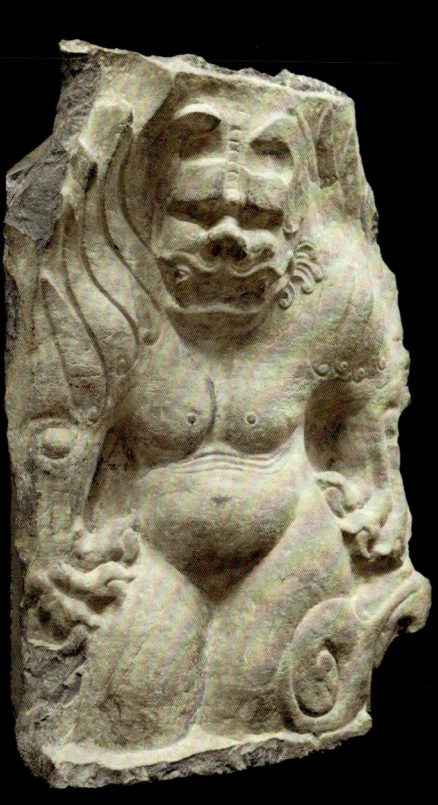

Winged monsters
China, Hebei Province, Handan, northern Xiangtangshan
cave temples, North Cave
Northern Qi dynasty, 550–77
Limestone
80.5 × 55.7 × 30.5 cm; 84.4 × 53.4 × 28 cm;
79 × 57.5 × 31.6 cm; 79 × 53.3 × 30.5 cm
Freer Gallery of Art, Purchase, F1953.86–87, Transfer from the National Museum of Natural History, Smithsonian Institution, F1977.8–9

These grotesque beasts are composite creatures, with humanoid bodies augmented by horns, claws, wings, and a snarling mouth. Although similar beings appear in sixth-century Chinese tomb murals, we know that these examples were intended for a specifically Buddhist context. A few identical monsters remain in the North Cave at Xiangtangshan, a Buddhist cave temple site created in the Northern Qi dynasty. The first Northern Qi ruler, Emperor Wenxuan (reigned 550–59), likely sponsored the cave: it is the earliest and most impressive construction of the complex.

Sixteen deep niches line the North Cave's walls. Originally, they were designed as jeweled pagodas occupied by images of the Buddha and bodhisattvas, which were supported by these kneeling winged monsters. At the time, popular belief held demons and ghosts responsible for all suffering. The subservient placement of the fanged figures showed the power of Buddhist wisdom to tame terrifying creatures and overcome superstitious fears. This also explains why the monsters are compressed, as if supporting a tremendous weight.

Unlike the deities above them, which were created as freestanding images from quarried stone, the monsters were carved from the living rock of the cave walls. Many were damaged or broken when removed from their original setting and have been reassembled.

KW

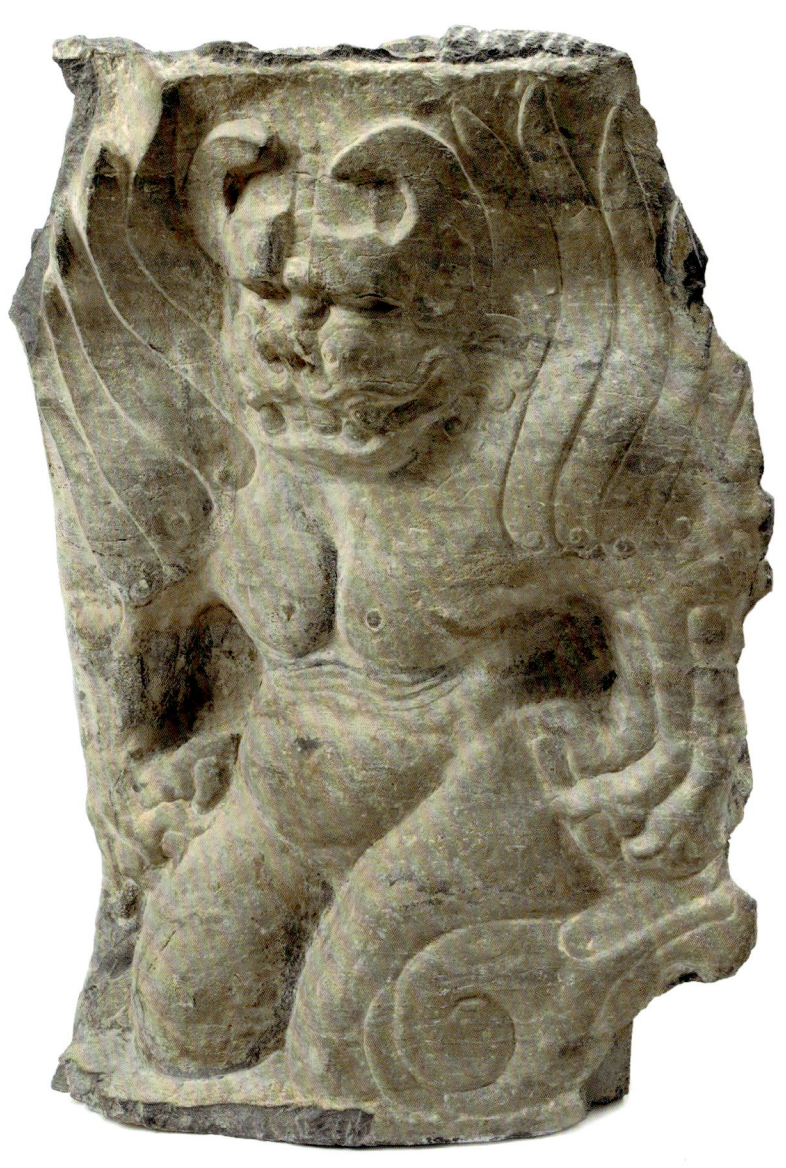

204 ATTENDANTS AND PROTECTORS

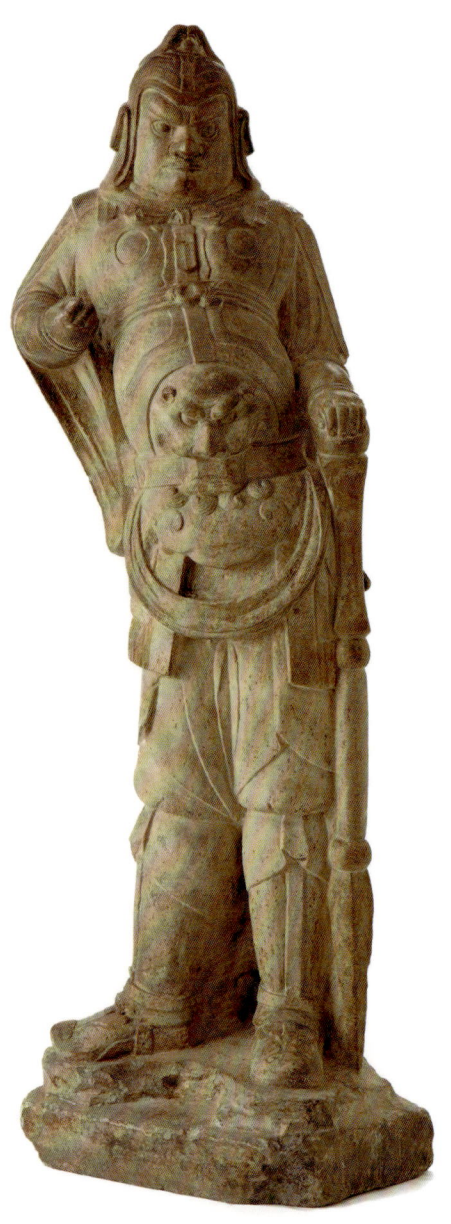

Guardian
China, Tang dynasty, 618–907
Limestone with traces of pigment
103.2 × 39.4 × 29.5 cm
Gift of Charles Lang Freer, Freer Gallery of Art, F1913.60

As protectors of the faith, military figures frequently appear in pairs at the edges of Buddhist figural groups. Shown with non-Chinese features, such soldiers wear full armor, leather boots, and elaborate helmets. This freestanding sculpture also carries a club-like weapon that resembles an elongated *vajra*, or thunderbolt. Thus, he has often been called a *vajrapani,* or thunderbolt bearer. Perhaps to emphasize his strength, this guardian is depicted with a strangely small head and short arms, but his massive torso and sturdy legs are planted firmly on a stony base.

KW

Vasudhara
Nepal, 1082
Gilded copper inlaid with semiprecious stones, traces of vermilion
20.9 × 16.1 × 14.9 cm
Gift of Susanne K. Bennet in memory of Felicja "Lusia" Arendt (1928–1942?), Arthur M. Sackler Gallery, S2012.2

Vasudhara (in Sanskrit, "bearer of gems") is the goddess of wealth, good fortune, and abundance. Seated comfortably and gently smiling, she holds emblems of her wisdom and power, including a cluster of jewels and a book of transcendental teachings.

The graceful bronze dates from the eleventh century, when the cult of Vasudhara first arrived in Nepal from India. Like her Hindu counterpart Lakshmi, the goddess of prosperity, Vasudhara usually wears a royal crown. Here, she is adorned with the crown of a tantric priest, which depicts cosmic buddhas on its panels and is topped with a four-pronged thunderbolt. The headgear's presence tells us that the bronze likely was commissioned for a monastery, where such crowns were worn during certain tantric rituals. Traces of gilt indicate that it was originally covered in gold; the goddess of abundance would have glimmered in the dim light of a monastic chapel.

This bronze is one of only twelve Nepalese sculptures with inscriptions dating prior to 1090. Beginning with the auspicious syllable *om*, the inscription tells us that a husband and wife donated the "venerable Vasudhara" in the winter of 1082. They were likely expressing a wish for children or gratitude for their wealth.

DD

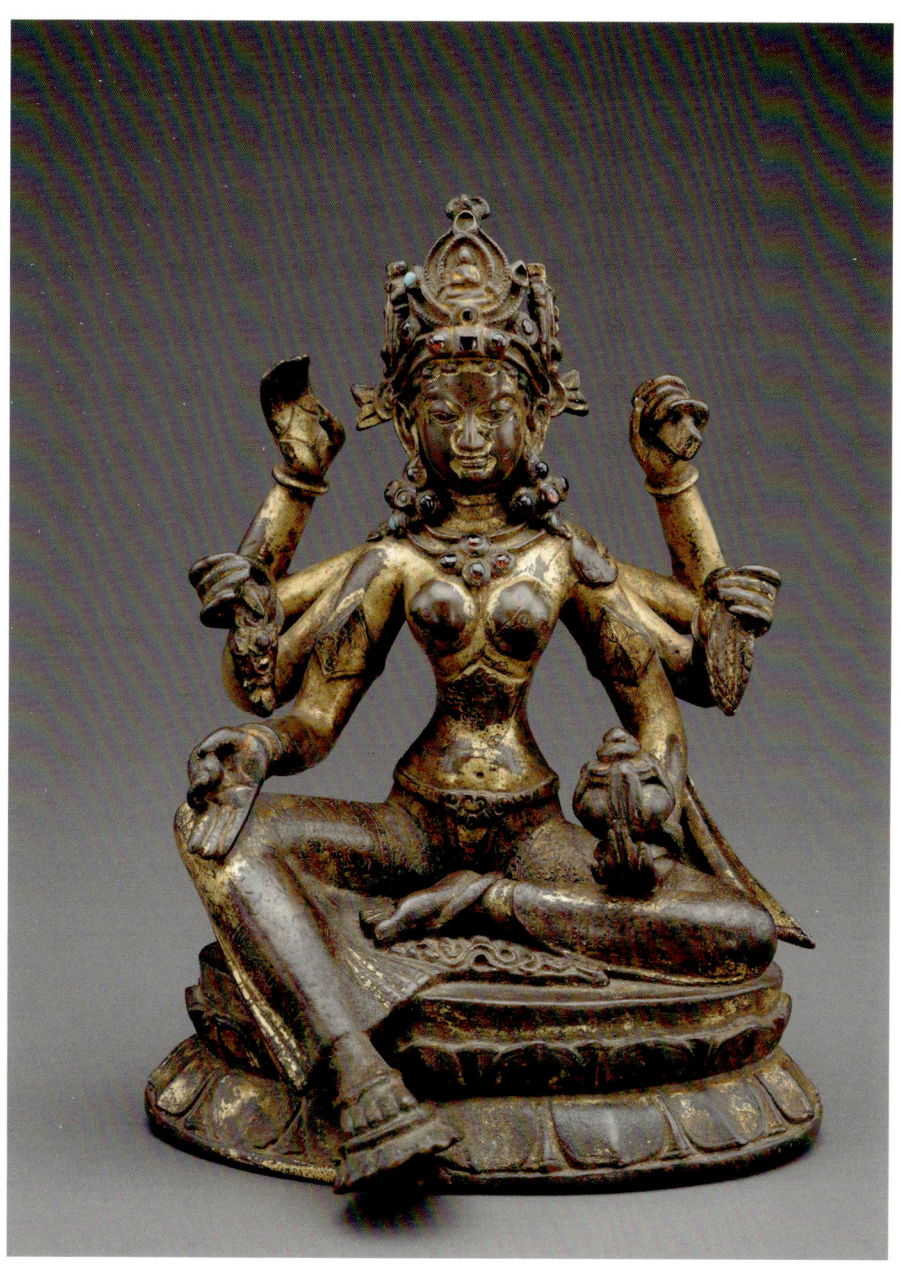

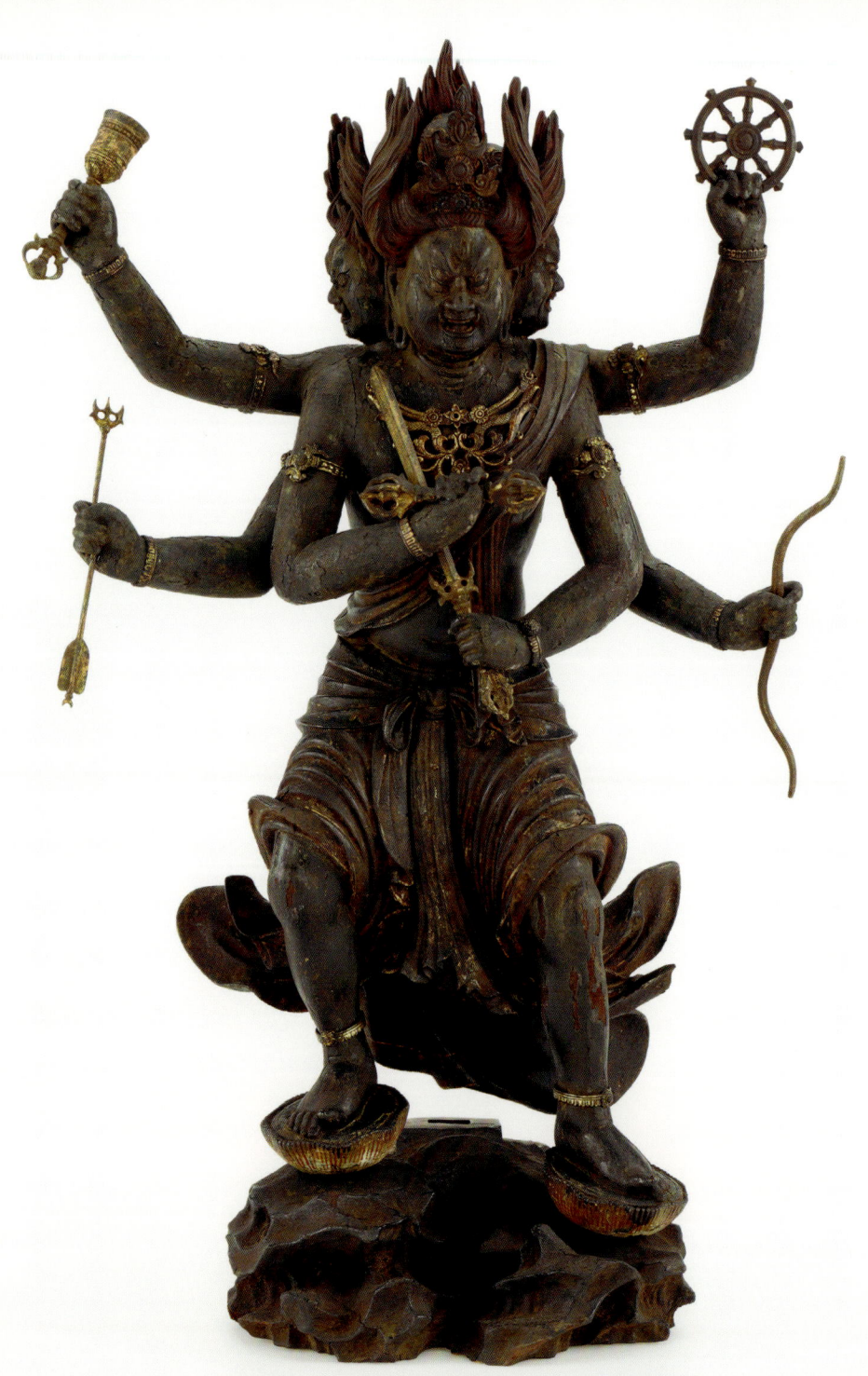

Vajrayaksha (Kongo Yasha)
Japan, Kamakura period, 13th century
Wood with color and gold; gilt bronze
43 × 27.6 × 15.4 cm
Gift of Charles Lang Freer, Freer Gallery of Art, F1909.346

Three fierce-looking faces represent Vajrayaksha (in Japanese, Kongo Yahsa), a guardian deity of esoteric Buddhism. This wooden figure, which still bears traces of gold foil on its robes, also has six arms wielding weapons and Buddhist symbols: *vajra* (thunderbolt), arrow, bell, chakra (wheel), bow, and sword.

Vajrayaksha is one of the Godai Myoo, or five radiant kings. These figures are a product of the complex doctrines and iconography of esoteric Buddhism, whose central effort is to help believers achieve enlightenment through powerful rituals and visualizations. In Japan, popular devotion to these fierce deities rivaled that for the benevolent intercessors of Pure Land Buddhism, such as Kshitigarbha (Jizo) and Amitabha (Amida).

Although ferocious in appearance, the five radiant kings are benevolent. Their task is to protect worshippers from external obstacles by frightening away evil spirits and from internal obstructions by destroying passion and ignorance. Here, the *vajra*-shaped bell handle symbolizes both protection and esoteric Buddhist teachings' capacity to cut through illusion, revealing the ultimate nature of reality.

JU

Zocho-ten, Guardian of the South
80 × 35 × 20.5 cm; F1974.20

Komoku-ten, Guardian of the West
66 × 33 × 19 cm; F1976.12

Tamon-ten, Guardian of the North
76 × 33 × 20.5 cm; F1978.28

Jikoku-ten, Guardian of the East
67.3 × 35 × 20.5 cm; F1977.19

Japan, Kamakura period (1185–1333)
Wood with polychrome, gold, crystal, or glass
Purchase, Freer Gallery of Art

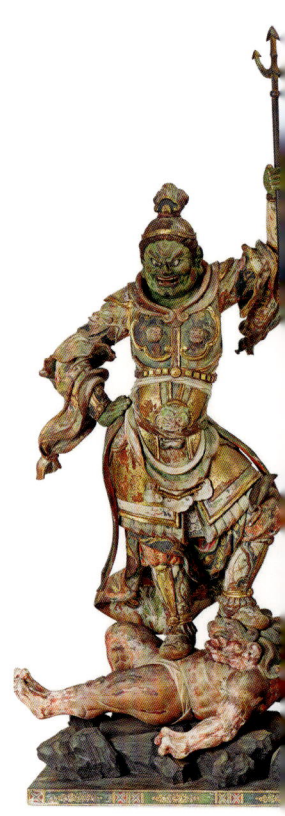

This quartet represents a Japanese interpretation of deities known as world-protectors (*lokapala*). They would have stood within a temple protecting a central Buddha at the cardinal directions. Komoku-ten holds a writing brush and sutra scroll. Tamon-ten carries a stupa in one hand and a spear in the other. Jikoku-ten and Zocho-ten raise their right and left arms, respectively, to provide a visual frame for the ensemble. Each figure stands on a writhing demon, symbolizing dominance over enemies of Buddhism.

These guardians have been part of the Japanese Buddhist iconographic repertoire since the seventh century. The four figures have been produced in many sizes, from more than double the size of a human to even smaller than the diminutive forms seen here. These lithe, animated figures, each less than three feet tall, are excellent examples of a hyperrealistic style that came to prominence in Japanese Buddhist sculpture during the thirteenth and fourteenth centuries. The exaggerated postures suggest both a sacred choreography and no small amount of humor, particularly in the contrast between the guardians' fierce bombast and the subdued demons' put-upon postures. Inset glass or crystal eyes and the violent billowing of their garments create a vivid sense of movement. The garments also feature colorful and detailed patterns, and extensive gilt is still visible on the guardians' armor.

JU

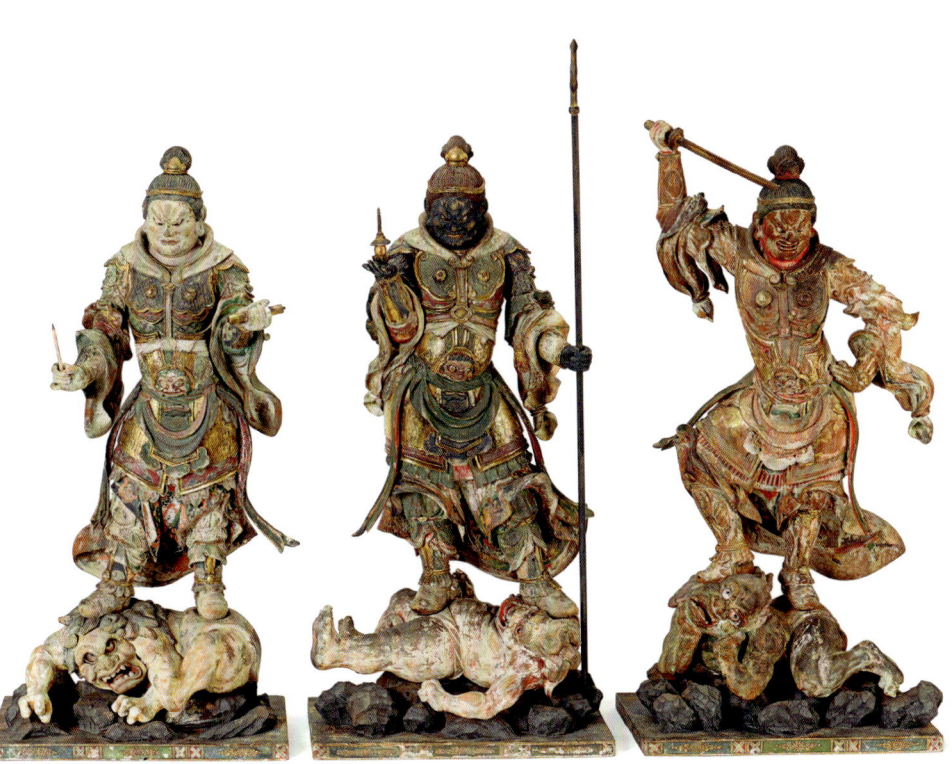

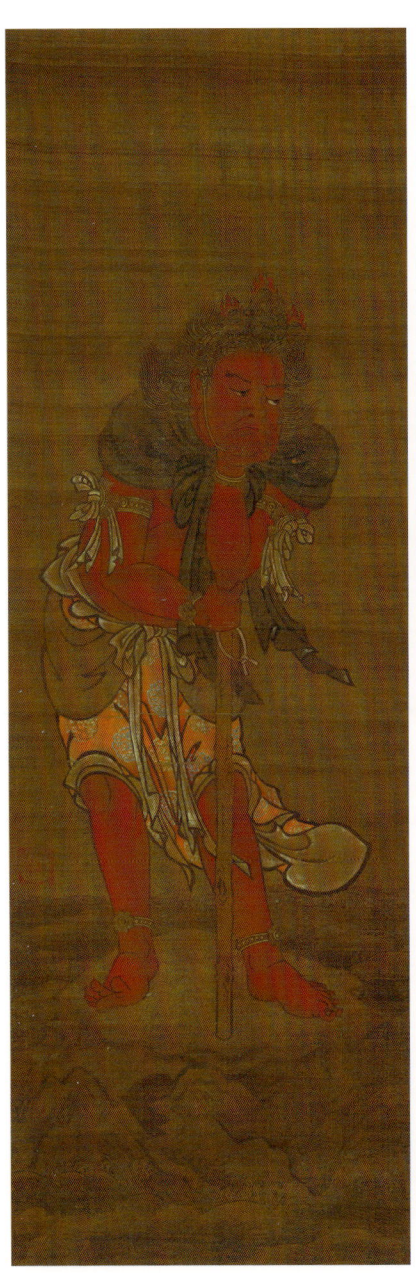
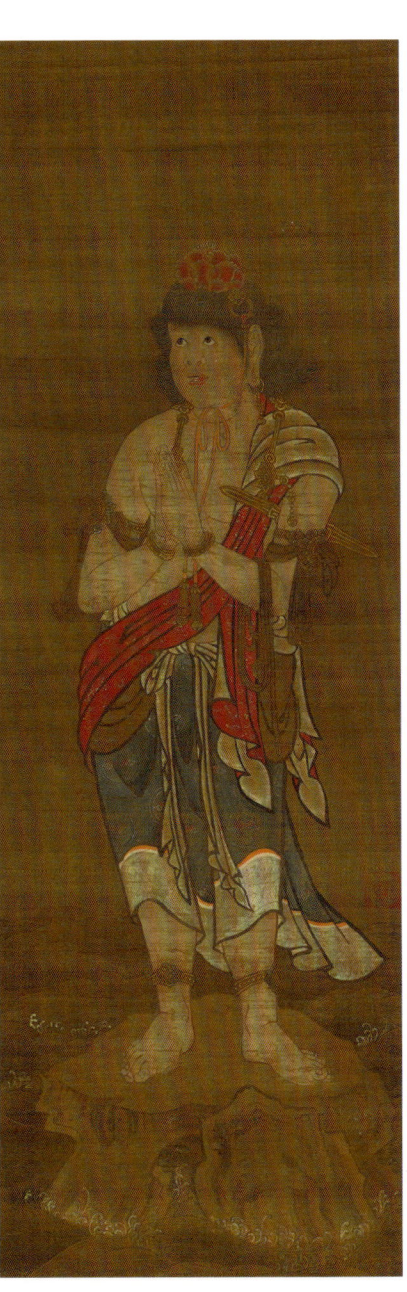

Seitaka-doji and Kongara-doji
Takuma Choga (act. ca. 1253–70)
Japan, Kamakura period, early 14th century
Hanging scrolls; color on silk
125.9 × 42.5 cm; 126.5 × 42.4 cm
Purchase, Freer Gallery of Art, F1970.28, .27

Seitaka-doji and Kongara-doji are attendants of Fudo Myoo, the fierce deity who protects the Buddhist law and guides those seeking enlightenment through the path of esoteric Buddhism. A painting of Fudo Myoo once hung between these two attendant figures, but the location of that central image is unknown. Sketches of a Fudo Myoo icon, also attributed to the artist Takuma Choga, in the great esoteric Buddhist temple of Daigoji may be the only hint of the image that would have completed the trio.

These paintings are unique in two respects. The trio of figures was usually presented in a single painting; this is the first known example in which they were depicted in three distinct paintings. Further, these works represent the first known example of a Japanese artist impressing his own seal on a painting.

A prominent esoteric Buddhist iconographer, Takuma Choga was regarded as one of the most talented artists of his day. He was active at a time when religious painters emerged from anonymity to be acknowledged as the creators of specific works. Here, the combination of a fierce, snarling Fudo Myoo with plump, boyish attendants hints at the painter's sense of humor.

JU

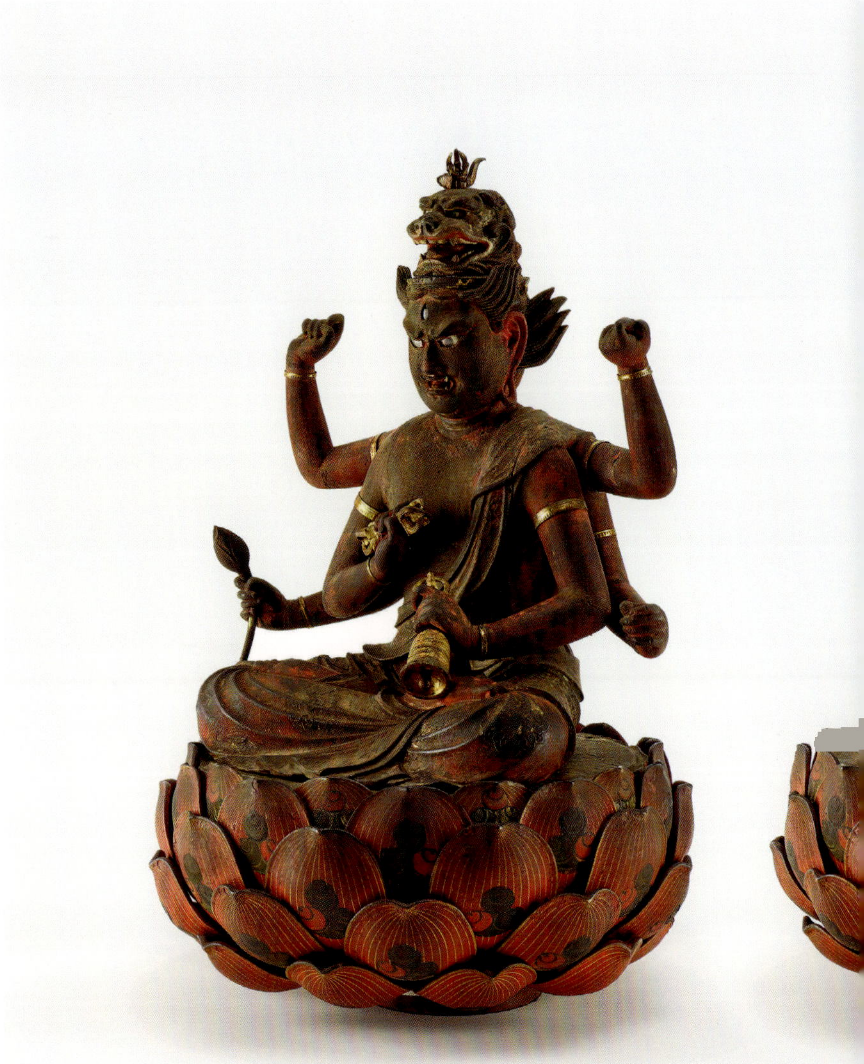

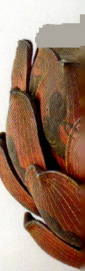

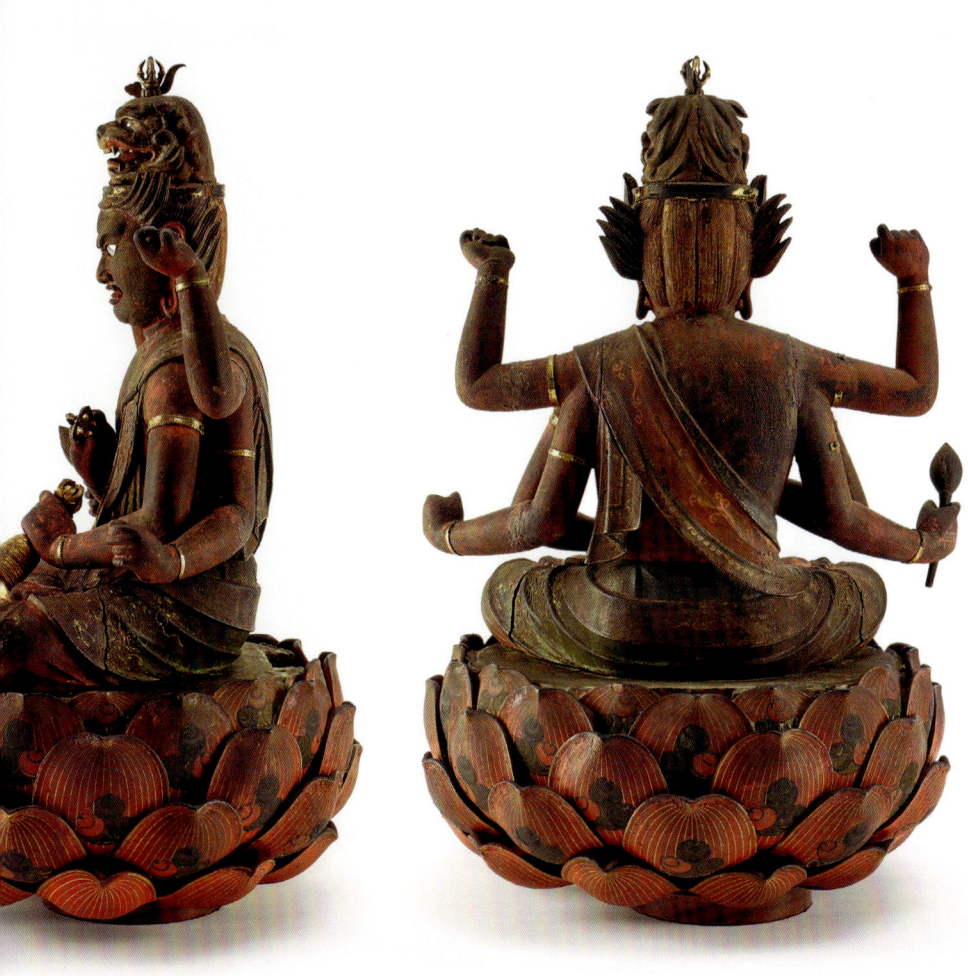

Aizen Myoo
Japan, Kamakura period, dated 1293
Wood with color and gold
43.1 × 32.2 × 29.9 cm
Purchase—Charles Lang Freer Endowment, Freer Gallery of Art,
F1974.21.1a–b

Aizen Myoo, whose name means "king of bright wisdom dyed in love," is the avatar of sacred lust in esoteric Buddhism. Here, his red body, six arms, glaring eyes, snarling face, symbolic weaponry, and bared-tooth lion headdress create a threatening image.

Myoo, deities that express the Buddha's wrath against evil, are prominent in the teachings of esoteric Buddhism. This school recognizes and emphasizes the confusing and disruptive power of sexual passion. It personifies this force in Aizen Myoo, turning lust's energy into a weapon in the struggle for enlightenment. Believers embroiled in matters of the heart popularly invoked Aizen Myoo in hopes of attaining guidance and calmness. And during the tumultuous years of the late 1200s, warriors in Japanese armies commonly invoked the deity as they fought against invasions.

JU

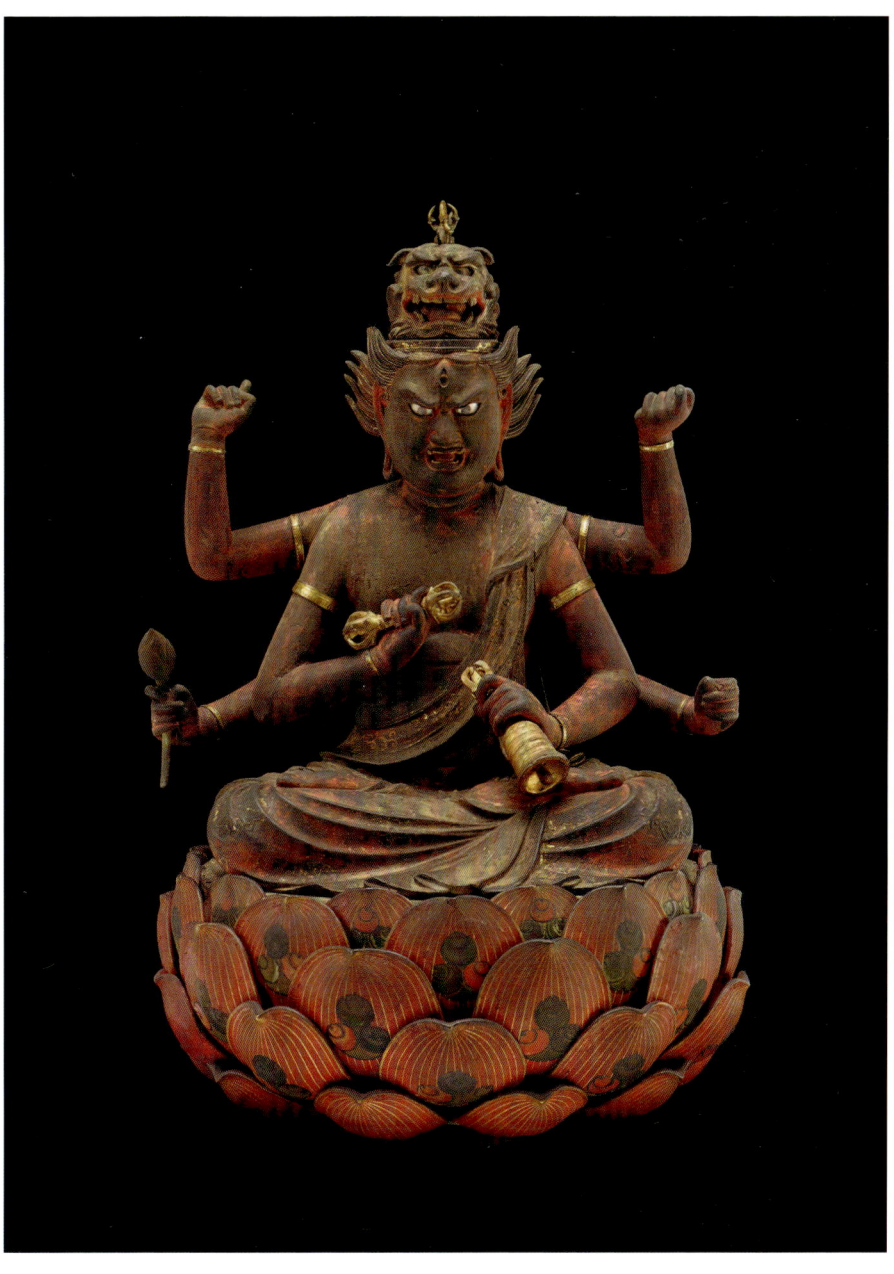

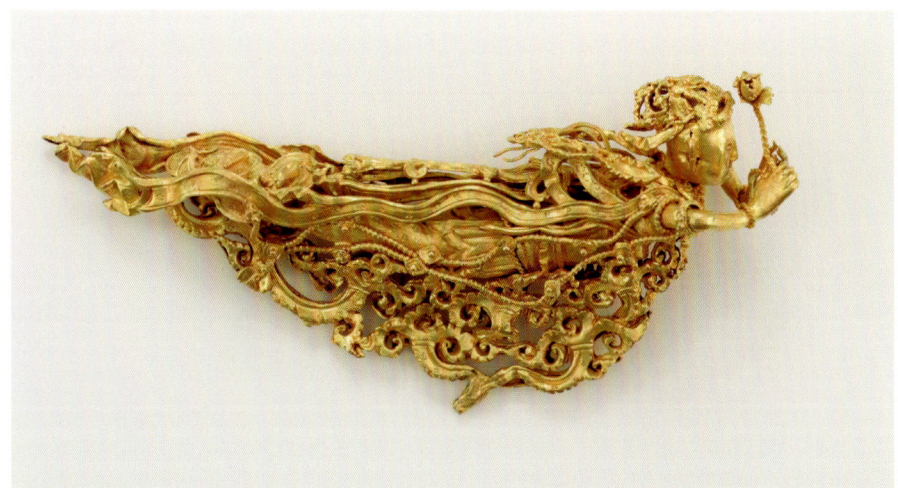

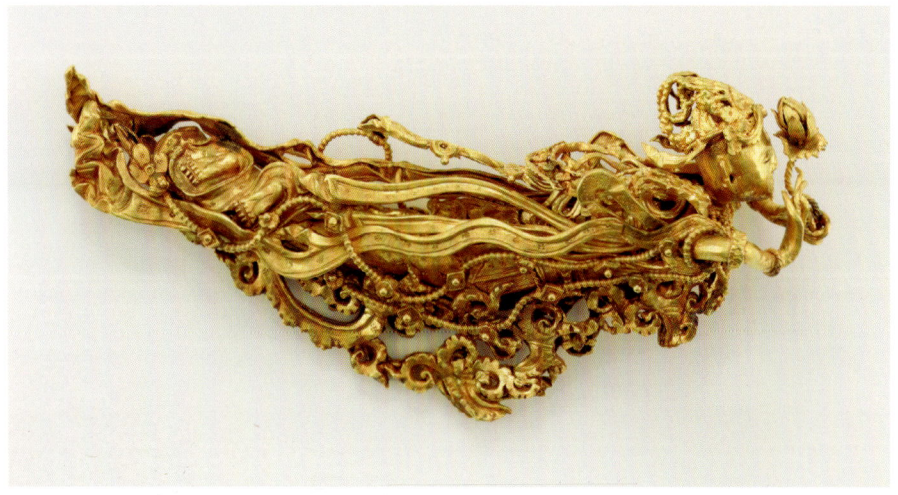

Apsarases (feitan)
China, Yuan dynasty (1279–1368)
Gold
4.7 × 2.3 × 8.8 cm; 4 × 2.3 × 8.1 cm
Purchase, Freer Gallery of Art, F1946.20 and .21

Representing flying celestials, or *apsarases*, these gold ornaments originally topped hairpins made to adorn an elaborate female coiffure. The wearer may have been a devout Buddhist, or a woman could have chosen this motif for its beauty and auspiciousness. Even though relatively little Chinese gold jewelry from any period remains, it was a highly desired luxury in many dynasties.

Modeled in the round, these delicate golden figures float on their stomachs with outstretched legs, bare feet pointing heavenward, buoyed by filigree clouds. They wear elaborate headdresses, wreaths of flowers around their necks, and jewelry, including long ropes of textured beads. Their flowing robes and extended scarves resemble the lines seen in celestial nymphs depicted in Yuan-dynasty Buddhist paintings. In the 1940s, when these *apsarases* were collected and before any archaeological evidence was available, they were dated to the Tang dynasty (618–907). The excavation of a Yuan-dynasty tomb with a nearly identical hairpin reinforces the current date.

Heavenly celestials are described in Buddhist texts as female divinities who reside in the sky but visit earth at will. In Indian tradition, they are married to celestial musicians. In Chinese tradition, they often play musical instruments themselves or carry offerings, such as the flowers they have here.

JS

About the Authors

Stephen D. Allee is the Freer|Sackler's associate curator for Chinese painting and calligraphy. He has curated or cocurated more than thirty exhibitions at the museums, including the popular *Painting with Words: Gentleman Artists of the Ming Dynasty* (2016).

Rebecca Bloom is a Freer Fellow with the University of Michigan, Ann Arbor. Her current research project is titled "Creating Context, Conjuring Experience: Innovative Approaches to Displaying Buddhist Art."

Louise Allison Cort is the Freer|Sackler's curator for ceramics. In 2012, she received the thirty-third Koyama Fujio Memorial Prize for her research on historical and contemporary Japanese ceramics, as well as the Smithsonian Secretary's Distinguished Research Lecture Award.

Robert DeCaroli is a professor of art history at George Mason University. His research has focused primarily on early South Asian Buddhist art. The author of numerous articles, his most recent book is *Image Problems: Art, Text and the Development of the Buddha Image in Early South Asia*.

Debra Diamond (content editor) is the Freer|Sackler's curator of South and Southeast Asian art. Her 2013 exhibition and catalogue titled *Yoga: The Art of Transformation* both received first place awards of excellence from the Association of Art Museum Curators.

Johannes Eijsermans is a Freer|Sackler curatorial fellow for Southeast Asian art. A doctoral candidate at Leiden University in the Netherlands, he is researching narrative Hindu and Buddhist art in temples in Southeast Asia.

Jan Stuart is the Freer|Sackler's Melvin R. Seiden Curator of Chinese Art. She has brought greater attention to the fields of Buddhist sculpture, Chinese portraits and court paintings, and ceramic and decorative arts of China through her research, publications, and exhibitions.

James Ulak is the Freer|Sackler's senior curator of Japanese art. A specialist in the history of narrative painting production in fourteenth-

and fifteenth-century Japan, he has developed and produced numerous exhibitions, most recently *Sotatsu: Making Waves* (2015) and *Inventing Utamaro: A Japanese Masterpiece Rediscovered* (2017).

J. Keith Wilson is the Freer|Sackler's curator of ancient Chinese art. Although his primary field of expertise is Chinese antiquities, he has researched and published broadly on a range of East Asian art historical topics, including Korean and Japanese art.

Ann Yonemura is the Freer|Sackler's senior associate curator of Japanese art. She has organized numerous exhibitions and has published on Japanese ink paintings, calligraphy, lacquer, prints, and printed books.

Objects in the Tibetan Shrine from the Alice S. Kandell Collection (see p. 153), as exhibited at the Freer|Sackler, March 13–July 18, 2010

ELS2010.4.2a–b, ELS2010.4.13, ELS2010.4.17, ELS2010.4.22, ELS2010.4.23.1, ELS2010.4.23.2, ELS2010.4.23.3, ELS2010.4.23.4, ELS2010.4.23.5, ELS2010.4.23.6, ELS2010.4.23.7a–b, ELS2010.4.34a–e, ELS2010.4.38, ELS2010.4.41, ELS2010.4.43a–i, ELS2010.4.44a–b, ELS2010.4.45, ELS2010.4.47, ELS2010.4.48, ELS2010.4.51a–k, ELS2010.4.53, ELS2010.4.54, ELS2010.4.56a–f, ELS2010.4.57a–f, ELS2010.4.64, ELS2010.4.65, ELS2010.4.66.1–6, ELS2010.4.67.1a–b, 8a–b, ELS2010.4.68a–e, ELS2010.4.69a–e, ELS2010.4.72a–h, ELS2010.4.73.1–7, ELS2010.4.75.1–2, ELS2010.4.76.1–2a–e, ELS2010.4.77.1–2, ELS2010.4.80a–k, ELS2010.4.81a–t, ELS2010.4.85a–c, ELS2010.4.86, ELS2010.4.87.1a–c, ELS2010.4.87.2, ELS2010.4.88.1–2, ELS2010.4.91, ELS2010.4.94a–c, ELS2010.4.95, ELS2010.4.96, ELS2010.4.98, ELS2010.4.99, ELS2010.4.101, ELS2010.4.105a–e, ELS2010.4.106a–e, ELS2010.4.107, ELS2010.4.108, ELS2010.4.109a–b, ELS2010.4.110, ELS2010.4.111a–c, ELS2010.4.123a–c, ELS2010.4.124.1, ELS2010.4.124.2, ELS2010.4.124.3, ELS2010.4.127, ELS2010.4.128a–c, ELS2010.4.133.1, ELS2010.4.133.2, ELS2010.4.134.1, ELS2010.4.134.2, ELS2010.4.136.1–2, ELS2010.4.138.1, ELS2010.4.138.2, ELS2010.4.140.1, ELS2010.4.140.2, ELS2010.4.143, ELS2010.4.144.1, ELS2010.4.144.2, ELS2010.4.149.1, ELS2010.4.149.2, ELS2010.4.152, ELS2010.4.154, ELS2010.4.155, ELS2010.4.160, ELS2010.4.163, ELS2010.4.164, ELS2010.4.165, ELS2010.4.166a–e, ELS2010.4.167a–s, ELS2010.4.168, ELS2010.4.169a–e, ELS2010.4.170, ELS2010.4.172a–f, ELS2010.4.173a–k, ELS2010.4.174a–b, ELS2010.4.175.1, ELS2010.4.175.2, ELS2010.4.177.1, ELS2010.4.177.2, ELS2010.4.179, ELS2010.4.180, ELS2010.4.181a–d, ELS2010.4.182, ELS2010.4.184a–d, ELS2010.4.185, ELS2010.4.186a–b, ELS2010.4.187a–e, ELS2010.4.188, ELS2010.4.189a–m, ELS2010.4.190a–e, ELS2010.4.191a–e, ELS2010.4.192, ELS2010.4.193a–c, ELS2010.4.194, ELS2010.4.195, ELS2010.4.196a–c, ELS2010.4.197, ELS2010.4.198, ELS2010.4.199a–c, ELS2010.4.202.1, ELS2010.4.202.2, ELS2010.4.204.1, ELS2010.4.204.2, ELS2010.4.205a–b, ELS2010.4.206, ELS2010.4.207, ELS2010.4.208, ELS2010.4.210.1–2, S2011.10a–c, S2011.11, S2011.12a–c, S2012.3, S2012.4a–e, S2012.5a–b, S2012.6, S2012.7, S2013.19a–c, S2013.20a–d, S2013.21a–e, S2013.22a–j, S2013.23a–e, S2013.24a–d, S2013.25a–c, S2013.26a–b, S2013.27a–b, S2013.28.1, S2013.28.2, S2013.28.3, S2013.28.4, S2013.29.1, S2013.29.2, S2013.29.4, S2013.30, S2014.18a–b, S2014.19, S2014.20, S2015.28.1a–b, S2015.28.2, S2015.28.3, S2015.28.4, S2015.28.5, S2015.28.6a–b, S2015.28.7, S2015.28.8, S2015.28.9a–c, S2015.28.10a–b, S2015.28.11a–b, S2015.28.12.1, S2015.28.12.2, S2015.28.12.4, S2015.28.12.5, S2016.26a–c, S2016.27, S2016.28, S2016.29, S2016.30a–b, S2016.31a–c, S2016.32, S2016.33a–b, S2016.34

Glossary

Key: **Sanskrit**/**Chinese**/**Japanese**/**Korean**/**Pali**

Amitabha/**Amituo**/**Amida**/**Amita**: literally, "Infinite Light"; the buddha of the Western Paradise. Widely revered in Mahayana Buddhist traditions, Amitabha enables his followers to be reborn into his paradise and attain buddhahood in one lifetime.

Ananda: literally, "Blissful"; a cousin and chief disciple of the Historical Buddha, Shakyamuni. Ananda remembered all words spoken by the Buddha and recounted them to the monks, who then recorded the Buddha's teachings in sutras.

arhat/**luohan**/**rakan**: literally, "worthy one"; a disciple of Buddha Shakyamuni who has attained enlightenment. Arhats are typically represented as monks. In East Asia, they are often depicted with exaggerated features and expressions.

auspicious: causing good fortune.

Avalokiteshvara/**Guanyin**/**Kannon**/**Gwaneum**: literally, "the Lord who Looks Down [from on high]"; the widely worshipped bodhisattva of compassion, who protects and saves all beings.

bodhi: literally, "awakening"; the emergence out of ignorance into a profound and complete understanding of the world. This leads to liberation from the cycle of birth, death, and rebirth, facilitating entry into nirvana.

bodhisattva: literally, "enlightenment being"; a person who, inspired by compassion, vows to become a buddha for the benefit of all sentient beings.

buddha: literally, "awakened one"; a being who has awakened to the true reality of existence and is thereby liberated from the cycle of birth, death, and rebirth. A buddha teaches others the path to enlightenment.

buddhahood: the state of being a buddha and the goal of all bodhisattvas.

Chan/**Zen**: literally, "School of Meditation"; a form of Mahayana

Buddhism that was established in China and traces its origins to the legendary fifth-century Indian teacher Bodhidharma. It is famous for emphasizing distinctive meditative techniques and for transmitting teachings from master to student instead of relying on sutras.

dharani: a condensed Sanskrit verse or string of syllables that encapsulates larger Buddhist teachings and has the power to effect change when correctly recited or written.

dharma: a term of unique importance in Indian culture that has several meanings. In Buddhism, it refers to the Buddha's teachings or doctrines.

***dharmachakra*:** literally, "the wheel of dharma"; a symbol used in art and literature to represent the teachings of the Historical Buddha, particularly his first sermon.

enlightenment: a common English translation of the Sanskrit term "bodhi," which more literally means "awakening."

karma: literally, "action"; the cumulative effect of all good and bad actions that a being performs over many lifetimes, determining his or her future suffering, happiness, and favorable or unfavorable rebirths.

Kshitigarbha/Jizo/Jijang: a bodhisattva particularly popular in East Asia, venerated for his ability to aid those reborn in hells and (particularly in Japan) to protect children.

***lakshana*:** literally, "mark"; all buddhas possess the thirty-two major *lakshanas* that are the identifying physical marks of a great man.

lama: a Tibetan Buddhist guru or teacher.

maha- : literally, "great"; a Sanskrit prefix that appears in a number of Buddhist terms, including Mahayana ("Great Vehicle") and Mahavairochana ("Great Vairochana").

Mahayana: literally, "Great Vehicle"; a major Buddhist movement that emerged sometime before the second century CE and produced a large body of sacred texts. Encompassing several schools of practice, Mahayana encourages practitioners to follow the bodhisattva path and strive to become buddhas.

Maitreya/Mile: literally, "the Benevolent One"; the bodhisattva currently waiting, in Tushita Heaven, to descend to earth and become the next Buddha. He is therefore known as the Future Buddha.

mandala/mandara: literally, "circle"; a palace visualized in meditation or drawn as a two-dimensional, blueprint-like representation. The palace belongs to the deity residing at its center, the structure's apex. "Mandala" also refers to a cosmic diagram representing the entire universe.

Manjushri/Monju: literally, "Gentle Glory"; a prominent bodhisattva in Mahayana Buddhism, regarded as the bodhisattva of wisdom.

mantra: sacred syllables that effect change when recited in their original Sanskrit; associated largely with tantric Buddhist practice.

merit: the product of good deeds, which may be accumulated over time to benefit oneself or others.

mudra: most commonly, a hand gesture with a consistent meaning, made during Buddhist ritual practice or depicted in Buddhist images.

Nikaya: literally, "group" or "collection"; now frequently used to refer to non-Mahayana Buddhist groups. Nikaya communities generally view becoming an arhat as the goal of Buddhist practice and do not accept Mahayana texts as authentic teachings of the Buddha.

nirvana: literally, "extinction"; having attained enlightenment, the state in which all past karma is destroyed and no future karma is produced, resulting in release from the inherent suffering of the cycle of birth, death, and rebirth.

parinirvana: literally, "final nirvana"; the stage that an enlightened being reaches at death, in which freedom from the effects of karma results in no future rebirths.

pratyekabuddha: one who gains enlightenment without following a buddha's teachings and who does not teach others.

Pure Land: the purified realm of a buddha; an auspicious place in which to be reborn.

Samantabhadra/Fugen: literally, "Universally Worthy"; a prominent bodhisattva in Indian and East Asian Mahayana traditions associated with protecting the dharma; in Tibetan Buddhism, a primordial buddha.

samsara: literally, "wandering"; the continuous and inherently unsatisfactory existence over countless lifetimes in a karmic cycle of birth, death, and rebirth.

sangha: literally, "community"; typically refers to the order of nuns and monks but sometimes refers to all Buddhists.

Sanskrit: the Indian language in which many Buddhist scriptures circulated. Texts in Sanskrit or known to have been translated from Sanskrit are considered authoritative.

Shakyamuni: literally, "Sage of the Shakya Clan"; an epithet of the Historical Buddha.

Shingon: traditions of Japanese esoteric (*mikkyo*) Buddhism that trace their teachings back to the eminent monk Kukai (774–835).

Shinto: literally, "the Way of the Spirits"; modern designation for the indigenous Japanese religion that is distinct from Buddhism.

Siddhartha Gautama: the given name of the Historical Buddha, Shakyamuni.

stupa: a Buddhist reliquary; ranges in size from monumental to handheld.

sutra: literally, "aphorism"; a scripture recording a sermon or teaching attributed to the Historical Buddha.

tantra: a ritual manual, ascribed to Shakyamuni or another buddha, detailing esoteric practices and teachings aimed at gaining superhuman powers, the highest of which is buddhahood.

Theravada: literally, "Way of the Elders"; a designation that now refers to the dominant form of Buddhism practiced in Sri Lanka and

Southeast Asia. These traditions are associated with study of the Buddhist canon that was first written in the Pali language in Sri Lanka at the end of the first century BCE, according to tradition.

Tiantai/Tendai: literally, "Terrace of Heaven School"; a Buddhist tradition founded in sixth-century China that focuses on the *Lotus Sutra*, an important Mahayana scripture.

***urna*:** a curl of hair on the forehead of a buddha; one of the thirty-two marks of a great man.

***ushnisha*:** a protrusion from the top of the skull of a buddha, sometimes depicted as a knot of hair; one of the thirty-two marks of a great man.

Vairochana/Pilushena/Dainichi Nyorai: literally, "Resplendent"; one of the five primary buddhas, considered in some traditions to be the cosmic buddha. He is significant in both the Mahayana and Vajrayana traditions, particularly in East Asia, and is frequently depicted as the central figure in mandalas.

***vajra*:** literally, "thunderbolt" or "adamantine"; both a common symbol and a ritual implement used in tantric Buddhism to express the power and indestructability of its teachings and the speed at which buddhahood can occur when these teachings are followed.

Vajrayana: literally, "Thunderbolt Vehicle"; also known as tantric or esoteric Buddhism, this tradition is based on practices, described in tantras, that employ mantras, mandalas, mudras, and meditative visualizations utilizing sexual and violent imagery. So potent are these practices that they are secret, requiring initiation by a guru and promising buddhahood in this lifetime.

***vinaya*:** literally, "discipline"; the code of conduct for monks and nuns.

Western Paradise: known in Sanskrit as Sukhavati, the Pure Land of Buddha Amitabha.

Index

Amitabha, 13, *36*, 37, *50*, 51, *58*, 59, *64*, 65, 66, *67*, 68, *69*, 74, 80, 92, *132*, 133, 161, 184

arhat, 9, 155, *162*, 163, 164, *165*, 166, *167*, *176*, 177, 186, *187*

Avalokiteshvara, 7, 13, *36*, 37, *50*, 51, 66, *67*, 71, *72*, 73, 74, *75*, 77, 80, *81*, 82, *83*, *86*, 87, *90*, 91, 92, *93*, 106, *107*, 112, *113*, 133, 173

bodhisattva. See Avalokiteshvara; Bhaishajyaraja, 161; Kshitigarbha; Mahasthamaprapta; Maitreya; Manjushri; Prajnaparamita; Samantabhadra

Buddha. See Amitabha; Bhaishajyaguru, 52, *53*; birth of, 30, *31*, 48, 49; buddhas, multiple; death of, 4, 5, 27, *30*, 31, 62, 63; dharma; Gautama, Siddhartha; Shakyamuni; Vairochana

buddhahood, 4, 9, 25, 32, 41, 56, 71, 109, 115, 173, 192

buddhas, multiple, 4, 6, 7, 9, 13, 15, 25, 32, 33, 42, 55, 68, 83, 131, 147, 173, 197, 199, 206

Buddhism
  conversion to, 3, 5, 55, 105, 192, 197
  in Afghanistan, 9, 30–31, 38
  in Cambodia, 19, 173
  in China, 9, 13, 15, 16, 32, 35, 37, 38, 41, 42, 45, 46, 51, 52, 56, 66, 73, 74, 79, 80, 84, 87, 88, 92, 101, 106, 112, 119, 123, 133, 140, 144, 147, 148, 157, 158, 163, 164, 166, 178, 187, 199, 202, 205, 219
  in Gandhara, 9, 30
  in the Himalayas, 4, 19, 91, 101, 153, 192. See Tibetan Buddhism
  in India, 2, 4, 9, 15, 16, 19, 27, 30, 35, 49, 52, 55, 73, 79, 87, 91, 126, 133, 157, 192, 197, 206, 219
  in Indonesia, 19, 52, 120
  in Japan, 1, 4, 13, 16, 49, 52, 59, 62, 65, 83, 95, 96, 99, 102, 105, 106, 125, 126, 131, 133, 137, 140, 158, 161, 169, 170, 174, 177, 178, 181, 184, 188, 191, 209, 210, 213, 216
  in Korea, 13, 66, 109, 123, 135
  in Myanmar, 194–95
  in Pakistan, 6, 30–31, 35
  in Nepal, 68, 101, 112, 143, 206
  in Sri Lanka, 4
  in Thailand, 19, 55, 77
  in Tibet. See Tibetan Buddhism

chakra, 55, 147, 208, 209

Chan, 13, 15, 16, 56, 88, 106, 163, 188. See Zen

collectors. See Charles Lang Freer, 177, 187; Alice S. Kandell, 153

demigod, 3, 38. See deva, 38, 199

dharani, 80, 126, 170

dharma, 1, 3, 7, 9, 13, 15, 25, 155, 163, 170, 177, 181, 191, 197

disciple, 4, 41, 51, 62, 157, 163, 181, 188, 191, 192. See Ananda, 41, 158; Kashyapa, 157; Mahakashyapa, 41

enlightenment, 1, 3, 15, 25, 32, 38, 41, 42, 56, 65, 68, 71, 115, 133, 143, 149, 157, 161, 177, 181, 188, 191, 209, 213, 216

esoteric, 4, 19, 125, 126, 131, 136, 140, 209, 213, 216. See tantric; Vajrayana

Four Noble Truths, 3

Gautama, Siddhartha, 2–3. See Shakyamuni

guardian, 4, 5, 16, 51, 112, 147, 164, 187, 197, *204*, 205, 209, 210, *211*

heaven, 3, 7, 25, 37, 49, 59, 65, 66, 99, 102, 133, 148, 166, 199

hell, 3, 38, 66, 71, 88, 102, 109, 184

Hinduism, 9, 206

Historical Buddha. See Gautama, Siddhartha; Shakyamuni

karma, 1, 3, 71, 197

Kshitigarbha, 7, 66, 71, 88, *89*, 102, *103*, *104*, 105, *108*, 109, 177, 209

lakshana, 6, 35

lama, 144, 147, 153. See Dalai Lama, 19; Phagspa, 101

laughing buddha, *2*, 7

lotus, 7, 13, 37, 41, 42, 45, 46, 49, 52, 65, 73, 79, 83, 87, 95, 99, 112, 115, 125, 126, 133, 144, 147, 148, 161, 173

Lotus Sutra, 13, 95, *160*, 161, *168*, 169, 170, *171*, 177, 178

Mahasthamaprapta, 36, 37, *50*, 51, 66, *67*, 74
Mahayana, 4, 9, 13, 25, 32, 68, 173. *See* Pure Land Buddhism
Maitreya, 7, 15, 25, 32, *33*, *40*, 41, 42, *43*, 77, 155, 170, 177
mandala, *116*, 117, 120, *124*, 125, *132*, 133, 140, *141*, *142*, 143, 144. *See* mandala of the adamantine sphere, 120; mandalas of the two worlds, *124*, 125, 140, *141*
Manjushri, 7, 71, 95, 98, 99, 146, 147
mantra, 80, 126
Maya, 30, 62
meditation, 2, 6, 27, 30, 42, 66, 68, 71, 83, 84, 115, 117, 125, 140, 143, 170, 178, 192
merit, 1, 123, 144, 157, 161, 184, 195
monastery, 1, 4, 9, 13, 15, 16, 91, 96, 101, 112, 136, 164, 166, 188, 191, 194, 198, 206. *See* Daitokuji, 191; Guangzhai, 80; Mount Koya, 99; Ngor Monastery, 143; Tenryuji, 188
monk, 1, 4, 9, 15, 27, 51, 52, 66, 79, 84, 91, 102, 105, 115, 123, 125, 135, 136, 140, 143, 153, 155, 163, 164, 170, 177, 187, 188, 194, 199. *See* Daoming, 88; Dharmakshema, 157; Kogetsu Sogan, 191; Mokuan Rei'en, 106; robe, 6, 7, *34*, 35, *44*, 45, *46*, 55, 68, 88, 106; Ryonin, 184; Saicho, 178; sangha, 4; Sunakshatra, 157; Tanyou, 166; vinaya, 123, 135; Xuanzang, 79
mudra, 6, 31. See *abhaya*, 46, 54, 55; *dhyana*, 68; *varada*, 92, 102; *vitarka*, 92, 47

Nikaya, 4, 9, 25. *See* Theravada
nirvana, 1, 3, 4, 9, 31, 42, 52, 62, 161

Padmasambhava, 19, 192
pagoda, 37, 51, 80, 131, 202
patronage, 9, 35, 73, 102, 109, 143, 161, 188, 199; imperial: Emperor Duan Zhengxing, 92; Emperor Qianlong, *146*, 147, 148; Emperor Shomu, 158; Emperor Wenxuan, 202; Empress Komyo, 158; Prince Shotoku, 174; Princess Li, 88; Qubilai Khan, 101; shogunate, 16, 96, 181; Wu Zetian, 80
Prajnaparamita, *172*, 173
pratyekabuddha, 41, 51
priest, 59, 131, 178, 181, 188. *See* Fayan Wenyi, 188; Getsuan Shuko, 181; Kenko Shokei, 188; Zhiyi, 178

Pure Land, 13, 37, 66, 99. *See also* Sukhavati; Western Paradise
Pure Land Buddhism, 13, 59, 109, 133, 209. *See also* Amitabha; Mahayana

rebirth, 3, 7, 42, 62, 65, 66, 88, 157, 161, 195, 197. *See* samsara, 3, 157

Samantabhadra, 7, 71, 94, 95, 99, 170, 171
schools. *See* esoteric; Mahayana; Nikaya; Pure Land Buddhism; Sarvastivada, 199; Shingon; tantric; Tathagatagarbha, 157; Tendai; Theravada; Tiantai; Tibetan Buddhism; Vajrayana; Yuzu Nembutsu, 184
Shakyamuni, 3, 5, 6, 7, 25, 27, 30–31, 32, *33*, 38, 41, 48, 49, 55, 56, *57*, 62, 95, 99, 158, 199
Shingon, 16, 99, 131, 136
Shinto, 105, 169
shrine, 27, 83, 91, 102, 152, 153, 157, 169
Silk Road, 9, 119, 199
stupa, 5, 27, 30, 77, 102, 148, *149*, 210
suffering, 3, 25, 38, 52, 59, 72, 80, 87, 88, 95, 102, 105, 133, 161, 170, 202
Sukhavati, 13, 36, 37, 51, 66. *See* Pure Land; Western Paradise
sutra, 13, 49, 65, 95, 99, 109, 147, 155, *160*, 161, *168*, 169, 170, *171*, 174, 177, 178, 210. See *Avatamsaka Sutra*, 38; *Lotus Sutra*; *Mahaparinirvana Sutra*, 156, 157; *Prajnaparamita Sutras*, 173; *Sutra of the Wise and Foolish*, 158, *159*

tantric, 4, 80, 117, 120, 192, 206. *See* esoteric; Vajrayana
Tara, *114*, 115
temple, 1, 15, *32*, 37, 41, 46, 49, 59, 62, 73, 74, 77, 80, 83, 84, 87, 96, 102, 106, 112, 119, 120, 126, 133, 136, 140, 153, 157, 158, 164, 166, 169, 170, 174, 177, 178, 187, 191, 199, 202, 210, 213. *See* Cisheng, 84; Daiganji, 95; Daigoji, 213; Daitokuji, 191; Enryakuji, 178; Gonxian, 73; Guangzhai, 80; Horyuji, 49; Kizil, 199; Mogao, 87; Seijoshin'in, 99; Shogenji, 49; Taimadera, 133; Todaiji, 158; Tofukuji, 177; Toshodaiji, 170; Xiangtangshan, 37, 51, 74, 202
Tendai, 16, 95, 131, 178. *See* Tiantai
Theravada, 4, 194. *See* Nikaya

Tiantai, 13, 178. *See* Tendai
Tibetan Buddhism, 1, 19, 68, 91, 101, 112, 115, 143, 144, 147, 148, 153, 192
Tushita, 15, 42. *See also* Maitreya

Vairochana, 38, *39*, *40*, 41, 120, 140
vajra, 99, 173, 205, 209
Vajrayana, 4, 9, 19, 173. *See* esoteric; tantric
Western Paradise, 13, 37, 51, 59, 65, 66, 74, 133. *See* Pure Land; Sukhavati

Zen, 1, 15, 16, 106, 177, 181, 188, 191. *See* Chan